TAKE ME TO THE RIVER

TAKE ME TO THE RIVER

A WAYWARD AND PERILOUS JOURNEY
TO THE
WORLD SERIES OF POKER

PETER ALSON

ATRIA BOOKS

NEW YORK   LONDON   TORONTO   SYDNEY

ATRIA BOOKS

A Division of Simon & Schuster, Inc.
1230 Avenue of the Americas
New York, NY 10020

First Atria Books trade paperback edition September 2007

ATRIA BOOKS and colophon are trademarks of Simon & Schuster, Inc.

For information regarding special discounts for bulk purchases,
please contact Simon & Schuster Special Sales at
1-800-456-6798 or business@simonandschuster.com

Manufactured in the United States of America

10   9   8   7   6   5   4   3   2   1

ISBN-13: 978-0-7432-8836-1
ISBN-10:   0-7432-8836-X
ISBN-13 978-0-7432-8837-8 (pbk)
ISBN-10:   0-7432-8837-8 (pbk)

For Alice (again) and for Eden River

CONTENTS

FOREWORD

These days, everyone you encounter is an expert at cards. That's what people will tell you, anyway. But in 1995, when I met Peter Alson, there were fewer than 200 regulars playing in New York City's underground poker clubs. This was before the WPT, before online gaming, before poker became a sport. Peter was among this select group of men, and a few women, who self-dealt Texas Hold'em to one another in underlit, underdecorated, illegal establishments until the sun came up or that week's suckerfish got broke. It was in these card rooms, the Mayfair on Twenty-fourth Street, the V.F.W. on Thirtieth and Madison, and the Diamond Club on Twenty-eighth off Seventh, that I learned Benny Binion's number one rule: Trust everyone, but always cut the cards. Peter Alson didn't need that or any other gaming lesson; it seemed he had them in his DNA.

In this era of the dilettante, the neophyte tournament contender, the computer kid, and all of them suddenly authors, Peter Alson has the bona fides. He has spent decades "in the action." For years, if someone on the East Coast was breaking the seal on a fresh deck of Kems, there was more than a fair chance that Alson was going to be cutting the cards. And back then, they were all cash games. There were no tournaments, no safety nets. If you got broke on the river, you couldn't rebuy, keep playing. You just went home, tried to figure out how you were going to pay the next month's rent.

My strategy when I began to frequent the underground card rooms was to watch the best players, try and learn from them. What I picked up studying Peter was a philosophy: Play your cards to the best of your ability. Win the hand, lose the hand, move on to the next hand. That's how the pros do it, and that's what Pete was: the first professional cardplayer I'd ever played against.

There are those who might say that Alson was not technically a pro. That he derived income by other means. Those are nitpickers; I have no use for them. Peter defined himself as a pro by his approach to poker. He thought about the game constantly. He was always replaying hands, re-thinking his bad plays, figuring out if he had maximized his good ones. I had my own poker-player aspirations at the time, but after spending just a few nights watching Peter close up, I saw the truth: I was a writer who liked to play poker. Pete was a poker player who wrote to pay the bills when he found himself on his uppers.

As you'll see, Peter certainly knows how to write. The pages of this book seem to race by as he brings the reader with him to the tables and hotel rooms and darkest nights of his journey to the World Series. But Alson is at his core a gambler. I use that word the way the old Texans do: as the highest compliment I can give a cardplayer. A man with gamble in him has the guts to make the right play no matter what the stakes, the guts to make the statistically wrong play when he needs to, the guts to walk away from the table when the cards just aren't running. The man with gamble in him is, by his very nature, set up for success at poker. If you've read Peter's first book, *Confessions of an Ivy League Bookie*, you already know that, while he might be able to match up with Woody Allen neurosis for neuro-sis on an analyst's couch, it'd be a fool's errand to try and sell him a bum line on a football game or give him short odds on a prizefight. And there's no place his nose for the angle serves him better than in a card room.

To the hustler, the world is divided into sharps and marks. I've been both. Believe me, so have you. The difference is simple: The mark only *thinks* he knows the play. Amid the morass of so-called expert opinions about the game of no-limit Texas Hold'em, here in your hands is a book written by a fellow who always knows what the shot is. Although it's not an instructional primer, there's plenty to learn here. If you're even thinking about making your own run at the World Series someday, and you don't want to feel like a first-timer, read this book and let Peter Alson wise you up.

—Brian Koppelman

TAKE ME TO THE RIVER

PROLOGUE

As a method for financing a wedding, a trip to the World Series of Poker would probably not be at the top of anyone's list (particularly when the wedding in question is one's own). Nevertheless, in early June 2005, I found myself on my way to Las Vegas for the start of the thirty-fifth annual tournament poker championship with that as my goal. My wife-to-be, Alice O'Neill, and I primarily made our living as writers, and were therefore almost by definition living beyond our means in New York City (which is to say we were in hock to several credit card companies). Our upcoming nuptials in Provincetown, Massachussets, were a scant three and a half months off, and though our less-than-wealthy families had agreed to kick in what they could, I did not have a clue—other than my getting lucky at poker—how we were going to pay the balance.

When I proposed my World Series idea to my future bride, it came cloaked in the premise of my writing a book about the venture, which on the surface at least (and because there was a modest advance involved) made it seem like a legitimate undertaking.

Of course I knew better, and I'm fairly certain she did, too. This was an essentially harebrained scheme—one that could easily take a turn toward disaster—and only someone (or two people) in the throes of serious denial could fail to see that. There were not merely two scenarios possible—i.e., my winning the money we needed or my not winning the money. There was a distinct third possibility—one that involved losing the advance and more. But that was a scenario we chose not to discuss.

In April, I had turned fifty, a milestone that was both shocking and sobering to me. I had lived my postcollege life, the preceding twenty-eight years, as if adulthood were a thing to be avoided at all costs. I had never gotten married, had kids, or held a steady job. I did not like bosses, authority figures, or anyone who thought he had the right to tell me what to do. I was my own man—albeit an only slightly more grown-up version of the type of literary-romantic subspecies Candace Bushnell had dubbed a Bicycle Boy in her book *Sex and the City*. Her description of this particular type, nearly all of them bachelors and freelance writers living in New York City, included the following: "They are smart, funny, romantic, lean, quite attractive" and in their "goofy glasses" somehow very charming, although she also added the caveat that they are not married and never will be, "at least until they give up their bikes."

I suppose I should credit myself with having given up my bike (though not the goofy glasses) sometime in my forties, but my reasons had more to do with my weariness of having my bicycles stolen by the ever-more-resourceful NYC thieves than it did with any burgeoning sense of maturity. Even without wheels, I was still too mobile and independent to be anyone's idea of a good mate.

Beyond that, and perhaps even more to my detriment than the bicycle spokes that still turned in my heart, was the fact that I played poker.

To my knowledge, Candace Bushnell never actually defined a subspecies of male known as Poker Blokes or Card Cads or the like, but I can't imagine that she would have conceived poker as a better preoccupation for a prospective husband than riding a bicycle.

Of course Alice didn't know the extent of my poker obsession when we first got involved. Or at least she didn't understand how deep it went.

The game and my passion for it had come early in my life—even before the training wheels on my bike came off. My father, a playwright, hosted an irregular nickle-dime-quarter game with a bunch of his theater cronies. These boisterous late-night affairs, which began in the wake of my parents' divorce when I was seven, featured heavy doses of drinking, smoking, gossiping, and storytelling. The game was, in a way, beside the point. There were wild cards, something called baseball in which threes and nines were wild, Black Mariah, high spade in the hole wins half the pot, and other crazy permutations that did not emphasize skill. My dad had the care of me every other weekend, and once a month, after he had tucked me away for the night in his guest room, his pals would come over.

How many times did I make up some excuse to wander out from the shadows of my darkened room and my supposed sleep to the dining table where the grown-ups were gambling? Eventually my father, with the overly indulgent guilt of a divorced parent, let me sit with them—or rather with him, on his lap, sweating his cards. Before long he was staking me to a few bucks, letting me play and stay up well past my bedtime. I was hooked.

It wasn't until the summer I turned seventeen, working as a service bartender (illegally, I might add—I was underage) at a famous Italian restaurant in Provincetown, that I got my first taste of a more serious game. The waiters played $1–$2 dealer's choice (mostly seven-card stud high and high-low, five-card stud high and high-low with a double replace) a couple of times a week after closing. One of them, Buzzy, made me his summer project, teaching me about life, women, and cards. He introduced me to Orwell's *Down and Out in Paris and London* as well as the concept of aggressive betting. His favorite phrase at the poker table was "If I can call, I can raise." He was always needling everyone, talking us into or out of pots, and he almost always won. I studied his every move.

By the time I got to college a year later (first attending U.C. Berkeley; then, after a junior-year transfer, Harvard), I had become good enough to make my weekly spending money playing cards. We had a regular game, at stakes of fifty cents and a dollar, and I won consistently. I knew that there were people out there who played poker for much higher stakes, but it wasn't until I read a story in *Sports Illustrated* about the still-nascent World Series of Poker that I became aware just how much higher.

The article described an elite group of larger-than-life Las Vegas characters who were willing to put up $10,000 to play a winner-take-all contest of a form of poker I had never even heard of—Texas Hold'em. These men, with names that instantly captured my imagination— Puggy Pearson, Sailor Roberts, Amarillo Slim, Texas Dolly—seemed impossibly removed from the tame little game that took place in our common room. I actually tried to introduce Texas Hold'em into our regular game at Harvard, but it didn't take. Hold'em—at least the limit version—seemed slow compared with our usual fare; it certainly didn't produce the kind of action that a game like Green Lantern, a wild-card variation of seven-card stud, did.

The concept of a World Series—a championship freeze-out tournament with a single winner—was another matter. Everyone responded to my suggestion that we pick a weekend and hold a tournament similar to the one in Vegas but sticking with the games we usually played instead of hold'em. In the late spring of 1976, seven of us regulars from the Harvard Co-op House Wednesday-night poker game had a three-day marathon with an escalating ante structure and an initial buy-in of $200 (a small fortune for a college student in the 1970s).

We arrived for the beginning of it dressed to the nines—just as the participants in the real World Series did back in those days. Bob McCoy wore a morning suit; Henry Sandow wore a red-and-white Huggy Bear pimp getup with six-inch platform heels; and Jeff Kristeller wore a bolo tie and lizard-skin cowboy boots. Someone, I can't remember who, read a proclamation christening the event, and we shuffled up and dealt. Three days later, Maurice Herlilhy, who would eventually graduate from Harvard with a degree in applied mathematics, claimed the $1,400 first prize. I finished third. The next year, we did it all over again, and the results were the same.

It was interesting to me because Maurice was not the best player in our weekly cash game. Without realizing it, I was getting an early lesson in the differences between a good cash-game player and a successful tournament player. Maurice, with his math skills, understood conceptually something about play within the structure of a tournament that the rest of us didn't.

My poker education continued during my first few years after college, when I moved out to L.A. to try my hand at screenwriting and wound up frequenting the card rooms in nearby Gardena, where I played five-card draw with the denture-wearing, chain-smoking retirees who made up the majority of California players at that time. It was while I was in L.A. that I first saw Robert Altman's classic 1974 gambling flick, *California Split,* about a friendship between characters played by George Segal and Elliot Gould based on a shared lust for action. There's a scene in which George Segal, having lost badly, comes out of an all-night poker game, into the raw, blinding glare of morning; it was so palpable, desolate, and familiar that it stays with me to this day.

When L.A. did not surrender to my screenwriting dreams quickly enough, I returned to New York, the city where I was born, and struggled to write a novel, keeping myself afloat with a new assortment of odd jobs. The extra money I was able to earn playing poker, though it probably amounted to only a few hundred dollars a month on average, made a difference. There was one game I found in the basement of a restaurant in Chelsea, another one at the East Seventies apartment of a garment district guy who was the neighbor of a magazine editor I knew. This was back in the days of cocaine and disco, and one of the regulars in that game, a diamond dealer from Forty-seventh Street, always brought blow to the game, which he shared freely, leaving an open bag in the center of the table for us to dip into with the edge of a playing card during the middle of a hand. It almost goes without saying that the game routinely lasted into the wee hours of the morning.

As our drug consumption escalated, so did the stakes. There was one particularly vicious variation of seven-card stud high-low that we played called Burn in which, if you decided to stay until the last card and then lost the hand, you were required to match the pot. Wins and losses grew to many hundreds—sometimes thousands—of dollars, and the previously congenial atmosphere got testy.

Mitch, the diamond dealer and drug purveyor, lost his mind one night and planted a nine-inch bowie knife in the tabletop, claiming that he was being cheated. This was nothing but cocaine paranoia, but it still took some quick talking and cool heads to keep the situation under control.

In the early 1980s, I went into therapy and abandoned writing my novel. I was nearing thirty, caught in a squeeze between my desire to be a successful writer and my fear that I didn't have what it took, and that if I didn't face up to the facts quickly and seek out a more stable career, I would wind up painted into a corner from which there was no escape. Poker served as a tonic for me during this time—at least when I was running good. It allowed me to have illusions, fortified by hard cash evidence, that I was possessed of at least some unique talent. It wasn't a huge stretch for me to fantasize about playing poker professionally, though this was less a fantasy to be acted out than it was an antidote to the agony of trying to write.

In 1982, the distinguished English man of letters A. Alvarez, who wrote poetry and criticism but whose "bravest book," as James McManus, his literary offspring, observed in his book *Positively Fifth Street*, was a meditation on suicide called *The Savage God,* published a two-part series in *The New Yorker* about the 1981 World Series of Poker.

The long article, which was later published in book form as *The*

Biggest Game in Town, galvanized my obsession with the World Series. By the late 1980s, having fashioned something of a career as a freelance journalist, I was going out to Vegas practically every year to write about the big event for such publications as *The Village Voice* and *Esquire.* I was also starting to fantasize about playing in it myself someday, though the fantasy at that time seemed outrageously far-fetched.

In the early 1990s my poker playing took its next jump (how plodding must this decade-by-decade education seem to the Internet-schooled players of today!) when I found my way to the New York underground clubs like the Mayfair and the Diamond and began playing in baby no-limit ($2–$5 blinds) games in which wins and losses frequently measured several thousand dollars.

At the point when Alice and I first hooked up, poker winnings probably made up half my yearly earnings, with the rest coming from my freelance magazine writing. On one of our first dates, I came back from a weekend tournament in Foxwoods with $22,000 stuffed in my pockets and took her out for a $600 dinner that I paid for in cash.

I was the kind of louche but intriguing guy Carrie Bradshaw might have fallen in love with for part of a season on *Sex and the City* before the writers forced her to come to her senses. Alice—who looked a bit like Sarah Jessica Parker though more beautiful, with a mane of golden butterscotch ringlets; high, rosy cheekbones; piercing blue eyes; a graceful nose; and a small, perfect kiss of a mouth—did the falling part but not the coming-to-her-senses part.

She was my fantasy Irish beauty, smart, talented, moody, but also reserved, controlled, careful in what she presented to the world, not that easy to know. In my romantic history there were two plot lines. In one, the girl would like me and want me, and I would keep her at arm's length before dumping her, the classic I-wouldn't-want-to-belong-to-any-club-that-would-have-me-as-a-member scenario. In the other, the girl would like me and then not want me, and I would obsess about her and pursue her until my heart got thoroughly stomped on.

When I began seeing Alice, I was forty-four and had vowed never to reenact story line number two again. Unfortunately, the last heart-stomping I'd suffered had pretty much walled off that poor, fragile organ entirely, and as much as I wanted to have a healthy relationship with a plotline-number-one kind of woman, I was still fighting a lifetime of neurotic patterning. This manifested itself with Alice in a kind of paralyzing ambivalence on my part, nearly six years of it, punctuated by her periodically breaking up with me out of frustration and despair.

Even now, having made the first and most important step toward actual commitment by asking for her hand, I was still confronted on a nearly daily basis by my doubts: she was too contained, too much like me in that way. I sometimes thought we'd both be better served by being with someone whose emotional energy could jolt us out of our comfort zones. I also worried that her writing career had not progressed as quickly as she wanted and that if that didn't change, she might wind up bitter and unhappy. More than that, my acquiescing finally, after all this time, hadn't seemed to quell her anxieties or brought her the peace and happiness she indicated all along it would. But then who could blame her? My continued ambivalence was obvious and ever-present. And here I was, flying off to Vegas for six weeks at this most vulnerable, emotion-fraught moment—a true test, if ever there was one, of her ability to accept me for what I was.

Alice put up a good front and went along with the basic premise. After all, the idea of my winning the wedding money, no matter how misguided, was certainly real enough. But did either of us really doubt what the trip represented on a deeper level? There were jokes about it being the world's longest bachelor party and the last gasp of my prolonged childhood, but the jokes only hinted at the true and precarious nature of the undertaking: that it still wasn't too late for me to fold the hand and leave the table.

1

Vegas from the Air

At Kennedy, with time to kill, I head into the Brookstone store and plop myself into a souped-up massage chair that not only begins kneading my back but wraps itself around my calves and goes to work on them as well. I'm a little bit more tense than I realized, and this Barcalounger version of the old Magic Fingers really hits the spot. As I sit in it, with my eyes closed, I think of Alice, the way she looked through the tinted back window of the black Lincoln Town Car that whisked me away down our quiet Brooklyn block a little while earlier: slender and blond; unbelievably pretty; wearing a green T-shirt, short skirt, and gray Reef flip-flops; waving good-bye in the dappled light of Second Place.

It's no wonder I'm tense. The wedding. The World Series. My bruised, fickle, and wayward heart. Impending obligations. Responsibilities. Money. I make up my mind that if I win the World Series, I'll buy one of these fabulous massage chairs for the living room of the fabulous West Village apartment that Alice and I will undoubtedly purchase. Check that. If I win the WSOP, I'll hire two strong Swedish women and keep them on call 24-7 (one for each of us, of course!).

Make no mistake, I'm excited to be going. The World Series of

Poker! Six weeks in Vegas! But I'm scared, too. The World Series of Poker! Six weeks in Vegas! A week in Vegas can seem like an eternity. In six weeks I could lose a lot more than my bankroll. Six weeks alone in a room at the semi-seedy Gold Coast hotel, the same place that was the last real residence of the poker legend Stuey Ungar before he died, his body worn out by too many late nights and too much crack—there's no telling what could happen. Thank God I have a book to write, a purpose beyond playing poker. At the same time, I feel the weight, the oppressiveness of having to do a book. I think of all my friends who are going to the Series simply to play poker. These are my friends who play for a living, who don't have a care in the world beyond the felt. I was like them once. Why do I need all this weight now after all those years without it? Maybe I'm not ready to get married.

Half an hour later, I extricate myself from the chair, a little wobbly-kneed, and browse the array of other cool gadgets that I have absolutely no need for but want anyway. One thing I find amazing is that Brookstone, Sharper Image, Hammacher Schlemmer, and all the other high-end gadget stores now sell the kind of quality poker chips in brief-case-style cases that used to be available only at gaming and casino equipment stores. It's all part of the insane poker mania of the moment. Everybody loves Texas Hold'em. For years only a subculture of mostly hard-core poker players and gamblers even knew about the game. Back in the old days—and hell, we're going back an eternity in this insta-culture, like almost two years ago—whenever it would come up at dinner parties that I played hold'em and went to Vegas, it gave me a kind of Rat Packy hipster cred. Now everyone's doing it. It's like yoga. My married friends tell me their preteen kids can't get enough of the game. "Jamie and Henry watch it on TV constantly," my pal David told me recently. "I bought them poker chips for Christmas and that's all they play with their friends now."

"Your seven-year-old kid is playing poker for money?"

"No, no, just for fun," he said. "Although," he added, as if the thought had just occurred to him, and a bit uncomfortably at that, "I have noticed a few toys around the house that I don't remember buying for them."

Apparently, the only thing left I have going for me in the cool department is that I've actually played in the World Series of Poker. I've sat at a table with Negreanu, Seidel, Hellmuth, and the rest of them. But even that is conferring less glamour on me than it once did. When I played in the World Series, the one and only time, in May 2001, there were 613 players in the main event. This year, if registration goes as expected, over 5,000 people will be able to say that they took part. *You're playing in the World Series? That's funny, so is my dry cleaner. He won his seat on Party Poker.*

Somehow I cannot manage to leave the Brookstone store without purchasing something. I have gotten it in my head that what I am really going to need when I get to the Vegas tables is a pair of Bose noise-canceling headphones. My friend Nicky Dileo, an artist-turned-poker pro, has told me that it will be the best $300 I've ever spent. "Dude, believe me," he said in his thick Boston accent, "you need to shut out all the moronic chattah. It's the only way to maintain your sanity." Another guy I know, Wes, says that in his opinion the Bose headphones and the iPod are the two greatest inventions of the past twenty years. "And the really great thing," he says, "is that they work *together*." Since my sister already gave me an iPod Shuffle for my birthday, I'm halfway home. What better time to purchase the crucial complement than before a long flight, where the headphones will pay the added dividend of dampening the obnoxious roar of the jet engines?

On the other hand, it's not as if I don't have a conscience; I am aware that I am living in a culture of pathological, materialistic narcissists, that there are people in this country without enough to eat or warm clothes to wear in winter. I wonder what my mother, a child of the Depression, would say about her son spending 300 clams on friggin' headphones when he already has the perfectly serviceable white Earbuds that the Shuffle comes with? On the other hand, why sweat $300 when I am about to invest $10,000 and possibly a lot more in a poker tournament?

In the end, I reach a compromise with my conscience and purchase a pair of Sennheiser noise-canceling headphones for a much more prudent $150.

Several hours later, I'm somewhere over the Midwest, buckled into seat 31F, my head enveloped by the sound of the Ohio Player's "Love Rollercoaster" (part of a mix that Alice put together for me). I gape out the porthole window at the green and brown patchwork quilt of Middle America slipping by below. I have been jotting down my thoughts in one of the five spiral notebooks I've brought along with me. It seems not at all coincidental that my two favorite books about the World Series of Poker, A. Alvarez's *The Biggest Game in Town* and James McManus's *Positively Fifth Street* both start out with the narrator/hero flying into Vegas, trying to make sense of the world he left behind—in Alvarez's case, England; in McManus's, Chicago—each of which is in the grip of cold weather and a very different reality. Alvarez, when he disembarks from his plane, and learns that in this new world $1,000 is called a dime, can only utter the words, "Welcome to Dreamland." McManus finds himself comparing the new experience with the virtual unreality of the Masque video game that he has been playing at home in Chicago all winter.

The truth is that there may be no other way to tell the story of a trip to Vegas and the World Series of Poker than by using the Joseph Campbell template of the classic adventure in which the hero leaves the known world behind and heads out into the unknown, there to do battle with a host of memorable pirates and scalawags while at the same time fighting the forces of good and evil within himself.

Although Alvarez did not actually participate in the action, his account of the 1981 WSOP makes extensive use of the first person, and for a reader aware of Alvarez's history (particularly an unsuccessful suicide attempt that was chronicled in his fine book *The Savage God*), his romantic take on the larger-than-life gamblers he encountered in Vegas can be seen almost as an antidote to the dark urges in himself. Poker exhilarates him in an uncomplicated way: so when the gambler Mickey Appleman tells him that poker proved to be a more successful cure for his own depression than psychoanalysis, Alvarez never for a moment doubts the notion's validity.

Unlike Alvarez, McManus, during his trip to the 2000 WSOP, which he recounts in his book *Positively Fifth Street,* does not stand on the sidelines observing but actually plays in the $10,000 buy-in main event. While he isn't the first writer to do so—Tony Holden took on the pros and described his experiences in his fine book *Big Deal,* ten years earlier, and Michael Konik wrote of his numerous WSOP experiences in the novella-length title piece from his collection *Telling Lies and Getting Paid*—McManus is without question the first literary man to make it to the final table of the Big One (where he finishes fifth and collects a healthy $247,000). His gripping account of the action, played off against his internal conflict, the battle between the two sides of himself (characterized as "Good Jim" and "Bad Jim"), shows poker to be a territory for explorations that go far beyond a deck of cards and some chips.

Interestingly, during an extended contemplation of Alvarez's book in the pages of his own, McManus gently chides the trailblazing master for devoting less attention than he might have to the kamikaze wunderkind Stuey "the Kid" Ungar, who wound up winning the 1981 WSOP. Since I myself found Ungar so compelling that I wound up writing a biography of him (in collaboration with Nolan Dalla), I'm inclined to agree. At the same time, I can see why a self-destructive soul like Stuey, who could not readily articulate or divine the nature of his psychic pain, might be less appealing to Alvarez than a self-reflective intel-lectual misfit like Mickey Appleman.

I might as well get something off my chest right at the outset of this adventure. It irks me that I am following in such well-traveled footsteps. Every writer wants to be the Magellan or Columbus of his subject. At the same time, it is also true that terrain can change—as the poker world most certainly has in the past couple of years—and that even in the familiar we can discover the new. Thus it was that before leaving New York, I decided that it would be a good idea, from a financial as well as a literary perspective, to try and win a seat online just as the past two world champions, the amateurs Chris Moneymaker and Greg Raymer, had done.

Moneymaker's 2003 parlay of a $40 PokerStars tournament into a $10,000 WSOP seat and then into a championship bracelet and a first prize of $2.5 million is near legend by now, probably the seminal event in the recent history of the game—and certainly, when combined with the powers of television and the Internet, responsible for the huge surge in poker's popularity. If you were going to create an eye for this perfect poker storm, you could do no better than to name it Money-maker. The message had been clear enough in 2002, when an amateur from Brooklyn, Robert Varkonyi, won, but the message, after Money-maker, turned into a scream, a yell, an invocation: "Anybody can win this thing! Anyone!"

You didn't even have to go to Vegas anymore to gain entry. All you had to do was get lucky in an Internet super the way Moneymaker did. So get off that couch, Bubba. Turn off the Packers game. Pull up a chair to your desktop and start betting and raising. Or hell, don't get off the couch. Stay right where you are and keep the game on. You can watch television and play poker online at the same time.

Remarkably, in just a few short years, Internet poker has become so hugely popular and lucrative that the biggest site, PartyPoker.com, and its parent company PartyGaming, were able to go public with an initial public offering that made billionaires out of its ragtag crew of founders and majority stockholders, one of whom got her start in on-line pornography and phone-sex lines. Of PartyPoker's $600 million in annual revenue and $350 million in profit in 2004 (think about those gross-to-net numbers), nearly 90 percent came from the wallets and bank accounts of American gamblers. Never mind that the U.S. government—rather than trying to regulate and tax online gambling—has been trying (unsuccessfully so far) to squash it. It's hard to keep a good vice down.

As for myself, I am not an Internet poker virgin. In fact, I was a relatively early participant, despite my basic aversion to technology. Did I say aversion? (Yes, I know—the Sennheiser headphones, the iPod Shuffle.) Let me correct myself: despite my love-hate relationship with technology (similar probably to the relationship alcoholics have to booze). The fact is that I love technology but suspect it is not healthy for me. I tend to abuse it. Several years ago, like any other 12-step candidate, I finally surrendered to my television set's power over me, admitted I was unable to regulate my watching habits, and canceled my Time Warner Cable account. While I still maintain a subscription to Netflix, I use the set now only as a video monitor to watch movies and last year's HBO (and, yes, the occasional porno). There are times—Sundays during football season particularly—when I miss live television. But I read all the time now. I get more work done. My brain is in better shape. I'm happier.

If television is like heroin for me, online poker is crack. I opened a PokerStars account several years ago, downloaded the program onto my computer (the same now-ancient computer on which I compose these words), and proceeded to play so much poker over the course of the next two weeks that I began to feel physically ill. Like too much of anything pleasurable but solitary (think masturbation), the activity was accompanied by a growing feeling of self-loathing—particularly when added to the fact that I couldn't seem to win. The other players, true to what I'd heard, were terrible, but still I managed to consistently lose to them in excruciatingly painful ways. Before I could get too caught up in conspiracy theories or paranoia, however, I obliterated the program. To have the game right there on my computer, the same computer on which I did my writing, was suicidal. I would never produce another word. In fact, I hadn't produced anything in two weeks. So I hit the delete key.

Now, two years later, I called my friend Shane Schleger to ask him if he'd let me play for a WSOP seat using my old account and his computer (my five-year-old VAIO, as I say, was now too old and decrepit). Shane— or "Shaniac," as he was known on PokerStars—was, at the age of twenty-eight, a full twenty-two years my junior. Along with a few other mostly younger players I knew, he had been having great success online. Smart, good-looking (think Jewish JFK Jr.), with a strong nose, square jaw, thick curly brown hair, and five-day stubble, Shane was also a bit of a lost boy and a stoner with a pre-poker résumé that included a drug-induced psychotic breakdown. His introduction to the poker world came courtesy of another poker friend of mine, Tristan Baum, whom he met at the Central Park tennis courts in the summer of 2000. Tri brought him to the PlayStation, an underground poker club on Fourteenth Street, which is where we first met. Shane was a poker neophyte at that point and seemingly without much aptitude. Over time, however, he got a bit better, his reckless style serving him well in the PlayStation's weekly Sunday tournament, where he began cashing in with a fair amount of regularity.

Ironically, he claims to have been inspired to play online by something I said to him during my two-week Internet submersion in 2002, though I can't for the life of me think what it was. Shane lost online at first, just as he was losing in live action. But he kept at it and improved. He improved so much, in fact, that he was able, after some months, to

Shane Schleger, better known on PokerStars as Shaniac, hard at work.

quit his job as a waiter at Blue Ribbon Sushi in Park Slope, Brooklyn. For the past year, Shane had been supporting himself solely by playing on-line tournaments and sit'n'go's, which are single-table tournaments with first-, second-, and third-place payouts. Though he didn't keep records, his big scores in the past twelve months included a couple of $18,000 wins in $200 buy-in tournaments; $10,000 in an $11 rebuy tournament that had a field of over 1,000 people; and, most recently, four $10,000 World Series of Poker seats (plus plane fare), three of which he had taken in cash, one of which he was going to use.

"I've made enough money to live on and live pretty well," he told me the week before I left for Vegas. He and his girlfriend, Sheila, and I were sitting in the living room of their cozy, art-filled one-bedroom Park Slope apartment. It was my first time meeting Sheila, a pretty brown-haired, blue-eyed Irish filmmaker/barmaid thirteen years Shane's senior.

"But you know what I'm like. I'm a gambler," Shane said. "As long as I can stay in action I'm happy. I travel, I eat well, I do pretty much what I want. So far this year, I've gone to the Bahamas for nine days, L.A. for two weeks, Lake Tahoe for a week, all to play poker. In the Bahamas, I started off sleeping on a friend's hotel room floor, but then I won ten thousand playing blackjack the second night, moved into a suite, and flew Sheila down."

Sheila and Shane first met at the bar at Blue Ribbon one night during the winter. Though Shane no longer worked there, he still dropped in occasionally for a meal. The night he met her, he had pried himself away from his computer screen long enough to walk over and grab a quick bite. Sheila was at the bar doing the same thing. They began talking, and before the night was over, they were on their way to becoming a couple.

I'd been hearing about her for the past few months, usually when Shane and I got together to play tennis in Prospect Park. As she left now for her job tending bar at Puffy's in downtown Manhattan, she regarded the two of us, bent over the liquid color screen of Shane's state-of-the-art Dell laptop and said, "Good-bye, you two poker nerds."

I had decided to take two cracks at winning a World Series seat in the $160 buy-in double shootouts, which were, according to Shane, the best value play. The way it worked was that you put up $160 and then had to beat a virtual table of eight other players. The winner went on to the next round, another table of nine players. All the players at the final table got their buy-ins back; the winner got a $10,000 main event seat plus a $1,000 in cash. Shane had lost track of how many of these he'd played, but the $40,000 he'd won had put him, after his entry fees, "quite a bit ahead."

I had been around poker long enough to know that he might just be riding a hot streak, that it could all go south for him at any moment. But maybe not. Maybe he had more going for him than luck. I was still somewhat dismissive of his skills, because of my experience with him in live games, but I was also aware that he'd played an awful lot recently, and that online poker can speed the learning curve exponentially. Where it once took years to play the number of hands required to gain a poker education, an online player can now cram it into a few months. Shane told me about friends of his, most of whom he first met in cyberspace, who were playing eight sit'n'go's at once and making $200 to $300 an hour, which translates into several hundred thousand dollars a year. Eight games at once! It boggled my mind. During my two-week experience online I got a headache trying to play more than two at the same time, jogging between screens.

"They're the compulsive types," Shane said. "They'll sit there ten hours a day."

"What about you?" I asked. "How many hours are you playing?"

"Probably fifty or sixty a week."

"Isn't that close to ten hours a day?"

"Yeah, I guess it is," he said with a laugh.

I found myself fascinated by the online poker world; it was its own strange subculture, with heroes and celebrities, villains and fools, a place where you could start with a clean slate and reimagine yourself not just once, but countless times—a new persona for each new site. At Empire Poker, you could be Loose Lester, the raising machine; at PokerStars, Sexxy Suzee, the femme fatale who liked to check-raise bluff. Even in live games, poker had always been an invitation to invent or reinvent a persona, to put on funny hats and weird sunglasses, but in Internet poker, you could stay in the shadows forever if you liked, growing your own myth.*

---

* At the 2005 WSOP, an Internet player who goes by the name of NeverLose would finish third in the $5,000 Limit Hold'em event, surprising many people who were previously convinced he was a bot (a computer program that plays without the need of human supervision). He is in fact a Chicagoan named James Kwon.

My own PokerStars handle, resurrected now on Shaniac's computer, was Mortallock, a sort of puffed-up version of "the nuts" with Tolkien and Dungeons & Dragons overtones. I wasn't sure what kind of reaction it had originally been intended to elicit, but if discouraging my opponents from contesting hands with me was one of them, it wasn't working: Five minutes into my first $160 double shootout, I moved in with middle set and got called by a player named KrackPot, whose top pair sucked out a runner-runner full house to relieve me of all my chips. On rec.gambling.poker, an Internet newsgroup devoted to discussions of poker, this is known as getting "PokerStarred." For me, it recalled the rash of similar bad beats I had received on the site during my abbreviated tenure three years ago.

"This is what always happens to me on this fucking site," I said to Shane.

"You're not one of those people who thinks it's rigged, are you?"

"No, I'm just saying it happens a lot."

"I thought you deleted the program after two weeks."

"I did."

"So how can you make that kind of assessment?"

I knew what I was saying made no sense. I couldn't possibly argue the point with him. It was just the feeling I remembered. A sense of the outcome somehow being predetermined no matter what I did. The deeper truth was, I had gone into this exercise without really believing that I would win a seat this way. Not because it was impossible or rigged, but because it wasn't my karma. I needed to suffer more. I needed to commit myself more deeply, and another $160 probably wasn't deep enough. Sure enough, my second $160 bullet resulted in another quick flameout (though this time it was more a case of user error than bad luck).

* * *

"We are beginning our descent into the Las Vegas Airport," the flight captain intones over the plane's intercom. I put down my pen and gaze once again out the porthole window. My descent into Las Vegas. Yes, that sounds about right.

Vegas has a skyline unlike any other American city. There are no skyscrapers, no business or financial center, just the glitzed-up gambling casinos of the Strip, which lie on the baked earth, as Alvarez described them, "like extravagant toys discarded on a beach." And the signs—the millions of signs!—flashing, eddying, twisting, revolving, pulsing with electricity and pixilated video images.

Seen from the air, the signs, and the edifices of the colorful, monolithic, monstrous 5,000-room hotels, the bright green facade of the MGM Grand with its sphinxlike entrance, or the fairy-tale magic towers of the Excalibur, or the black modern-day pyramid of the Luxor (which if it were night would project a single white beam of light from its pointy apex to the heavens), can stir the blood of even the most jaded sophisticate.

When Alvarez landed at McCarran in 1981, he found the airport almost empty. It was a Tuesday and the weekend rush was over. In the summer of 2005, the old rules no longer seem to apply. It doesn't matter what day of the week it is, or what season; the airport is always bustling, crowded as if for the holidays, with a jangly, giddy, casinolike energy. As always, I find myself marveling at the desperate suckers spinning their quarters and dollars into the airport slot machines. Everyone knows by now that the slot machines at McCarran give the lowest payouts in the entire city, but these withdrawing slot junkies still can't stop themselves from taking one last crack at ringing the bell and leaving town a winner.

By the time I get to baggage claim, a crowd has assembled around the carousel. Ten minutes go by. Restless, I look around to see whom I've just been traveling with. Several young guys are standing together. They're wearing T-shirts, jeans, baseball caps, sunglasses. The new poker uniform. One of them says, "Ten bucks my bag comes off first." Another says, "You're on." Finally, the siren sounds and the conveyor belt rumbles to life. To my amazement, maybe for the first time in the history of my life, my bags—all three of them!—are the very first to tumble down the chute. *Give me some of that action!* I want to shout to the young poker studs.

I'm a little embarrassed to admit that I believe in omens. I mean, I don't *really* believe in them; empirically, logically, I know better. At the same time, I can't stop myself from taking the first-off arrival of my bags as an auspicious sign for the success of my mission here. The *Oxford American Dictionary* defines this kind of thinking as "a belief that events [read: my poker results here in Vegas] can be influenced by certain acts or circumstances that have no demonstrable connection with them." The part of me that is susceptible to this sort of thinking finds further reinforcement at the Alamo Rent-A-Car lot when I am upgraded from a Geo Metro to an electric blue PT Cruiser.

I once had a girlfriend who saw omens in everything this way, and it so appalled me—offended me, actually—that it was one of the things that I used to rationalize breaking up with her (I'm not proud of that, but then I've broken up with women for infinitely more ludicrous reasons).

So how does a supposedly serious poker player get caught up in patent nonsense like omens and superstition? In a word—luck. The luck factor. It's such a huge part of poker that it sometimes actually makes me hate the game. It makes me question the most basic elements of what I'm doing. Like: Is there too much luck? Am I deluding myself into thinking that my skill can compensate, that it is as much of a factor as I would like to believe? For years I used to dismiss the uninitiated who foolishly talked of poker in relation to luck. Poker, I insisted, was a game of skill. I could say this because I consistently won. And other skilled players I knew also consistently won. Bookies consistently win, too, in a similarly random environment. The slight edge the vig gave them over bettors (5 percent) equates roughly to the edge superior skill gives a winning poker player over his opponents. But bookies can lose. They can lose for extended periods. Sometimes they lose so much they have to leave town. Poker players are vulnerable to the same fluctuations. (The truth is that poker is a game of luck—with a component of skill. Football and baseball? Those are games of skill—with a component of luck. Chess? Purely a game of skill. No luck at all. Skill counts in poker, but as Nassim Taleb writes in *Fooled by Randomness,* it "counts less in [a] highly random environment than it would in, say, dentistry.")

In poker, particularly in the short term, luck will annihilate skill. You can totally outplay an opponent, get your money in as a 60-40 favorite, and four times out of ten your outfoxed opponent will beat you—statistically, is supposed to beat you. But if luck inordinately favors him—and luck, for the purposes of this discussion, shall be defined as a short-term statistical variance during an ongoing series of events— he might win all ten.

Let me repeat that: You can outplay your opponent ten straight times, and ten times running he can get lucky and beat you. I've seen it happen. It's happened to me. It's unlikely. The odds are against it. But it can happen. It's not going to happen in tennis or golf, but it can happen in poker. Why? Luck.*

---

* If you go online and type in "What is luck?" some interesting things come up. On one blackjack site, I read the following definition of luck: "An imaginary substance believed by many players to aid in winning. Should not be relied upon in place of skill."

No, it should not. The skilled poker player, assuming that luck breaks roughly even, will always beat a player of lesser skills. But in a single poker tournament or even a series of tournaments over the course of six weeks (such as the World Series of Poker), luck will not "even out." It will have neither the time nor the number of results required to even out. How much time does it take for luck to even out? The simple answer is: a long time. In an even-money proposition, such as a coin landing heads or tails, only as you approach infinity will the number take on its expected shape. In the shorter term— that is, anything short of infinity—fluctuations are a given.

Since luck fluctuates, collecting randomly in runs both good and bad, it defies prediction. But since most of us like predictions (a lot of weathermen would be out of jobs if we didn't), especially when we are about to participate in endeavors requiring luck, we often find ourselves looking to unrelated phenomena to get a handle on our receptivity to luck. Are we under a black cloud? Yes? Then we're probably not going to be lucky (and we might get wet to boot). Is Dame Fortune smiling on us? Does the good but otherwise nonrelevant thing that just happened mean she's smiling, or is it just a slight grin?

Omens are what we look for in the universe to help point the way and let us believe that there is a plan. They are also often a means of finding justification for what we want or need to believe. Lord, I need a sign. Show me a sign. In Vegas signs are all over the place, flashing and pulsating in a rainbow of neon.

Superstitions are related to omens, but also quite different. They're meant to attract good luck, or to avoid repelling it. "You've been incredibly lucky today." *Oh, shit, don't say that.* Better knock on wood (or I'll scare the good luck away and attract the bad).

Some people (like me) are more prone to believe in omens than they are to practice superstitions. But if you consider all the things you do in the course of your daily life that might actually be deemed superstitious, you could well be surprised. I've noticed, for example, that if I wear suede, it's almost sure to rain. If I carry an umbrella when rain is forecast, it won't rain. If I talk about something before it's official, it'll fall through. These have become superstitions of a sort, in that I notice them, I think about them. I don't have a lucky rabbit's foot or a talismanic coin. But plenty of gamblers and poker players do. Not just the suckers, either. The great Johnny Chan, aka the Oriental Express, who has won the World Series of Poker twice, and has seven other bracelets in his safe-deposit box, kept a "lucky" orange next to him during his two championship runs (and during several subsequent attempts—

although he now seems to have abandoned it, having perhaps decided that its luck got used up). Did Chan really believe in the power of the orange? Probably not. But as the actor and comedian Lou Jacobi likes to say, "It couldn't hurt." Besides, the perception that Chan created with the orange that he *was* lucky gave him a psychological edge over his opponents.

Mike Caro, aka the Mad Professor, the author of numerous poker manuals, including *Caro's Book of Poker Tells,* advises his students that he doesn't believe in superstition and isn't a fan of affirmations. On the other hand, he does end his seminars by teaching his students an affirmation—"I am a lucky player. A powerful winning force surrounds me"—that is intended to combat "one of the worst things you can do at a poker table," which is to complain about bad luck. "Complaining about bad luck," Caro writes, "doesn't win you any sympathy. All it does is make your opponents think, 'Hey, there's someone even unluckier than me—someone I can beat.' What you need to do," he continues, "is the opposite. There's nothing [your opponents] fear more than luck, not even skill. The luckier they think you are, the more they will fear you."

Like Chan with his orange, it's the *idea* that luck favors you that you want to convey. On the other hand, it doesn't hurt if the idea that luck is favoring you finds a little bit of reality to support it. Like your bags coming off the chute first. Or an unexpected upgrade to a PT Cruiser. Or a beautiful woman back in New York having foolishly agreed to marry you.

2

HEART OF ICE

I drive straight to my hotel, temporarily spared the midday 102-degree heat by air conditioning and tinted windows. The Gold Coast, my residence for the next six weeks, is off the Strip on Decatur Avenue, in the shadows of the shimmering red and blue–mirrored glass towers of the Rio casino, the new home of the World Series of Poker. I pull up under the hotel's low-slung stucco portico, leave my PT Cruiser with the valet and my bags with the bellhop, and head to the front desk to check in. It's a little weird not being downtown, although this place definitely has the downscale, cater-to-the-locals feeling of the Fremont Street hotels, complete with cheesy-looking Western fixtures, a haze of cigarette smoke, and the sound of a lounge band playing a cover of "Boogie Down Tonight" from somewhere around a corner out of sight.

This will be the first time in history that the World Series of Poker has not been at Binion's Horseshoe casino (except for last two days of the Main Event, when they'll move to the Horseshoe to play the final two tables). I could say I'm a little sad about it, and that would be true, but it's not the place itself I'm nostalgic for so much as the time. The precorporate, pre–poker-boom, noncommercial time.

*   *   *

When Benny Binion came up with the idea for the WSOP in 1970, poker as it was played in most casinos was still regarded as a game of hustlers and sharpies, and smart tourists and home-game players kept their distance. Binion was hardly a likely candidate to confer respectability on the game or its image. An uneducated bootlegger and numbers racket man who had moved his family to Vegas from Dallas in the 1940s to evade his enemies and the authorities, he bought the Eldorado Club in 1949 and transformed it into a no-frills gamblers' joint of the sort to appeal to his pals, and christened it Binion's Horseshoe. Benny's joint might easily might have remained just another downtown gambling hall, if Benny's knack for gimmicky promotions hadn't resulted in his staging of a marathon poker game among his road-gambling cronies. He dubbed it the World Series of Poker, and invited the public and the press to come watch.

The first one, in 1970, lasted about ten days, at the end of which the nine players voted Johnny Moss the champion. The event drew curiosity seekers but lacked drama and a measurable resolution. The next year, the concept of a "freeze-out" was introduced, with each player ponying up $10,000 and playing until one man had won all the chips. Moss was the victor again, this time without a vote, and the WSOP, in a form pretty close to what it is today, was off and running.

If you can ever get your hands on a tape or DVD of the 1973 WSOP won by Puggy Pearson, which was filmed cinema verité–style and narrated by notorious oddsmaker and CBS sportscaster Jimmy "The Greek" Snyder, do so. It will give you an idea of what the Horseshoe and the World Series were like in the early days, in all their smoky, one-step-removed-from-a-saloon romantic glory.

The truth is, though, that I and most of my poker friends considered the Horseshoe a dump even in its prime. We had affection for it because it was the birthplace of the WSOP and had a full deck of history contained within its walls. But it wasn't place you ever wanted to *stay*. The only time I had stayed there in recent years, I'd been appalled to discover that management's idea of a nonsmoking room consisted of a maintenance man spraying some probably toxic liquid on the curtains to "take care of the smell." When I'd first gone out to cover the World Series, back in the late '80s, the Horseshoe's fortunes seemed to be on an upswing. The WSOP was making the name Binion famous and helping to increase revenues. In 1987, Benny's son Jack, who had taken over management of the casino along with Benny's other son Ted, owing to Benny's problems with the law, bought the adjacent Mint Hotel and merged it with what was the old Horseshoe, more than doubling the size of the place.*

By the mid-to-late '90s, despite the fact that the WSOP kept growing bigger, it was clear that the Horseshoe's best days were behind it. All of downtown had been out-Stripped by the corporate theme dreams of Las Vegas Boulevard—which were conceived, as A. Alvarez writes, "not as places to stay but as Hollywood sets, each offering their guests the chance to star in the movie of their choice." If your tastes ran toward *Ben Hur* or *Gladiator,* Caesars Palace was the place to stay; if they ran toward *La Dolce Vita* then it was the Bellagio. Every one of these mammoth 3,000- and 4,000-room hotels was a world unto itself, with nightclubs, spas, gymnasiums, world-class restaurants, theaters, zoos, art galleries, malls, and, of course, ultralavish casinos.

Binion's didn't go in for the frills. A carpet instead of sawdust was

---

* The same Mint Hotel was the scene of Hunter S. Thompson's classic book *Fear and Loathing in Las Vegas,* which sprang out of an assignment Thompson got from *Sports Illustrated* in 1971 to cover the Mint 400 motorcycle race. Thompson never got around to attending the race: instead, he described in hallucinogenic prose his week of near-heroic drug bingeing and the series of lunatic misadventures he and his 300-pound Samoan attorney got into. In the process, he gave birth to a new form of journalism, called gonzo, in which the writer did not just participate in the story but *became* it.

Benny's idea of entertainment. No ceiling on the limits, the best odds on craps, cheap food, clean rooms—what else did a gambler need? The prevailing wisdom in Benny's day had been, "Get 'em into your joint, give 'em rooms for nothing, and watch 'em lose it back with interest at the tables." Then came the visionary Steve Wynns and the Harvard Business–schooled corporate types, who realized that you could get 'em at the dice table *and* the dining table. You could sell luxury at premium rates. In the new Las Vegas, gambling accounts for only 40 percent of revenues.

Benny Binion died in 1989, the same year Steve Wynn opened the Mirage casino on the Strip. In 1994, Benny's wife, Teddy Jane, followed him to the grave, and an ugly estate battle that would last for years erupted among Benny's surviving children. In the end Benny's daughter, Becky, and her husband, Nick Behnen, wrested control of the Horseshoe away from her brother Jack, who had been running things since before Benny's death. But the fight was costly, and combined with the slow decline of downtown, put the Horseshoe on a collision course with bankruptcy. I could see the difference in the place every time I went back. Each year the carpets got more threadbare and dirty, the crowds sparser, the staff's morale lower. The irony was that, despite the staff and players' increasing dissatisfaction with the venue and the way things were being run, the World Series was getting bigger every year, with larger fields, more money, and an ever higher profile.

In May 2003, Chris Moneymaker beat 838 other competitors, the largest WSOP field in history, collecting a first prize of $2.5 million. It was the year poker really blew up big, drawing eye-opening ratings on TV and a massive influx of players to the Internet sites. Ironically, it was also the last year that Benny Binion's creation, and the casino that was its home, would belong to an actual Binion. In January 2004, just five months before the 2004 WSOP, U.S. marshals and IRS agents shut down the Horseshoe and seized its assets. Two days later, with poker players around the world worrying about the fate of their beloved tournament, Harrah's Entertainment announced that it had struck a deal with Becky Binion Behnen to buy the Horseshoe and the WSOP for $40 million. The casino itself was of little interest to the gambling corporation. In fact, it immediately sold the physical premises to another corporation that would manage the property. What Harrah's Entertainment kept was the WSOP brand, a commodity that, had Becky been able to hold on to it, probably would have turned her into a billionaire. Some might look upon this as a bad beat. But if you were me you could also think about how sweet $40 million would look in *your* bank account.

A young, eager bellhop leads me across the casino floor of the Gold Coast, wheeling my luggage on a cart past a phony-looking old-time ice-cream parlor and a security podium by the elevator bank manned by a sleepy blue-uniformed guard. The elevator doors open on the second floor, and we trek down a grim corridor that, if anytime in the next six weeks I start feeling suicidal, will be the thing to push me over the edge. The lighting is supplied by tired fluorescent panels spaced at ten-foot intervals, as if the architect had been directed to save money on electricity. Even a Motel 6 tries harder than this.

My actual room is slightly better. It's drab shades of brown and tan, and has two full-size beds and a comfortable amount of space. When I cross to the windows and yank open the curtains by their hanging plastic sticks, however, I'm confronted with a blank white stucco wall about ten feet away, across a narrow shaft. This is my view. Simultaneously, I'm slapped in the face with an awful stench—a mixture of ripe sweat socks and stinky cheese—the source of which seems to be the moist, frigid air coming out of the noisy air conditioner.

"Jesus," I mutter to the bellhop, who is unloading my bags. "Do you smell this?"

"What?" he says, at least for the moment fulfilling his role as a company man.

I am already trying to process my options. My room here at the Gold Coast is ridiculously cheap at $45 a night, whereas the rooms at the Rio are several hundred a night (and sold out, from what I hear), but it is clear that I cannot live in this environment for the next six weeks.

"Come over here," I say.

He steps closer.

"Smell it now?"

He sniffs, and his nose wrinkles. A tell.

"See?"

"Yeah, that's bad. I don't know what that is," he says.

"I'm here for six weeks. You gotta help me."

"Let me see what I can do," he says. He picks up the phone and dials. "Hi, Cindy, this is Manny. I'm here with Mr. Alson in room 263. There's something wrong with the air conditioner in this room. It's got a smell. . . . Yeah, a smell. Is there another room I could take him to?"

I point my finger up to the ceiling. "On a higher floor," I stage-whisper. "And with a view. I don't want to be looking at a wall."

Manny sweet-talks Cindy like a pro, earning himself a double saw-buck on top of my gratitude. A few minutes later, we hike down a similarly depressing hallway to my new room on the fourth floor. At least it doesn't smell, and it's got a view with some sky in it even if what lies below is the single-story parking structure for the housing development next door. There's a round white laminate table by the window, which is where I set up my laptop, plugging the dial-up port into the phone outlet with a twenty-foot extension cord that stretches across the carpet and the corner of one of the two double beds.

I reset the time on my Wenger wristwatch (a birthday present from Alice two years ago), spinning it back three hours from 6:30 p.m. Brooklyn time to 3:30 p.m. Las Vegas time. I'm anxious to get over to the Rio to check out the tournament room, but more than that I want to connect with Nolan Dalla, my coauthor on the book about Stuey Ungar, who is going to lend me $15,000 in cash, two-thirds of which I am planning to use as my buy-in to the Main Event.

I should explain: In the weeks before I left New York, I began to panic, thinking that I might get shut out of the tournament. All sorts of rumors were flying around on the Internet. On rec.gambling.poker, a number of posters were reporting that the Rio had already received 4,000 entries and possibly more, but it didn't have enough staff to have processed them yet. Worse, tournament organizers had decided to cap the field at 6,600, nearly three times the record 2,576 of the previous year. That seemed like a reasonable number, but with the current poker mania and all the rumors, I was afraid a bank-run mentality might take hold. It seemed quite possible, when you started to factor in the hundreds and thousands of seats that the Internet sites were awarding, that the 6,600 might be reached before the preliminary events had even begun. Since I had a contract to write a book about *playing* in the tournament, that could prove to be a problem.

As June approached, I reached out to Nolan. In addition to being my collaborator on Ungar's bio, and a poker player himself, Nolan was also the media relations director of the WSOP. He was quick to reassure me that there had been "no run on the bank" and that I had nothing to worry about. I worried anyway, calling him every few days leading up to my flight to check on the status of things. It was amazing to me that there was no good way of obtaining this most basic information. What was it like for Joe Poker in Duluth or José Poker in Costa Rica who couldn't call Nolan Dalla? It occurred to me that Harrah's actually might be encouraging the rumors to create a panic and ensure a sellout. Who knew?

My original plan had been to try and play a number of super satellites and win my $10,000 entry, but now that seemed too risky. I conferred with my friend Nicky Dileo, who had driven to Las Vegas from Los Angeles at the end of May and was staying at the Maloof brothers' Palms Casino Resort across the street.

"If I were you," he said, "I wouldn't take any chances. Are you definitely playing the Main Event?"

"Yeah."

"Then buy in as soon as you get here. That's my advice. Not only because you might get shut out, but because it'll take the pressure off you. When I played last year, I bought in as soon as I arrived, and then when I played in the supers, I was incredibly relaxed because I already knew I had a seat. That's really why I think I won so many of them. Trust me on this, dude. You'll thank me."

Since Nicky had won six $10,000 super satellites the previous year, his argument was fairly persuasive. On the other hand, he was one of those people who expressed opinions forcefully, and I was sometimes perhaps too easily swayed (witness my purchase of the noise-canceling headphones). That didn't mean he was wrong, of course. The problem, in this case, was that I didn't have the ten grand in cash or credit. The first part of the advance on the book, a little over twenty gees, had been promised to me by June 2, the day of my departure, but, typically, it hadn't come through on time. When I had mentioned this to Nolan during one of our conversations, he offered to lend me whatever I needed until my check arrived. My literary agent, who was also Nolan's agent, had assured me the check would be in my hands in two weeks at the latest, so Nolan wasn't taking any real risk. Still, I had never borrowed the kind of money we were talking about from anyone in my life.

"Are you sure about this?" I asked Nolan one last time before leaving New York.

"I'll have fifteen grand in cash for you when you get here."

* * *

Propped up on one of the beds in my room at the Gold Coast, with ESPN going silently on the television, I try calling him now, but reach only his voice mail. My next call is to Nicky.

"Peter!" he says. "You're here, dude! Where are you, at the Gold Coast?"

"I just checked in."

"What's the matter? You sound disgruntled."

I tell him about the suicide-inducing hallways and the overall desperate-loser mood of the place.

"Too bad you can't get a room here," he says. "The Palms' poker rate is ninety-nine bucks a night and the rooms are great. The only problem is, they're sold out after tomorrow night. I was actually hoping I might be able to crash with you."

I look over at the other bed, which I'm currently using as a luggage rack, and say, "Sure, it's okay with me."

"It's probably just for a night or two," he says. "Unless Betsy leaves and gives me her suite at the Rio." Betsy is Nicky's friend and sometime patron, a rich poker-playing retired businesswoman from Los Angeles.

"Have you been over there yet?"

"The Rio? It's insane, dude. There was a huge line to register already last night. That's just to get your player card. Then you have to stand in another line to buy in to the tournaments."

When I tell him that I'm planning to play in the first WSOP event, a $1,500 buy-in no-limit tournament (which he's playing in, too), he tells me I'd better get on line *now*. By tomorrow morning it's going to be sheer chaos.

"I guess I'll go over there, then," I say. "I've gotta find Nolan Dalla before I can do anything, though. He's got my money."

"I'll go with you. I'll pick you up in my car in a few minutes."

"Your car? Isn't the Rio next door?"

"Yeah, but the poker room is on the other side of the casino. It's a sixteen-minute walk door to door from the Gold Coast. I've timed it. It's much easier to drive around and park on the other side. I've got it all figured out. I've researched all the angles."

Five minutes later, I step out of the hotel into the baked desert air just as Nicky pulls up in a white Porsche SUV. He's wearing aviator sunglasses and a sixties retro-style lavender-and-white-striped shirt looking in his Moby-like baldness more Williamsburg, Brooklyn, than Vegas Strip.

"When the hell did you get this?" I ask, sliding into the buttery leather passenger's seat.

"It's Betsy's," he says, fingering his shades and peering in the rearview mirror.

"She just lets you have her car?"

"Dude, she's got a garage full of cars. She doesn't like the idea of me leaving Em and the baby in L.A. without transportation, so she always lets me borrow her Porsche when I come here."

"Doesn't Em ever get jealous or suspicious? What's she think of this arrangement?" Em is Nicky's wife, Emily, who along with their two-year-old daughter, Catherine, is back home in Los Angeles.

"She thinks Betsy's entertaining. She knows nothing's going on between us. I mean, I can see how some people would assume there is, but Em knows better."

Nicky and Betsy met in the poker room at Hollywood Park. The two of them traveled to Foxwoods last winter for the World Poker Finals; that's when I first met her. She's close to fifty, a gravel-voiced blond who wears lots of expensive jewelry and designer clothes. I can't say I quite understand her relationship with Nicky, although I'm certain that he's being truthful when he says it isn't sexual. There's definitely some sort of commerce involved, though, even if it's not sex. My best guess is that she wants to soak up his poker wisdom. Nicky's a brilliant player. But it's more than that. She wants a reality check, and Nicky—with his scalding take-no-prisoners wit, generally nihilistic outlook, and low tolerance for bullshit—gives it to her.

I find it interesting that he would be drawn to someone as purely L.A. as she is, but he says she's one of the few people he can stand in the city, and I think it's because there's an integrity to her L.A.-ness: She's unashamed, a doyenne in her world, which in a perverse way he respects. It also doesn't hurt that she's generous with him (her money comes from a wildly successful business involving 900 sex numbers), though her patronage, sadly, is for his poker playing, not his painting.

In a way, this is the source of most of Nicky's current angst, because as talented a poker player as he is, what truly feeds his soul is painting. When I first met him, seven or eight years ago, at the Diamond Club, an underground poker parlor (long since shut down) in New York City, he would show up to play in old work boots and paint-speckled jeans. He was odd-looking: balding, with large ears, dark brown eyes, and an ex-pression that most of the time was half quizzical, half amused, as if the world was a joke—but what if it wasn't? I didn't like him at first. When he picked up his cards or bet, his hands would shake. His movements were herky-jerky, speed-freaky. He took offense easily. I couldn't figure out if it was real or an act designed to annoy his opponents into making bad plays. I dubbed him Nervous Nicky, and much to his dismay, the name stuck.

Later, after we became friends, he told me how much he hated the name, so I stopped using it. By then I had discovered that he was a kin-dred spirit, a neurotic artist nutcase and tortured good soul, who loved poker/hated it/loved it/hated it with a passion to match my own. Like many friendships forged over chips and cards, ours developed out of a recognition of our shared obsession along with a respect for each other's skills. Gradually, the scope expanded beyond the Diamond Club (and the clubs that followed in its wake). There were road trips to Foxwoods, Atlantic City, and Las Vegas; introductions of girlfriends; and the discovery that, beyond poker, we both had a keen interest in books, art, and politics. I learned that the work boots and paint-streaked clothes came from Nicky's "other" life as a painter and constructor of both houses and art. He and Emily, to whom he was not yet married, lived in a rented ground-floor apartment in Park Slope with a separate painting studio. His work was big, colorful, sardonic, but as yet unrecognized.

As his poker skills developed and he began to make a living off the game, he was able to quit taking the construction jobs that had supported him previously. Poker also gave him the time to continue painting, although still without much commercial success. Then, in 2002, he and Emily got married and she got pregnant, and everything changed.

At that point I considered Nicky one of the top two pot-limit no-limit (known as "big-bet") hold'em players in New York. Despite that, when he talked about supporting his family by playing poker, I became anxious for him. No matter how good you were, there were times when you were going to run bad. At some point, he would have one of those bad runs, and if his bankroll got short, he'd start thinking about the money. The minute that happened, his edge would be gone. Nicky's greatest strength was his fearlessness, his ability to make reads and act upon them decisively. There was nobody else in New York I feared at a poker table the way I feared Nicky when he was on top of his game. But when I heard that Em was pregnant, I couldn't shake the bad feeling. You had to have a heart of ice for that kind of pressure not to affect your play.

After the baby was born, the three of them moved from Brooklyn to Los Angeles. Em's mother had a guest house in Santa Monica. The plan was to live next to her for a year while saving money for a down payment on a house of their own. Nicky had accumulated a bankroll of about

$60,000. He began playing a big pot-limit game at Hollywood Park. Like a lot of players these days, he had a strategy that involved playing cash games to build up his bankroll, then using a portion of his winnings to go for the big score in tournaments. In the WSOP, the Bellagio Five Diamond, and other WPT events, Nicky kept getting close, but he just couldn't make the big breakthrough, the $200,000 or $300,000 score that would take the pressure off. The responsibility of staying solvent was so overwhelming to him that he stopped painting. He didn't have a studio to work in, but it was more than that. He felt he had to spend every free minute taking care of his family.

Depriving himself of the thing he loved most exacted a steep cost. Whenever he talked to me about playing poker, there was now a measure of contempt in his voice, particularly for the other players. They were degenerates and lowlifes, and it pained him to be spending so much of his life among them. He began getting into altercations. The trouble would start with a needling remark and escalate from there. Nicky couldn't believe the stupidity he was encountering, the lack of erudition. The other players, in turn, hated his condescension, his conviction that he was somehow above them. The fact that he was taking their money made it worse. There were a couple of near dustups. Complaints were lodged against him. Casino management didn't like him, either. Winning was one thing; pissing off the fish who made the game was bad business.

When he told me about his problems, it was always him against the assholes. I was sympathetic at first, but after the second or third incident, I said, "Nicky, this shit doesn't keep happening by coincidence. What do you think is really going on?"

"Peter, these people are so stupid. They just can't stand losing to me."

"You know what I think? If you're beating people, it's part of your job to make them like you. Look at Persian Steve." Persian Steve was the only guy in New York whom I had considered Nicky's equal at the card table. Where Steve had a huge edge over Nicky was in public relations. He had the remarkable ability to kick people's asses and charm them simultaneously. To be sure, Nicky and Steve achieved similar financial results. Bad players would pay Nicky off because he got under their skin and they wanted to beat him, whereas bad players would pay Steve off because they liked him and wanted him to like *them*.

"You really buy Persian Steve's bullshit?" Nicky said.

"I think you could learn something from him."

Underneath it all, what I really thought was that Nicky could feel part of himself dying from spending all his time in casinos. I passed no judgment on the people who did that. But Nicky wasn't meant to be one of them. He was angry at himself because he knew that. And he was angry because he hadn't figured out a way to create some breathing room for himself, to get himself off the edge. Maybe it was healthy for him to take out that anger on the people he was playing against rather than on himself. It was also self-defeating.

We drive over an assortment of speed bumps and turn right out of the Gold Coast.

"The Rio's the other way, isn't it?"

"Trust me, dude. I know what I'm doing."

"Just making sure."

He lowers his aviator sunglasses and looks at me. "How's Alice? Is the wedding still on?"

"Yeah, it's on."

"You don't sound certain."

"Have I ever?"

"Dude, this is not a joke. You don't go into something like this halfway."

"You're saying this as one fucked-up guy to another?"

"Let me ask you something. In all seriousness, why are you getting married?"

"Well, let's see, I proposed to her and she said yes."

He's shaking his head.

"Look, I'm fifty," I said. "Last fall she stopped using birth control. Which I was okay with, or at any rate philosophical about. I told her if she got pregnant we'd get married. The thing is, as far as I know, I've never gotten anyone pregnant. So who knows if it can even happen. But she started getting serious about it, making a point of us having sex when she was ovulating. And that's when I thought, 'This is silly. It's the tail wagging the dog. Either marry her or don't marry her, but make a decision.' So I made a decision."

"Very romantic."

"Hey, you know what? All romance ever got me was a lot of pain and heartache. This is the healthiest relationship I've ever had with a woman. I'm not going to apologize for that. Last Christmas, we drove out to Race Point Beach in Provincetown at sunset. It was freezing cold and windy but beautiful. The beach was deserted. There was this pinkish red streak in the sky and you could hear the waves crashing."

"You had a ring?"

"Kind of. I bought her something on the street for twenty bucks."

"You're getting her a real ring, though, right?"

"As soon as I can afford it."

"Dude, you gotta get her a real fucking ring."

"The point is, I told her she made me happy. And it's true. That doesn't mean that there's been some radical alteration in my character. I have very mixed feelings about the institution of marriage—and I probably always will."

"And Alice knows this?"

"Of course she knows. She's been with me six fucking years. Besides, she's got her own ambivalence. If she didn't, she never would have hooked up with someone like me to begin with."

"You've got a point there."

He turns into the entrance of a large parking lot, and we drive around looking for a spot as close to the back entrance of the Rio as we can find, which winds up being about the distance of a football field. The air outside is like hot breath. It makes my skin prickle. I'm dressed too warmly in jeans and a Lacoste shirt, but it's for the air conditioning inside. Nicky's adopted a similar strategy. In addition to his retro shirt, he's wearing jeans and what look like white Italian dance shoes. We reach a set of stairs leading to an outdoor terrace at the end of which are glass doors that lead into the Pavillion Center, home of the Rio's convention halls.

As we approach, we pass several guys on their way out to the lot. I don't recognize them except in so far as it is clear they are poker players; you can tell from the pasty complexions, the baseball caps, and the Starter jerseys. Inside the glass doors, there are even more players milling about, wandering up and down a long, wide hallway off which are the various convention ballrooms. In the distance, about 100 yards ahead, I see a solid mass of people, a human bottleneck. A cloud of cigarette smoke hovers above them.

"Holy shit," I say. "Is that a line?"

"I'm telling you, dude," Nicky says. "It's going to be even worse tomorrow."

The line is currently about 200 people long. We take a spot at the back of it. Now I begin to recognize some of the faces. There's T. J. Cloutier, who has won more poker tournaments than anyone else in history, but never the Big One, though he has twice finished second; there's the Englishman Mel Judah, a former hairdresser, who finished third to Stuey Ungar back in 1997 and has lately gotten a lot of television time on the World Poker Tour, including winning the Legends of Poker for over $500,000 in 2003; and here comes the two-time world champion Doyle Brunson riding a glossy red motorized cart. He has to keep stopping to sign autographs, but he doesn't seem to mind, flashing a toothy grin from underneath his trademark cowboy hat.

In 1988, I persuaded the *Village Voice* to send me out to Las Vegas to write a story about Amarillo Slim's Superbowl of Poker. Even though poker players were not yet television stars then, I still had to pinch myself seeing Brunson, Stuey Ungar, Chip Reese, and Puggy Pearson in the Caesars Palace poker room. In the course of my young journalism career, I had rubbed shoulders with Patrick Ewing and Marc Jackson in the Knicks locker room at Madison Square Garden and with Mark Gastineau and Joe Klecko at Jets training camp. But meeting Brunson, Ungar, and the rest was different, like finding out that a character from a favorite novel actually existed—Jake Barnes or Holden Caulfield come suddenly to life.

Brunson is seventy-three now, the most famous poker player alive, but in '88 it was the self-destructive genius of Ungar that most captured my imagination. When the thirty-four-year-old man-child ended up winning the '88 Super Bowl of Poker, collecting a first prize of $210,000, I was among the throng of mostly local reporters crowded around him as "Amarillo Slim" Preston presented him with the prize money. Ungar was jumpy and uncomfortable, tugging at the chain of a Caesars medallion that a costumed Cleopatra had hung around his neck. When the chain snapped, Ungar flung the medallion into a nearby garbage can.

Doyle Brunson was there watching. The two were good friends, an odd couple if there ever was one. Seeing Ungar's discomfort, Brunson came over to rescue him from the press. As the big man hustled the little man away, I asked if the two of them were going out to celebrate. "Nah," Ungar replied with a mischievous smile, patting the fat sack of money. "Goin' to Doyle's to watch the Lakers game." More than fifteen years before I would get involved in writing his biography, I remember thinking how palpable Ungar's anxiety was even in that moment of glory, and how certain I was that the money he'd just won would be gone in short order.

My own anxiety revolves around more mundane issues. Like how long am I going to have to stand on this goddamn line? I try to imagine Stuey Ungar standing in a line like this. Forget about it. He'd pay someone to hold his place. Besides, back in 1988, a $10,000 buy-in tournament attracted only about fifty entrants. Here, less than twenty years later, the number is likely to be more than a hundred times that many.

Nicky, who has no reason to stand on this line other than to keep me company, decides to go have a look at the live games.

"Come find me when you're done here," he says.

"Yeah, thanks."

After he leaves, I try calling Nolan again. This time he answers. When I tell him about the long line, he says, "I wish there was something I could do to help you, buddy. I don't know what to tell you." He's in the media room at the end of the hall. He tells me to call him when I'm finished. We'll meet up and he'll give me the money.

Forty-five minutes later, I reach the registration desk, where one of the three women stationed at computers issues me a bar-coded identification card and makes me sign a waiver stating that I am granting Harrah's and ESPN the right to film me for television. It seems as if that's every poker player's dream nowadays, to play on television, but just out of curiosity I ask if anybody has objected to signing the waiver.

"Not yet, hon," comes the cheerful reply. "But there's always one troublemaker in every crowd."

"What'll you do if somebody refuses?"

"Why, we won't give 'em a card, of course."

Of course.

I sign the release and hand it to her. She hands me my card, which is a piece of flimsy cardboard the size of a picture postcard. It's got my name printed on it and the serial number 00000003583, which I'm assuming means I'm the 3,583rd person to register so far, here on the eve of the first tournament.

I call Nolan again, and he tells me to meet him in the hallway that forks off just to the left of the registration desk, outside the Amazon Room. Standing at the mouth of the hall is a statuesque blond in a red miniskirt and a bustier hawking the official World Series of Poker program, which used to be given away but is now just another cash-making opportunity. Behind her down the corridor is a row of booths on either side. Here, among other things, you can buy WSOP T-shirts, get a shiatsu chair massage, sign up for a subscription to *CardPlayer* magazine, or sample a Havana Honeys cigar proffered by a scantily clad model in fishnet stockings. The marketing of poker paraphernalia reminds me of what happened with rock concerts in the 1960s and the U.S. Tennis Open when it moved from Forest Hills to Flushing Meadows in the 1970s.

Nolan comes up behind me while I'm looking at a video interview with Phil Hellmuth on the monitor in the *CardPlayer* booth.

"Don't spend this all in one place."

I turn around and he's standing there in a snappy blue pin-striped business suit with a big grin on his ruddy, hirsute, friendly bear face. He's holding out a wad of cash for me that's the size of a roll of Charmin. There are few public places other than a Las Vegas casino where you would feel comfortable making a handoff of fifteen thousand in cash this way, but here in this crowded corridor at the Rio nobody bats an eye. I riffle the paper without counting, then shove the whole massive wad into the pocket of my jeans. It creates a bulge that would make Dirk Diggler envious. One of the Havana Honeys winks at me as we walk by. Or maybe that is just my imagination. The sad thing is that I will not be endowed this way very long.

* . * . *

As soon as Nolan and I part ways, after promising to find time some-where in the next few weeks to get a meal together, I head into the Ama-zon Room through a set of double doors and take my place on another long line that snakes around by the gated windows of the cashier's cage. The Rio has transformed a convention space the size of a football field into what must be the world's largest card room. Stretching out before me in this cavernous airline hangar are row upon row of poker tables, as far as the eye can see; 200 tables, to be exact, with numbered signs hang-ing from globed white lights that are suspended from a tubular grid at-tached to the ceiling. The names of various corporate sponsors are also suspended from the grid, plastic pennants advertising Knob Creek bourbon, Honeywell, and Milwaukee's Best Light.

Nicky comes up and nudges me. "You get your money?"

I tap the bulge in my pocket.

"I've been trying to get in touch with this friend of Betsy's who's supposedly hooking me up with a backer. I don't know what's going on with it, though."

Last year, Nicky made a tidy profit for a backer who put him into a bunch of supers and a number of tournaments. A lot of people sell off pieces of themselves. It's become a common practice. In fact, last year's winner, Greg Raymer, wound up paying multiple backers $2.4 million of his $5 million purse, and Chris Moneymaker paid out probably half of his $2.5 million.

"Look around," I say to Nicky. "Can you believe what's happened? None of these people were even playing poker two years ago."

"Dude, you know what the worst part is? That two smart, enterpris-ing guys like us haven't been able to capitalize."

The crazy thing is that in 2001, Nicky and I actually sat down and wrote a proposal for a poker TV show called *Final Table* that would use lipstick cameras to show the players' hole cards. Nicky had seen tapes of the BBC show *Tuesday Night Poker* that used the technique and was certain that it would translate to American television. I agreed with him. So we wrote up a proposal, used whatever Hollywood contacts we had, set up a bunch of meetings, and then suffered one turndown after another. The response was pretty much the same. None of the TV execs "got it."

At the same time we were pitching our show, Steve Lipscomb and Lyle Berman were getting ready to launch the World Poker Tour without even having a network behind them. When the Travel Channel decided to pick their show up, we thought that killed us. Little did we know that over the next couple of years, every network and its brother would air a copycat version. The problem was that they didn't need us then. Our idea was no longer original, so they weren't even stealing; they were just doing what they do, lifting the tried-and-true concept of another show. For me and Nicky, it was like sitting at the table with the world's biggest sucker and watching everyone else get some of his money while we got none of it. That's what it felt like.

Of course, all of this, my reporting of this, is just another bad beat story. Poker breeds bad beat stories. But at least making some money off the boom would have taken away some of the sting of seeing the game we love mainstreamed, seeing its special aura of mystery and romance turned into just another product by the corporate marketing money machine.

Nicky goes back to his game, and I finally reach the cashier's window after another forty-five-minute wait. I pass my registration card under the metal grille, telling the pretty Asian cashier, whose name, according to her Harrah's badge, is Susie, that I want to buy into both the Main Event and tomorrow's $1,500 no-limit. She types my request into her computer, which spits out two postcard-size entry stubs, and tells me

I owe her $11,500. I extract the wad from my pocket, which deflates immediately, like a collapsed lung. Since I know that the wad is $15,000, I simply count off thirty-five bills and hand her what's left.

The act causes me physical pain. One moment I have fifteen grand in my hand, and the next it's all but gone; in its place are a couple of very expensive lottery tickets. One of them is for event 2, tomorrow, June 3 (event 1, which is taking place at this moment on the far side of the room, is the employees' tournament), and the other is for event 42, the Big One, on July 8. Oh, yeah, and I also have two $10 food vouchers, Harrah's idea of giving a little back to the players, who by the end of the next six weeks will have paid them nearly $8 million in entry fees.

But I'm in. I've got a seat in the Big One for the second time in my life. I didn't win it on the Internet, the way 96 percent of the field will. I paid for it in cash, the same way the big boys did in the old days.

3

A Thin Slice of Nothing

Unfortunately, there's another way to look at the transaction: Less than three hours after stepping off a plane, I am down $11,500 without having played a single hand of poker.

When I call Alice to tell her that I've landed and already miss her, I do not mention this demoralizing interpretation of my trip to date. I just tell her that I've got my seat already, and that I'm happy to have that bit of anxiety quelled.

She is, at this point, not much interested, anyway. Back in New York there are things like bridal showers and invitations to worry about. She needs my guest list so she can get a head count. "I need you to make some decisions," she says.

"I will."

"I know you don't want to think about it, but I need to know."

"I know."

"Please don't make this into a thing where I have to keep bugging you."

"I won't."

I meet Nicky over at the Palms for a late dinner. I first go up to his room, which is night and day from my room. Not bigger, just much nicer, with luxurious linens and hip modern furnishings that are the polar opposite of the tacky, no-frills economy-motel trappings of the Gold Coast.

"You really ought to try and get a room here when Alice comes to town," he says.

I have mentioned to him that she is going to fly out for three days near the end of the month, after which I'll fly back to New York with her for several days so I can be around for the filming of a television pilot I wrote.* Until this moment, I haven't really thought about finding a swankier hotel for her visit. But he's right, of course. It's a strategic move.

"I just hope I'll have the money," I say. The pain of coughing up the nearly twelve grand is still with me.

"Forget the money, dude. Make the reservation now. Put it on your credit card. It may already be too late to get something here. But if so, take her somewhere else. You can't stay at the Gold Coast."

"I hear you."

"Just bite the bullet."

"I'm agreeing with you."

---

* Called *Nicky's Game* (and, yes, partially inspired by Nicky Dileo), it's a project that came together quickly and unexpectedly after my friend Matthew Strauss called me at the beginning of May and told me that if I could quickly create a story about underground poker in New York, he and his partners at LaSalleHolland, a film management company, had a producer willing to pony up some cash to film it. I wrote a draft in a week for virtually no money, and Matt was now back in New York casting for a shoot that was scheduled to run June 24–28. John Ventimiglia, who plays Artie Bucco on *The Sopranos*, had agreed to play Nicky; and Burt Young, probably best known as Paulie, Sylvester Stallone's brother in the *Rocky* movies, had signed on to play Nicky's father. From a financial standpoint, I looked at the pilot as one more long-shot lottery ticket. But I wasn't thinking about the money. I had written a number of scripts for money and none of them had ever been filmed. This one was going to be filmed.

It is funny, in a way, to be getting this kind of advice from Nicky. He is hardly a poster boy for the model husband. But by necessity he has learned some useful tricks to compensate for his deficiencies, and sharing this hard-won knowledge with me probably makes him feel a little better about the things for which he is compensating.

No matter how you slice it, though, we are here in Vegas, away from his wife and my wife-to-be; and although it is useful for everyone involved to believe that we are here working, we are not tractor salesmen and this is not Iowa.

Downstairs in the Blue Agave restaurant, we take seats at the bar and order drinks and look at menus. There is a lot of bare young flesh squeezed into shiny dresses wandering around.

"What did I tell you about this place?" Nicky says.

There are two women sitting to our immediate right. They have drinks and a plate of half-finished fried shrimp, and they are alone. Nicky leans over and says something to one of them.

"Excuse me?" she says.

"I said, are you going to finish those shrimp?"

The two girls look at each other and laugh.

"Nick, what the fuck are you doing, man?" I hiss at him.

"I'm just fucking around," he says. "And I'm starving." He turns to the girls again. "You don't mind, do you?"

The girl closest to him shrugs.

He picks up one of the shrimp, dips it into what appears to be an aioli sauce, and chomps on it. "Not too bad. What is it, coconut?"

And with that, he is talking to them.

To my dismay, they talk back. Without a graceful way out, I soon become part of it. Even in the days when I would have been open to something like this, I would have known that this particular evening was not going to lead anywhere. Nick knows, too. He's just fucking around, as he says. When the amusement factor wears thin, I take advantage of a break in the conversation to ask Nicky a question about the backer he was supposed to hook up with earlier.

"I don't know what's going on with it," he says. "The guy is just jerking me around."

Since I'm not familiar with the backstory, he fills me in. It seems that there is this friend of a friend of Betsy's, a big Vegas sports bettor, who's heard that Nicky's a good player. "The guy talks big. He says he'll buy me into twenty thousand dollars worth of events, including the main event. But when it comes down to actually giving me the money, he starts acting cute. Who needs it? It's not worth it to me to prostrate myself to try and convince this guy I'm worthy."

"What are you going to do if he doesn't come through?"

"My bankroll's down to about sixteen dimes. Em and I have had a lot of expenses, and I've been on a cold streak. What do you think I'm going to do?"

"Play?"

"I'm here, aren't I? It'd be nice not to be taking the risk, though."

In the five minutes that we spend ignoring the two girls, a couple of guys from the opposite side of the bar get up and move in on them. *Thank the Lord.*

"I'm gonna call it a night," I say, determined to make my getaway before something else happens. "I'm still on New York time. I want to be rested for tomorrow's event."

"Why don't you come back here in the morning before the tournament?" Nick says. "There's a good breakfast place upstairs with an outdoor patio. Afterward, I'll drive you over to the Rio."

We agree on a time, and I tell him I'll call when I'm leaving.

Back in my room, I get into bed, douse the lights, and turn on the television. The addict in me is thrilled to have these next six weeks to indulge my tube craving. I flip around for a while and—what a shocker—come upon poker, ESPN rebroadcasting last year's WSOP finale. It's near the climax, and even though I know what happens, I stay up watching anyway. Down to head's up play, David Williams, a young African-American and virtual unknown, bets $300,000 pre-flop with A-4 offsuit; and Greg "Fossilman" Raymer, a rotund patent attorney, who with $17 million in chips is about a 2-1 chip leader, calls, holding pocket eights. The flop comes 4-2-5 with two diamonds, and Raymer check-raises Williams's bet of $500,000 another $1.1 million—which Williams instantly calls. It's hard to imagine what Williams is thinking here. He's got a pair of fours and a gutshot straight draw. If he thinks his fours are good, he should probably reraise and commit to the hand right here. More likely he's hoping his call will slow Raymer down. When a second 2 falls on the turn, Raymer bets another $2.5 million, and again Williams calls in a flash. Okay. Let's review. Williams's call of the reraise on the flop didn't slow down Raymer. If that had been his hope, he now has to think that Raymer may actually have him beat. While the 2 on the turn doesn't hurt Williams's hand, it doesn't help it either. So what's he thinking when he calls? *Maybe I'll hit an ace or a three on the river? Maybe my call will stop Raymer from betting the river?* As I say, it's easy to second-guess when you're watching on television and you see what both players are holding. But still. Now comes the final card of the tournament. A third deuce on the river. Raymer, without too much consideration, moves in.

Williams, who has twice called, hoping maybe his pair of fours is good, hoping that his calls would have slowed Raymer down, sees a river card that doesn't appreciably change things. Either he was good the whole time or he was behind the whole time. *The problem is that he never made a decision.* At a certain point, in poker and in life, you have to make decisions. You have to commit. He played this hand with utter passivity. Watching now, it's easy to be critical of Williams's play, particularly of his all-in call on the river, but I wonder what would have been his best strategic move as the hand progressed. Could he have gotten

Raymer to fold at any point? Should he himself have folded at any point? Obviously, knowing what they both had, he should have, but without knowing, what should he have done? What would I have done?

I close my eyes for a moment pondering it. Suddenly, I am head's up at the final table, and my opponent has put a clock on me. There are only seconds left to make my decision. Then the timer is going off. What am I going to do?

The ringing continues, and I suddenly become aware that it is a phone. I am not at the final table. I am in my room at the Gold Coast. It's my wake-up call. I reach out toward the night table in the flickering light of the television, groping for the receiver. When I press it to my ear, I hear a recorded voice. The television is sounding the *duhduh duh, duhduh duh* theme from a repeat of last night's *SportsCenter*. And that's when it comes to me: Williams should have moved in when Raymer check-raised him on the flop. That was his only chance to move Raymer off the hand. *Make a read and go with it. Be decisive. And when in doubt, be aggressive, always be aggressive.*

I lie in bed for a while watching *SportsCenter*. It's mostly baseball and the NBA playoffs. Eventually, I get up and go through my ablutions, which include shaking up a powdered wheatgrass drink and downing a bunch of vitamins and supplements that I've been taking to combat sinusitis and a migraine.

I meet Nicky on the patio of the 24-7 Cafe, over the Palm's pool, from which we have a prime view of bikini-clad twenty-year-olds baking in the morning heat. We wash down platefuls of bacon and eggs with big glasses of fresh orange juice, then collect his bags from his room to take over to Betsy's suite (she's decided she's leaving), driving to the Rio by Nicky's circuitous back-road route.

Betsy's suite is on the eighteenth floor. We wheel and carry Nicky's belongings down the hall and knock on the door of room 1845. A minute goes by. Nicky knocks again. Another thirty seconds pass. Finally the door opens. Betsy's boyfriend, Peter, a fast-talking Queens guy, greets us, saying, "Come in, come in." We follow, walking into near darkness. The drapes are closed. The only source of light comes from one of the reading lamps over the bed. Betsy is in the bed, propped up like a queen, a sleep mask pushed back on her forehead. She's holding a Big Gulp in one hand, a giant, sweating paper cup of soda and ice, sipping it through a straw. Her dyed blond hair is loose and wild. Diamond rings flash on her fingers. There are clothes and magazines strewn everywhere. She tells us to sit. I'm anxious to leave, but Nicky takes a seat on a couch that faces her, and I realize that it will be rude if I don't join him. As the two of us sit there, Betsy remains in bed, holding court, sipping her Big Gulp, while Peter bops around the room, plucking items of clothing off the floor. After ten minutes of poker gossip, I look at my watch and say, "I think we'd better go. The tournament starts in twenty minutes." And with that we make our getaway.

"That was very strange," I say to Nicky, as we head for the elevator.

He shrugs. "It's Betsy."

In the hall leading to the Amazon Room, yesterday's crowds are dwarfed by the mad crush of those who have descended for today's tournament. What's incredible to me is how few of the players I recognize. There was a period of several years when I would show up at a poker tournament and recognize at least two-thirds of the players from the year before, or the year before that. Now there is no year before. A lot of these players weren't even playing poker a year ago; they were watching it on television. Or if they were playing, it was on the Internet, and this is their first time in a brick-and-mortar casino.

Nicky and I shoulder our way through the noisy, smoke-filled hallway, running into Adam Schoenfeld, whom we both know from New York. Adam is slender and thirtyish, with a newly grown mustache and

The Amazon Room in full swing.

goatee. The expression on his long, narrow face typically alternates between a kind of mournful amusement and ironic detachment. He could be the model for the Hugh Grant character in the movie *About a Boy*. He's funny, charming, rich (he made millions during the Internet boom of the '90s), and steadfast in his belief that every man is an island and should act accordingly. Since he got bitten by the poker bug several years ago, he has devoted himself to becoming both a top-notch player and a poker celebrity. His success in becoming the latter has been more notable thus far: He wrote a column for *CardPlayer* for a while from the perspective of a neophyte, risking humiliation by keeping a public record of his wins and losses as he learned the game, and he also conducted a fairly public romance with top woman pro Evelyn Ng, who had previously been Daniel Negreanu's girlfriend. But I shouldn't minimize his improvement at the poker table. He has had numerous tournament cashes and made it to the television table of a World Poker Tour event (something neither Nicky nor I have done), winning $170,000 before having a brain freeze and blowing off all his chips on a stone-cold bluff.

It's a quarter to twelve, and the tournament starts at noon. I want to locate my table, number 154, seat 9, so that I'm not running around looking for it at the last minute. Entering the Amazon Room, I have to catch my breath. I have never seen so many packed poker tables in one room. The final count will be 2,305 players, forcing us to play eleven per table with another 105 alternates who will get seats as players bust out. In terms of numbers, this is the biggest field in WSOP history, second only to last year's final event.

Just before Nicky, Adam, and I head off in separate directions to find our tables, we agree to trade 2 percent of each other, or in the vernacular, "take a piece of each other." Trading pieces is a common practice among tournament players, a way to hedge one's bets, and it goes hand in hand with backing arrangements, where players may actually sell significant pieces of themselves to reduce their risk.

For me, there is another, much more important element to these trades: The sense of camaraderie I feel with my poker friends is an enormous part of the experience of spending time at a tournament. It is, I imagine, how Olympic boxers must feel when they travel to far-off places as a team. Even though you are engaged in a solitary quest, you feel love and solidarity for the other members of your tribe. You pull for them, and their success makes you feel stronger because it makes your own seem more possible. If they can do it, you can do it. You may have only a couple of percent of them, but it intensifies your stake in them, and lets you literally share in their victories. In this case, if Adam or Nicky wins any money, I'll get 2 percent of it, and if I win any money they'll get 2 percent.

Of course not all players are honorable. I've heard stories of players not paying their investors or the players with whom they've traded pieces, and also of cases where, à la *The Producers,* a player has sold more than 100 percent of himself and then had to lose in order to reap a

profit. In that vein, I've even heard about one name player who tried unsuccessfully to dump chips, and then just said to hell with it, and went
on to win the tournament even though he knew he was pieced out for
more than 100 percent.

Table 154 is in the far back corner of the room, a definite handicap
for older players or those with weak bladders. The one small bathroom
is a good three-minute sprint from here, and during the ten-minute
breaks that occur every couple of hours, there will be a mad rush for the
restrooms and then a long line. Beyond that, there is an obstructed view
of the two giant hanging screens that display the time left in each round,
the amount of the blinds, the number of players left, and other such useful information—though as it turns out, this is of little consequence,
as the screens are actually able to supply only the most basic and rudi-
mentary information. According to one rumor making the rounds, the
programmer who invented the software and was supposed to run it
asked Harrah's for a free room during his stay and was turned down. As
a result, nobody on Harrah's staff knows how to operate its more
sophisticated functions.

We're waiting for play to start when I see Shane and wave him over.
He's searching for his table, and he looks a little out of it. Turns out that
he flew in yesterday and didn't get much sleep last night. Something
about a party next door to the apartment that he and another young
Internet player are renting together. Looking at him, I don't give him
much of a shot, but that doesn't stop me from trading a couple of points
with him, too.

As Shane wanders off, I glance around the table, sizing up my competition. You hear players talk all the time about what kind of table they
drew. "Not a single name. They're all nobodies or online players." Or,
"Christ, you cannot believe the table I'm at. I've got Phil Ivey and Men
'The Master' on my left, and Erik Seidel and Johnny Chan on my right."

At table 154, the only player I recognize is Steve Zolotow, better
known in gambling circles as "Stevie Zee," a wiry, balding guy with a Fu

Manchu mustache and a dry, sardonic wit. The son of the late Maurice Zolotow, a writer who had the dubious distinction of having created the modern celebrity bio (he was the answer to the Trivial Pursuit question "What is the name of Marilyn Monroe's first biographer?"), Zee is, among other things, one of the most respected sports bettors in the country. His knack for winning basketball and football games in the last minute is so uncanny that it has become known as the Zee Factor. One year, according to a bookie I know, he won over 75 percent of the games he played, a phenomenal rate, earning himself somewhere in the neighborhood of $10 million (enough to buy a palatial Las Vegas estate of the sort usually associated with movie and recording stars). He's one of a number of old-school poker players who made their bones at New York's Mayfair Club, and although he hasn't quite achieved the same level of success or fame as some of the Mayfair alumni (whose ranks include Dan Harrington, Erik Seidel, Howard Lederer, Jason Lester, and Noli Francisco), he is still considered a top-rank professional.

Every other player at my table is unknown to me, as doubtless I am to them. As I say, this used to be a good thing. Back when I first started playing tournament poker in the early 1990s, if you didn't recognize a player, you could make the assumption that he lacked experience, and beyond that probably wasn't very good. In those days, the only way to get real tournament experience was by playing in the dozen or so major events in this country and in Europe, or by playing in the small buy-in daily tournaments that many casinos ran (and still run). By and large, when someone showed up at a major, if you hadn't encountered him anywhere before, such assumptions about him would be accurate. No longer. Now a player may have played hundreds or even thousands of tournaments online by the time he decides to step out of the virtual shadows and into the brick-and-mortar world. It's like one of those old martial arts movies where the hero has been perfecting his art for years in seclusion, and now he shows up at a competition where nobody knows him or takes him seriously and he winds up kicking everyone's unsuspecting ass.

What I am trying to say is that my edge at a tableful of strangers used to be much bigger. I could reliably count on at least two or three of them being transparently inferior. This one overvalued top pair; that one was tight-weak and could be pushed off a hand; this one didn't raise enough to protect against draws; that one raised too much with medium-sized pocket pairs. Somewhere along the way they would make a glaringly obvious mistake, and I would be able to take advantage.

These days such gifts are rarer. Terrible players still exist, but there are proportionally fewer of them and it has become harder to determine who they are. The mere fact that I have never seen a player before is no longer a reliable clue. I must make decisions based on subtler and less obvious signals.

This process of sizing up something or someone on the basis of very little is what Malcolm Gladwell calls "thin-slicing" in his book *Blink,* which someone gave me recently, assuming, correctly, that I would be interested in a work that examines pattern recognition and intuitive decision making. As Gladwell outlines it, thin-slicing is not about analytical thinking but rather about the instantaneous reaction to subliminal clues that results in what we call "snap decisions," or what he describes as "knowing without knowing."

As an example he describes an incident in which the Getty Museum purchased, in 1983, an incredibly rare Greek statue dating back to 600 B.C. It was not an impulse purchase. Before committing to buy it, the Getty spent many months carefully inspecting the statue's documentation and verifying its provenance. Additionally, the museum hired a respected University of California geologist to analyze the marble to see if it was really as old as it was supposed to be. Only after fourteen months of careful deliberation did the Getty go ahead with the purchase. In the fall of 1986, the statue went on display in the museum for the first time. *The New York Times* covered the unveiling on the front page and deemed it one of the events of the season. At the Getty, there were congratulations all around.

What followed, however, was not quite so glorious. First one outside expert, then another, seeing the statue for the first time, experienced an immediate and strong feeling that something was amiss. The word that popped into the head of Thomas Hoving, the former director of the Metropolitan Museum of Art in New York, upon seeing the statue for the first time was "fresh"—not a particularly reassuring word for what was said to be a 2,000-year-old statue. Another expert felt cold. Another one felt a wave of "intuitive repulsion."

Initially, the Getty stood by its painstaking assessment of its purchase; but over time, as evidence mounted that both the seller and the statue were fraudulent, the Getty was forced to admit that a mistake had been made. And so we are left with a seemingly baffling question: How were a number of experts able to understand in an instant what the Getty and its consultants could not process in fourteen months? The answer, Gladwell tells us, is that these particular experts had perfected the art of thin-slicing. They were able to instantaneously filter out the few factors that really count from an overwhelming number of other variables. In fact, Gladwell maintains, if mastered, the art of thin-slicing is actually a much more effective decision-making tool than a careful, deliberate, and thorough analysis of mountains of information.

I read the book with great interest, as thin-slicing seemed directly applicable to poker, and I hoped that I might learn how to improve my thin-slicing skills. Unfortunately, *Blink* was not particularly illuminating in that regard. It identified the phenomenon and gave anecdotal examples, but overall left me feeling, as John Malcovich puts it in *Rounders,* "extremely unsatisfied." Where it was most useful was in reminding me to trust my instincts. It is easy to overthink things at the poker table or focus on the wrong details. As in life, there is a tendency to hear not just one voice but several different voices in your head, telling you what to do. *Call. Think of all the money you'll have if you're right.* Or,

Fold. Better to play it safe here. Or, *The pot is giving you two to one, and your opponent could be bluffing.*

Sometimes it is hard, with so many disparate and conflicting voices, to screen out all but the most important one, the one that *just knows* what is the right thing to do. I have been in some sessions and some tournaments where I have achieved a Zen-like communion with that voice, where my decisions have been dictated not by fear or desire or prudence but rather by something that I can't even articulate but that comes through in simple declarative sentences: *I'm beat. I'm ahead. He's got nothing. He wants me to fold. He wants me to call.*

This is the state I want to be in now, as the dealer swivels in his seat and spins out the first hand of the tournament. Each of the players at my table has $1,500 in tournament chips, which is dollar-for-dollar what we have paid to enter. The blinds begin at $25-$25* and increase at one-

---

* Perhaps this is the time to explain, for the uninitiated, how Texas Hold'em is played. It's a relatively simple game in its mechanics. Each player is dealt two hole cards, facedown, which he will ultimately use, in conjunction with the five community cards that are dealt faceup in the middle of the table, to form his best five-card poker hand. To instigate action, there are blinds, forced bets from the first two players to the left of the dealer that create a pot before the cards are even dealt. The dealer in most casinos is supplied by the house, and a plastic disk, called the button, is rotated clockwise around the table to signify the player who would have been the dealer for that particular hand in a self-dealt game. The player directly to the left of the dealer, the small blind, has to pay a portion, usually half, of the opening bet, while the player to his left, the big blind, must post the full opening bet (in tournament poker, the blinds and antes are increased at regular intervals, forcing players to risk larger and larger portions of their stack without knowing their cards). After two cards are dealt to each player, the action falls on the player to the left of the big blind, who must either fold, call (limp in), or raise. When the action comes back around to the blinds, they then have an option to call, fold, or raise (in the case of the small blind), or check, fold, or raise (in the case of the big blind). When the betting is completed, the dealer turns three cards faceup in the center of the table (the flop), after which there is another round of betting. A fourth faceup card, called the turn or fourth street, is then dealt, followed by a third round of betting. One last up card is dealt, the river or fifth street, which is followed by a final round of betting, after which the remaining players show down their hands, with the pot being awarded to the best five-card hand.

hour intervals. As always, the first few hands are nerve-racking. I'm happy not to find anything playable. J-6. *Muck.* K-8. *Muck.* 5-3. *Muck.* Larry Phillips in his excellent little book, *The Tao of Poker,* says that one can derive great strength from folding, and it's true. His number one rule (out of 285) is not to dig yourself a hole when you first sit down. "Start slow," he writes. "Observe for a while." It's like just keeping the ball in play in tennis while you develop a sense of the court and your opponent and the rhythm of the game. Once you have that, you can begin to go for your shots, to try and put a little pace on the ball.

After two orbits, it seems clear to me that everyone at the table is playing tight, that there are no obvious maniacs. On the button, with 8-10 suited, I make it $125 to go after a couple of players limp from middle position. I get one caller, which is one more than I was hoping to get. On a flop of 7-3-K, my opponent, a skinny geek in a PartyPoker hat, checks, and I make what Dan Harrington and Bill Robertie refer to in their latest book, *Harrington on Hold 'em,* Volume 2, as a "continuation bet" of $225.

Harrington, who is known on the circuit as "Action Dan," an ironic reference to his image as a "tight" player, has won a number of major no-limit poker tournaments, including the 1995 WSOP Main Event. He has also reached the final table three other times, most recently in 2003 and 2004. His game-theory skills, which have helped him become a chess master and world-class backgammon player, make him a kind of poker Obi Wan Kenobi; and *Harrington on Hold 'em* and its sequel, Volume 2, are probably the most important instructional books to hit the poker world since Brunson's *Super/System.* To make what Harrington defines as a continuation bet, three conditions are required: "1. The player making the bet was the betting leader before the flop; 2. After the flop, no other bets have yet been made; 3. The player making the bet missed the flop. Under these circumstances," he writes, "the pre-flop betting leader can consider making a continuation bet, even though the flop didn't help him." The purpose of the bet, obviously, is to pick up the pot even though you don't have a hand, on the basis of the power you represented with your initial bet. "Since you indicated strength before the flop, your opponent probably assumed you had a better hand than he did, and if he missed the flop and you now bet, it would be natural for him to lay down his hand."

When I make my continuation bet, I'm indicating that I have a king with an ace or queen kicker, and my opponent, even if he has a king with a jack kicker, would be forced to make an uncomfortable call.

He folds.

Score one for the good guys. After a couple more orbits, I've chipped up to about $2,000, when I get involved in a hand with Steve Zee. Oddly, since he is probably the best player at the table, I am not unhappy. Zee is the one player I can count on not to do something stupid or off-the-wall; at this stage of the tournament that is precisely what scares me most about my other opponents—they might.

Zee's still got close to his starting stack, maybe $1,400, and from late-middle position raises the pot the standard three-times-the-blind bring-in of seventy-five dollars. It's folded back around to me on the little blind, and I look down and find a pretty A-Q of spades.

"I raise," I say, and pluck two black $100 chips off my stack, adding them to the green twenty-five-dollar chip that's already in front of my cards.

Steve Zee arches an eyebrow and studies me. My heart is racing. Is he going to reraise? If he does, I'll have to fold. He shuffles his chips for an excruciating few seconds, then tosses in two black chips. A call.

The dealer knocks the table, burns a card, and spreads the flop. An ace, along with the three and six of spades. I've made top pair with a queen kicker. Even better than that (as if that's not good enough), the two spades on board, combined with the two in my hand, give me the nut flush draw.

This is a huge flop but also a somewhat dangerous one. If I make a bet and Zee reraises, it'll be pretty clear that he's either flopped a set, or, more likely, has ace-king. But at that point, even if I'm right and he does have either of those two hands, I'll be forced to call. I'll still have a lot of "outs"* to improve and win, and the money odds (certainly in the event that he has ace-king) will make a call obligatory. On the other hand, a check might induce a bet from a hand like kings, queens, jacks, tens, or nines that he would otherwise probably fold to a bet.

Although that would be a good play, maybe even the best, I decide instead to make what looks like a defensive bet, as if *I* have pocket kings or queens but I'm afraid of the ace and I'm testing the waters. Two hundred seems like the right amount.

Zee looks as if he wants to raise me, but instead he just calls. What could that mean?

My stomach is starting to tighten as the dealer thumps and deals the turn card. I'm already considering my next move, what I'll do if I don't improve, when the best possible card arrives: the nine of spades. Suddenly I've gone from a guy who might be in trouble to a guy with the nuts. And Zee doesn't have a clue. If anything, from the way the hand has unfolded, it seems more likely that he's the one on a flush draw. So that's how I play it. As if I'm thinking he might have hit the flush and I'm afraid. I rap my knuckle on the felt. Check.

---

* An out is any card left in the deck that will improve your hand, turning it from a loser into a winner. In this particular hand, if my opponent has ace-king, there are twelve cards left in the deck that will win the hand for me, and I have two shots at getting them, one on the turn, one on the river. The twelve cards or "outs" that I have are the nine remaining spades and the three remaining queens. Thus, I have what is called twelve outs twice, or twenty-four chances out of the remaining forty-five cards in the deck with which to win. Twelve outs with two cards will, without getting into the math of it, improve roughly 45 percent of the time. Thirteen outs will improve 48.1 percent of the time. And fourteen outs will improve 51.2 percent of the time, making your hand a slight favorite.

From Zee's perspective, the time has come to protect what he thinks is the best hand. It's possible I have a spade, and he certainly doesn't want to make it cheap for me to see the river. He bets $500.

"I'm all in," I say.

This surprises him—and not in a good way. Really the only time that you want to hear an opponent say "all in" is when you know you're ahead. At this point Zee's got only $425 left. He knows he should fold, but there's too much in the pot. His voice is resigned as he says, "Call."

We flip over the cards. The bad news for him is confirmed. He's drawing dead with his ace-king. "Sorry, Zee," I say, as he gathers his things and stands up. The final, now irrelevant, card is dealt. I am fully aware that I got lucky on the turn. I could just as easily have lost the bulk of my stack if a spade hadn't come. But I also know that it is from such luck that a tournament is won. I'll need a lot more before the day is over.

By the time the second round is ticking down at 2:15 p.m., I've worked my stack up to a little over $6,000. I make a mad dash for the men's room, which is halfway down the hall outside the Amazon Room. Others with the same idea are hurrying along with me. There's already a line stretching out the door and into the hall by the time we get there, but it's manageable. Behind me and in front of me all the talk is of misfortune and narrow escapes, a trading of vital statistics. *"I'm at thirty-five hundred. Where you at?" "Four thousand, but I'd have twice that if this donkey hadn't sucked out on the river against me."*

On the way back to the poker room, in Trinket Alley, I grab a cheeseburger sheathed in a tinfoil bag. It costs nearly seven bucks and tastes like warm cardboard. Another example of Harrah's largesse. Back at my table, the dealer sits on guard, but none of the other players have returned. While I'm loitering, Englishman Harry Demetriou, a middle-aged retired clinical scientist, comes over, carrying a hefty rack of chips, about $10,000 worth by my estimate.

"They keep moving me," he says.

"It doesn't seem to have hampered you much," I say.

I've seen Demetriou on television a couple of times, and I tell him I admire his comportment. He never ruffles and always conducts himself like a gentleman.

"I've only been playing for three years," he says. "I've been very lucky."

"I'm guessing it's not all been luck."

He ducks his head modestly.

When all the players have returned from the break, Johnny Grooms, the tournament director, announces that because of the size of the field the decision has been made to expand the tournament from two days to three. A murmur of approval spreads through the room.

No sooner have we resumed play than I make my first misstep. With the blinds at $50-$100, I make it $300 to go from late position holding the 5-3 of spades. A loose Asian player, recently arrived at the table, calls from the big blind.

The flop is A-2-6 rainbow. He checks, and I bet $450, representing a big ace. Obviously, I'm hoping to take the pot down right here, so I'm not thrilled when he calls. My guess is that he has some kind of weak ace, A-7, A-3, A-4, in that neighborhood, or some kind of pair, eights or lower. The problem I'm faced with is that I know that he's likely to call any bet I make on the turn. One of the biggest mistakes many players make in tournaments is to try and bluff players who can't be bluffed. I've learned my lessons the hard way and done my share of Phil Hellmuth impersonations in the aftermath: *"You called off all your chips with middle pair?"*

The thing is, there's no sense in getting mad at people who play badly. Just don't try to bluff them.

On the turn, the dealer flips up a nine of spades that gives me a flush draw in addition to my gutshot straight draw. Against a different opponent, I'd probably bet again to try and pick up the pot. Not against this guy. When he checks, I check back. The river jack unfortunately does not fill either of my draws. Once again, the Asian Action Player checks. Now, I'm in a quandary. I've got five high. The only way I can win here is by betting. There's $1,500 in the pot. Do I check and just concede? Or do I bet and hope that I'm wrong about his weak ace or small pair and his stubborn refusal to fold? Maybe he was on a draw, too.

I decide to bet $600, thinking that he might even fold a small pair to that bet. Unfortunately, he's got A-4 and calls.

And just like that, I'm down to $4,650.

I'm still hovering around that mark when the round comes to an end. The blinds are still $100-$200 but now the antes kick in. Twenty-five per man. Since we're playing ten-handed, that now means that there's an extra $225 in each pot before a card is dealt. Interestingly, the customary first raise stays the same, a three-times-the-big-blind bet of $600.

Stuey Ungar often said that not long after the antes kicked in during the WSOP, he would have all the $25 chips on the table and then would have to make change for the other players. What he really meant was that he recognized a golden opportunity when it came up. While the perception had not changed among most players, Stuey understood that for the same $600 opening bet that minutes before might have netted you a pot of $300, you could now collect $525, a significantly better return on your money. So he'd get much more aggressive, raise a lot more, and take advantage. Even if somebody reraised him and he had to muck, he could make up the lost $600 by raising again the next hand. And sometimes when he got reraised, he'd have something, and then he was likely to win a really big hand.

Maybe it's because I've just finished writing a book about him and his ideas have rubbed off on me, or maybe it's just because the idea makes sense, but I try adopting the same strategy. By the end of the round, I have $7,600 and most of the green chips on the table.

Fifteen minutes into the next round, more than five hours after we started, I'm up to $8,500, and a glance at one of the big hanging screens reveals that we are down to 800 players. That means that we've lost nearly two-thirds of the field in a little over five hours. Eight hundred players is more than the starting field of the Main Event that I played back in 2001 (even if now it doesn't seem like that many bodies to get past). The truth is I need to get past only 600 more of them to make the money.

My hopes for doing that soon suffer a setback. My misfortune starts, as is so often the case, with a woman. Two women, actually. I look down in the hole and find two lovely queens staring back at me. This is the best hand I've seen all day, and my heart rate speeds up. When the action comes to me the cutoff position (last player to act before the button), in a thus-far unraised pot, I throw in the standard three-times-the-big-blind raise of $900.

The player to my immediate left, on the button, a clean-cut, handsome fellow in his early thirties, who has been nursing a short stack for a while, moves all-in for $3,600. Everyone folds, and the action comes back to me. It's a relatively easy call. There are five likely hands that he might be holding: aces, kings, ace-king, jacks, or tens. Of the five, I'm trailing two, dominating two, and a coin-flip proposition with the third. It's $2,500 to win the $4,950 already in the pot—or almost 2-1—so it's a virtual no-brainer.

"I call," I say.

We flip up our cards. He's got jacks. Though I can't help letting out a worried sigh, scarred from the many wounds I've received at the hands of the poker gods, it's also hard not to get ahead of myself. If I win this hand, in which I'm a 4-1 favorite, my stack will be up over $12,000. The average stack right now is $4,500. What this means is that I will be boss man at the table, a force to be reckoned with, and unless I screw up badly or get unlucky, a good bet to make the money.

My little daydream does not survive even the flop, as a jack falls, turning the tables as surely as day changes to night. My opponent, who apologizes to me the way I apologized to Steve Zee earlier (there are those of us—definitely a minority—who feel remorse when involved in an injustice, even one that benefits us), doubles up to over $7,000 while I'm reduced to $4,900. It's by no means a death blow, but it darkens my mood.

During the course of a tournament, these are the times that most test your character. If you are the sort of person to brood or fret over things you can't control—such as luck—then this is where you lose your shit. Psychologically, it's very difficult to adjust to a sudden swing from good fortune to bad. One moment you were on top of the world; in the next, a cruel turn of the deck changes everything. Even if you aren't in dire shape, it *feels* as if you are, or should be. And so you panic. You "tilt," in the parlance (an expression that comes from the world of pinball, where a too-violent shove of the machine causes everything to freeze up until your ball is down past the dead flippers and gone).

I don't exactly tilt after this hand, but something happens, and it isn't good. The very next deal, again in late position, I make it $900 with A-3 suited. But when the chip leader, who is on the button, makes it $2,000 more, I'm forced to fold (I'm not that far gone). Before I know it, my stack has dwindled to $2,300. Again, I take a firm grip on my psyche. *You're still alive. Don't give up.* Picking my spots carefully, I bluff my way back to $5,000 without showing a hand.

At 7:30 p.m., we take another break, and none too soon. I run to the piss line, winding up about midway down the hall with seventy or eighty people ahead of me. The last hour was frustrating as hell. From the point I worked my way back to five grand, I've been gradually blinded back down to $2,900. The good news is that there are only 428 of us left, 228 players away from the money. The bad news is that the blinds are about to go up to $200-$400 with a $50 ante, which means that each round is going to cost me $1,100 (which is also how much is in each pot to start). After one round, if I don't do anything, I'll be down to $1,800. To let myself be blinded off any lower than that will rob me completely of whatever dwindling leverage I might still have.

Dan Harrington and Bill Robertie explain this concept in Volume 2 of *Harrington on Hold 'em.* The first volume of the set came out prior to the WSOP; the second, which I have managed to get hold of early, is scheduled for release in the next couple of weeks. Having access to it ahead of publication is a bit like having the test questions to the exam the night before it's administered.

The truth is that players like Nicky and Mike May and myself, not to speak of the top name pros like Negreanu, Cloutier, Seidel, Ferguson, etc., wish Harrington had kept what he knows to himself. Most of what the book reveals are things that we ourselves either already knew intuitively or have broken down empirically. So what he is accomplishing, from our standpoint, in articulating these things, is enabling our competition to catch up on the cheap. (I realize that it's an act of hubris to include myself in the above-mentioned company, but what separates me from them is not, at least for the most part, a technical understanding of the game, but rather the kinds of subtle and intuitive talents that cannot be learned but are due to innate brilliance.) Perhaps the most useful (and therefore most annoying) revelation of Volume 2 of Harrington and Robertie is what they call the "theory of inflection points," which as they describe it is a strategy for proper play as "your stack decreases in relation to the blinds." Using italics for emphasis, they add, *"Be advised that playing correctly around inflection points is the single most important skill of no-limit hold 'em tournaments."* Apparently Harrington and Robertie have never heard the expression "Don't school the fish."

The analogy these coauthors use in underscoring the exact nature of an inflection point is that of a football game. "When the score is close and there is plenty of time remaining, a football coach has his whole range of offensive options available to him. . . . He's not in any way constrained by the clock." But as time runs down, if he's trailing in the game, his options become more and more limited. Eventually, as the seconds tick away, he gets to a point where he can't run, he can't pass up the middle, and by "the last few seconds, his choices are reduced to a single play—the Hail Mary bomb into the end zone."

Using a simple formula that they credit to the eccentric but brilliant backgammon and poker whiz Paul Magriel, Harrington and Robertie provide us with a way to gauge the changing inflection points. "The single most important number that governs your play toward the end of tournaments is M," they write, "which is simply *the ratio of your stack to the current total of blinds and antes.* This number is crucial, and you must develop a facility for calculating it quickly and easily at the table. You don't need to know it to two decimal places; a rough approximation will work just fine, but you need to know your M at all times."

They then give a couple of examples of M in a question-and-answer form: "Nearing the end of a major tournament. The blinds are now $100/$200, and the antes are $25. Nine players remain. Your stack is $1,600. What is your M?

"Answer: With nine players left, there are $225 in antes in addition to the blinds, so the total amount of the blinds and antes is $525 per hand. Your M is $1,600/$525, which is about 3."

The significance of these numbers is that by calculating and knowing your M in the latter stages of a tournament you can adjust your play properly. Harrington divides the M numbers into color zones. In the Green Zone you have 20 or more times the size of the starting pot. In the Yellow Zone you have 10–20 times the size of the pot. In the Orange Zone the range is 6–10 times. And in the Red Zone it's 1–5 times. As with the football coach, your options decrease as the time or money runs out. By the time you're in the Red Zone, your only move is to pick a hand (your starting requirements are now much lower) and move in with it. I won't get into all the other ways in which your tool kit is reduced as you move down in zones (buy the book!), but suffice it to say that you never want to get into what Harrington and Robertie call the Dead Zone, which is where your M falls below 1, or less than the size of the pot. This is when "you appear to be alive but you're not. You're a pokerwraith, not a player anymore but a gnat to be swatted. . . . You should never allow yourself to get in the Dead Zone by having your chips blinded away."

For this contribution to poker strategy alone, Harrington and Robertie should be knighted by the unenlightened and flogged by the rest of us. Intuitively, I have known and practiced the inflection-point theory for quite a while, but to have it articulated and codified in the way that they do gives me a slightly more precise method by which to execute it.

The first round after I get back from the break, I pay the blinds and antes for three hands; this means I'm $750 poorer. I have a measly $2,200 left—or 2M. It's become move-in time; I can't afford to pay the blinds again, so I'm looking for a hand where I can be first to act and thereby increase my chances of winning without getting called (the first few players to act immediately after me will be wary of a player *behind them* reraising).

My best opportunity comes when it's folded around to me in the cutoff* and I find K-Q offsuit, a truly excellent hand given that I was ready to move in with any two cards. Unfortunately, after I delicately place my chips in the pot, the little blind, who has me covered and then some, makes an easy call with A-Q, and whatever suspense is possible with a hand that's dominated is ended when an ace hits the flop.

I'm done.

As disappointed as I am by this long journey to nowhere, I shake the feeling off quickly. I played well, after all. I just got unlucky when

---

* The cutoff is the player directly to the right of the button.

my queens didn't hold up against jacks. I call Nicky to tell him I'm out. He's across the room, playing a mega satellite, which is a $1,000 buy-in event that they're running every night. For every ten entrants, they will award one seat into the Big One. I wander over, catching sight of his orange Index 5 cap* from a distance. He's at a table with Mike May, another New York player I first got to know at the now defunct Diamond Club.

"Aww," Mike says, his face scrunching up in sympathy when he sees me. "What are you doing here? You're supposed to be over there." Mike isn't wearing his usual Hawaiian shirt, and his once shoulder-length hair has been coiffed in a short fashionable 'do, but at least he's still sporting his trademark red Converse hightops.

"It doesn't seem fair, does it?"

"I mean, they should at least give you a Kewpie doll," he says. With his high forehead, horn-rims, and impish delivery, Mike reminds me a little of Dana Carvey from his *Saturday Night Live* days.

"What are they down to?" he asks.

"About four hundred."

"Any New Yorkers still left?"

"I think I was the last of us."

"They're paying two hundred?"

"Yeah."

---

* Adam Schoenfeld had a bunch of these caps made up after Nicky coined the phrase one day during a game. Adam was admiring a play somebody had made and Nicky said, "Yeah, that's Index Five."

Adam said, "Index Five?"

"It's a level of sophistication. There's Base One, Locus Two, Rubric Three, Matrix Four, and Index Five."

Adam said, "Really?"

Nicky said, "No, I just made it up, but it sounds good, doesn't it?"

Adam went nuts, thought it was brilliant, had the hats made up, and pretty soon there were all these New York poker players walking around wearing Index 5 caps.

He shakes his head. He knows. It's disappointing to get that close.

"You gonna play tomorrow?" Nicky asks.

"I wasn't planning to. What is it, the fifteen-hundred-dollar pot limit?"

"Yeah. It's gonna be a good event."

He's right. Pot limit is what we played in New York for years. It's got subtleties to it that you don't find in no-limit, mostly having to do with controlling the size of the pot, knowing how much to bet, and so on. Big pairs are much more vulnerable than they are in no-limit, and players lacking experience can get into all sorts of trouble with them—this makes the event attractive to someone who understands that.

"Maybe I'll take a shot at a one-table," I say.

"You're here, why not?"

Why not? Well, let's see, I've lost $1,500 today; I've invested another $10,000 in the Main Event; I've decided I'm going to play in the Senior's Event, which is yet another $1,500; my airfare was $634 round-trip; my hotel is probably going to run me a couple of grand; the rental car is going to be close to $800; meals are going to cost me at least a few thousand—oh, fuck, what's another $175?

I walk over to the satellite area and see a table that's almost full. There are two cards still sitting facedown in front of the dealer, along with two stacks of gray and green chips. I grab one of the cards, a six, sit down in the 6 seat, and whip out my roll, peeling off two honeybees.

I've always been a strong one-table satellite* player. I attribute this

---

* A satellite is a smaller buy-in tournament, whose winner receives, instead of cash, a voucher or a lammer (see footnote, page 76) entitling him entry into a bigger tournament. In a single-table satellite, for example, in which everyone buys in for $110 dollars, the winner would receive the equivalent of a $1,000 in the form of a buy-in to a larger tournament, with the extra hundred dollars in juice going to the house. A super satellite is a multitable version of a single-table satellite. In the nightly supers that the WSOP has traditionally run, a $220 buy-in event with rebuys, a number of $10,000 seats are routinely awarded.

less to my own aptitude than to other players' fundamental misunderstanding of the proper strategy for the format. Basically, it's an accelerated version of the Harrington-Robertie M formula. You want to play tight at the beginning, when the blinds are small, then open up when the blinds are worth stealing, even if you're sometimes getting in with the worst of it. I'm always surprised how few players follow this template. Most tend to play too fast in the beginning and too slowly at the end.

This table turns out to be no exception. By minding my own business and staying out of trouble, folding most of the time and playing only when I have a very strong hand, I watch six of the ten players bust out. With four of us left, I'm the short stack, but I now begin moving my chips around aggressively. I steal the blinds a couple of times, and this alone practically doubles my stack. Then, with enough chips to cripple someone, I twice move in after the pot's been raised in front of me and take down the gelt without showing a hand. Sans showdown, I go from short stack to second in chips.

Before long I'm head's up with a cocky, talkative player from Los Angeles.

"You wanna make a deal?" I ask. He's got me almost two to one in chips.

"I'm willing to talk."

"We're playing for sixteen-twenty? How about I take seven hundred and you get nine-twenty?"

"I've got you nearly two to one."

"That can change in one hand."

"Let's play then," he says.

This kind of negotiation is common in satellites and tournaments, particularly in situations like this, where it's winner take all. With steep blinds and antes, fast play becomes a necessity by the time it's head's up, and the outcome is pretty much of a crap shoot. It's certainly this guy's prerogative to turn me down, or negotiate for more money, but there's something about his cockiness that bugs me. I can get stubborn, too.

"Fine, let's play," I say.

On the very first hand, with the blinds $400 and $800, and our respective stacks at $9,500 for him and $5,500 for me, I'm on the button* and I make it $2,000 to go, holding K-J off. He immediately moves in, and I make a crying call, knowing I must be trailing but pot-committed. Sure enough, he's got A-9, which makes me a 57 percent to 43 percent underdog. But what do you know? The poker gods are smiling. I flop a jack, and just as I warned him, our positions have more than flip-flopped in one hand. I've got $11,000 now and he's got $4,000. Three hands later, it's all over, when I call him down with A-10 and he's holding A-3.

He gets up, grumbling about his luck, and I have to bite my tongue. What I want to say is that he could have locked up $920 a few minutes ago, but he let his ego override his judgment. I can't help feeling that justice has been served, though I know that's a dangerous way to look at it. The cards have no conscience.

What I do know for sure is that I'm playing in tomorrow's event, and when you deduct the $120 I've received in cash to go along with the three $500 lammers† I just won, it's going to cost me only $55.

---

* In head's-up play, the button, or dealer, is also the small blind; this means that he's first to act pre-flop. After the flop, he's last to act.

† A lammer is a special chip given to the winner of a satellite tournament, who can then use it as a complete or partial entry or buy-in to a larger tournament. Although the chip can be used only to buy into a tournament, it can be sold to another player for that purpose. For example, with my three $500 lammers, I can buy into any $1,500 event at this year's WSOP; I can also win three more lammers and buy into a $3,000 event, or use my three lammers plus $1,500 in cash for the same purpose. Additionally, I could sell them to another player for face value or less. The name lammer probably came from the original material, laminated plastic.

I stop back at the mega satellite area, hoping to share my little triumph with Nicky and Mike May, but only Mike is still there.

"Yeah, Nicky ran into an underpair that caught up on the river."

"Ouch."

"This gentleman here has his chips." Mike gestures toward an old guy in thick glasses and a T-shirt that says, PLEASE DON'T CALL (MY CARDS SUCK). The old guy grins.

"How'd you do over there?" Mike asks.

"I won a seat."

"Exxx-cellent! Did you chop it?"

"I wanted to but he wouldn't make a deal."

"Even better." Mike clucks. "Don't these people know by now that it's bad karma?"

"That's what I tried to tell him."

"Well, congratulations," he says.

"Are you playing tomorrow?"

"Of course."

"You want to trade two percent?"

"I thought you'd never ask."

As with many of my poker friendships, my experience of Mike May is almost entirely restricted to time spent in card rooms with him. I've known him in this way for probably ten years, and I have always and instinctively liked him even as he's remained something of a cipher to me. It's difficult not to like Mike May. He's incredibly friendly, funny, a bit diffident, with a stuttering delivery like the Warren Beatty of *Heaven Can Wait*. Famously barred from the big no-limit game at the Mayfair by one of the owners, who called him a "self-deprecating hustler" (a characterization that, like the question "Do you beat your wife?" is brilliantly unanswerable), Mike has often been an object of rumors and speculations. There has always been a sense that there is some Big Story underneath it all. That he is the heir to some great American fortune.

Or that he is into S&M and frequents bondage clubs. He is notoriously difficult to pin down, very good at asking questions but much less forthcoming when on the receiving end. Few people seem to know how to get hold of him. He doesn't have a cell phone. He disappears for weeks and months on end. Then he reappears without saying exactly where he was. But even when he is present he is elusive, there but somehow distant, hiding in plain sight. The mysterious Mike May.

4

THE TROGLODYTE ON THE COUCH

I'm dozing off in the garish colored light of the television when my cell phone rings. It's on the floor on the other side of the room, plugged in and recharging. I consider getting up to answer it, but instead just let it ring.

Five minutes later, I'm drifting back off when it begins to ring again. Fuck. This time, I drag myself out of bed to answer. It's Nicky.

"Dude, did I wake you up?"

I grunt. It's one in the morning, and I'm still on East Coast time, but it's hard to get too upset with him. If the cutoff hours for most people are after nine-thirty or ten in the evening and before nine in the morning, for a poker player in a casino hotel they're more like after two a.m. and before noon.

"I wouldn't have called," he says, "but it looks like I'm going to need a place to crash." From what I can follow, Betsy missed her flight to Chicago and couldn't give him her suite at the Rio as she had earlier promised.

"Uh-huh," I mutter, not really taking it in. "As long as you come over right now, it's fine."

"That's the thing. It's going to take me at least an hour. I've gotta get my bags from her room and take care of some other shit."

"An hour?"

"Is that a problem?"

"Dude, I'm trying to sleep. What am I supposed to do? Wait up for you?"

"All right. Fuck it," he says testily. "I'll figure something else out."

"What? You think I'm being unreasonable?"

"No. It's fine. I'll find something else."

"Look, if it's your only recourse, then obviously."

"No, that's fine. I got it covered."

I go back to bed feeling guilty but also angry. What the fuck does he want from me? I'm jet-lagged and I've got a tournament to play in.

He calls me at nine-thirty the next morning.

"Look, I'm sorry about last night," he says.

"No problem."

"I want to make it up to you by taking you out to breakfast."

"You don't have to do that."

"No," he says. "I do. It's as much for me as it is for you."

Twenty minutes later, we're in Betsy's Porsche, miles from the Gold Coast. The landscape of Las Vegas, once you get away from the Strip, is very much like Los Angeles: flat, paved, concrete desert; side streets and endless boulevards lined with drive-through businesses and strip malls; mountains and blue sky lying beyond like a mirage.

"I've been buried like this so many times that I should be used to it. But every time I manage to climb out from under, I swear that it'll never happen again."

"So where'd you end up staying last night?"

"After I spoke to you, I ran into these two kids I know from Holly-wood Park who let me crash on a foldout couch in their room. It would have been fine, but at three in the morning, they came back to the room

with a couple of girls. These two guys are twenty-one, they're here having the time of their lives. It's all a big adventure and a goof for them
being at the World Series. They bring these girls back, and the girls
see me on the couch in this dimly lit room, groaning and making un-
welcoming noises, and they start getting skittish. 'Who's the guy on the
couch?' 'What's going on here?' I mean, as if things aren't bad enough
for me, I also have to confront the fact that I'm basically this old
troglodyte lying on a pullout couch."

I'm laughing.

"So now all I'm trying to do right is keep from drowning," he says,
taking a right turn on Decatur. "Which is why we're driving around trying to find an IHOP."

Nicky has decided that the German lemon-butter crepes at IHOP
are one of the few things in the world this morning that might give him
hope that life is actually worth living. It's what I love about him. He can
be on his way to the dark side but still laugh about it and find hope in the
unlikeliest places.

"I don't know how you do it," I say. "I don't know if I could with a
wife and baby."

"Actually, I couldn't do it without them," he says. "Em'll say, 'That
sucks,' when I tell her what's going on. But she's seen me be down ten
thousand in a week and come back from it plenty of times, and she reminds me of that when I get down too low."

Nicky cranks up the volume on a Bob Dylan song playing on a CD.

I was born here and I'll die here against my will.
I know it looks like I'm moving, but I'm standing still.

"It's not dark yet but it's getting there," Nicky sings along, looking
over at me, his expressive eyebrows arched. None too soon, we find
the peaked blue-shingled roof and pull into the parking lot of IHOP.

Nicky's got his bags and his computer in the back of the Porsche. The plan is to drop everything off in my room at the Gold Coast after breakfast. But when he tries to lock up with the electronic key, nothing happens. He pushes the button several times. Nothing.

"You're turning into the character William Macy played in *The Cooler,*" I say.

"I can't fucking believe this," Nicky says, laughing along with me, continuing to punch the button on the key.

"Can't you lock it manually?" I say.

"No. These goddamn Germans. They make this genius car, but one little battery dies and the whole thing turns to shit."

We wind up carrying his three bags and expensive laptop into the restaurant with us. It's crowded as hell inside: a Saturday-morning throng of regular-looking people, the kind you might see in any chain restaurant anywhere else in the country. There's something soothing about that, about being jolted temporarily out of the poker cocoon, and remembering that, yes, well, there is another reality. Maybe even more than the crepes this has a salutary effect on us—although the crepes aren't bad either.

Afterward, we drive back to my room and drop his stuff off. We make it over to the Rio with only fifteen minutes to spare before the start of the pot-limit event, but our spirits, absurdly, are fortified by our little trip. I trade a 2 percent piece with him and the same with Shane, whom we run into while searching for our tables. When I locate table 74, it's still a couple of minutes before noon, so I take the opportunity to call Alice.

"Hi," I say when she picks up. She's at her office at the cosmetics company where she works as a copywriter—her day job. During the nearly five years she's been there, she's managed to write three screenplays, a number of short plays, and a full-length play. One of the short plays had a run at a downtown theater with Janeane Garofalo playing the lead, and it was also later turned into a short film. One of the screen-plays was set to be optioned by Gabriel Byrne, the Irish movie star, but hit a snag at the last minute when it came to the attention of his produc-tion company that a similar script had been bought by another studio. There have been other near misses for her with fellowships and grants and productions, all of which have given her an appreciation for the meaning of the poker term *bad beat*. She well understands the frustra-tion of putting time into a thing, doing good work, and not being able to catch the break you need to get to the next level, or catching a bad break that prevents you from getting there.

"Where are you?" she asks.

"In the poker room at the Rio. The tournament is just about to start." I apologize for not calling earlier, tell her about Nicky and the German crepes, and try to focus, amid all the ambient noise and com-motion, on what she's telling me about her upcoming bridal shower. In the middle of it, the dealers are given the "shuffle up" command, and I tell her I have to go.

I can tell she's irritated by my abruptness. But what can I do?

"Well, good luck," she says.

I close the phone, feeling slightly assholic and guilty. But the feeling quickly evaporates. The field is smaller today than yesterday, though still enormous. There are over 1,000 players. As I look around my table, the only player I recognize is Billy Baxter, who was Stuey Ungar's main backer and is someone I've talked to on the phone a few times. "Billy," I say. "Peter Alson."

He looks at me without recognition.

"I wrote the Stuey bio with Nolan."

"Oh, that's right, sure," he says in his soft Southern drawl.

"Have you seen it yet?" I ask him.

"No, I didn't even know it was available."

"It's not in stores, but Nolan has copies. If I see him, I'll get you one."

"That'd be nice," he says.

When the guy sitting to my right hears this conversation, he introduces himself, because of course he's a writer, too. "Bob Burton," he says, sticking out his hand (everyone at this table but me seems to have the initials B.B.). A lengthy conversation ensues, during the course of which I discover that among other things, Burton and I have at one time shared the same literary agent. There are other confluences. Burton's an old-schooler like me who lives in the Bay Area, which is where I went to college for a couple of years in the '70s before I transferred to Harvard. He played, as did I, in Emeryville, California, when draw poker and lowball were the only games spread, and the Emeryville clubs, the Key and the Oaks, were populated strictly by retirees and pensioners.

The cranky old cowpoke in the black Stetson in seat number 1, who looks as if he might have been one of them, is clearly annoyed by our nonstop chatter. He keeps giving us dirty looks and finally just comes out and tells us to shut up. I'm actually happy for his admonishment. I need to pay attention to what's going on. This isn't some friendly low-limit game, after all. This is a world championship event, the winner of which will be awarded a gold bracelet and some measure of poker immortality.

Lip zipped and attention now focused, I soon get involved in a four-way pot. I'm holding pocket sevens, and after an early raise and two calls ahead of me, I call, too. The flop comes 8-J-3 and two diamonds. It's checked to me. I figure if nobody can bet, my sevens might be good, so I take a $300 stab at it. I get one caller, which of course I'm not happy about. The turn is a four of clubs, and my opponent, a bearded fellow in a white satin Golden Nugget jacket, checks, and I check back. The river is an ace. Now he bets $500.

My immediate impulse is to fold. I have only $1,100 left and he's saying the ace hit him. Maybe he started with A-3 or A-8 and he just made two pairs. Maybe he started with A-K or A-Q. These are reasonable assumptions. For some reason, though, I don't give him an ace. I'm looking at him, staring him down, and I can't say exactly what it is, but something in his posture is unnatural. The hand that released the chips is still extended, as if he couldn't retract it, and now doesn't want to because it might arouse suspicion. Whether it's that or something else, I just feel that he doesn't want me to call. This means he's trying to steal, because if he doesn't have an ace, then he can't possibly have risked a bet. He certainly isn't betting a pair of eights or jacks. I decide he was on a draw with a hand like 9-10.

"I call," I say.

He zings his cards facedown into the muck. *Yes.* I show my pocket sevens and rake in the $2,000 pot.

"Wow," one of the other players says. "I'm not going to try bluffing you."

These words are gratifying to me on more than the ego level. One of the hidden advantages of making a big call, particularly if you're right (being right shows acumen in addition to stubbornness), is that it discourages opponents from trying to bluff you in the future. Once you begin to take weapons away from them, you have succeeded in giving yourself an edge.

Unfortunately for me, before I have an opportunity to exploit this, a floor man comes around and distributes seat cards and clear Lucite chip racks. Our table is breaking. I put my chips, which I've worked up to $3,200, into one of the racks and head off to find my new table.

Getting moved is one of the most difficult aspects of tournament play. You hear players complaining about it all the time. *I was at a great table and I was just getting a good feel for it when they moved me.* It can work both ways, obviously. You can be at a terrible table and get moved to a good one. More often, though, it's a negative, and more so for a good player than a poor one. Not only has a good player invested time and concentration on getting a read on his opponents; he may also have worked to develop a table image of his own that he was about to exploit (like me showing that I'm willing to call with an underpair to most of the board). As soon as he's moved, all that's lost. For the bad player, who mostly just plays his own two cards, oblivious of who his opponents are, the past (his old table) and the future (his new table) are pretty much interchangeable.

At table 129, seat 4, I don't recognize a soul; but as I've said, this doesn't mean as much as it used to. After one orbit, I get a beautiful pair of pocket kings under the gun. The blinds are now $50 and $100, which means that the maximum raise is $350. With kings, I want to make it as expensive as possible, so I bet the max. The chip leader at the table, a stocky Korean in an MTV Jackass visor, calls me from the button. I've watched him play fewer than a dozen hands, but it's obvious to me that he's a tricky, aggressive player.

The flop comes down 8-9-3 with two clubs. It's what I call a trap flop. He can easily have a club draw or a straight draw, and if I bet and he raises, that would be a natural assumption. But he might also have flopped a hand that has me in deep trouble: a set or two pairs. So instead of betting the pot, I bet $450 to see what he does.

He calls.

The turn card is a four of diamonds. I'm certain that it didn't help him, and I'm pretty certain that my hand is good. The obvious play is to bet the pot here, and I'd probably do that against a different kind of player, an ABC player. Against this guy, I'm thinking more about how I can use his aggressiveness against him to maximize my winnings. I check.

He riffles his chips a few times, then bets $800.

Again, I consider my options. I've got $2,400 left. I could move in and probably should, but for some reason, I just raise him back $800, leaving myself a way to survive the hand if he moves in on me and I decide he's got me beat. He calls the $800.

As I reconstruct the hand now, it's obvious to me that he was on a draw, but for whatever reason at the time I gave him an overpair to the board. Queens, jacks, or tens. When a ten hits the river, I move in for my last $800. Obviously, I'm not going to fold, so if the ten gives him a set, I'm just out of luck. By the same token, he'll have to call with queens or jacks. Writing this now, though, as I say, I see clearly that he was on a draw, and I probably should have checked on the river and given him a chance to bet, since betting was his only real way to win at that point. Instead, I gave him a chance to fold and save $800, which is what he did.

Still, despite my questionable play of the hand, it puts me up well over $5,000, which leaves me in good shape with 800 players left and the average stack around $2,600. Less than twenty minutes later, though, the table breaks and I'm moved again. This time my new table has a couple of familiar faces, one of them famous, one of them not. The famous face belongs to Erik Seidel, a Mayfair Club alum, whom I've known for many years. Erik is without doubt one of the best players and nicest guys in poker, a former Wall Street trader, who got creamed by Black Monday, the stock market crash of 1987, and subsequently turned to poker, which he has found to be a less tumultuous and more enjoyable occupation. A tall, gangly Ichabod Crane, with a soft-spoken, direct, no-bullshit manner and a pragmatic albeit sardonic take on things, Seidel is the costar of the most famous poker sequence ever captured on film, the final hand of the 1988 world championship, in which Johnny Chan, aka the Oriental Express, flopped the nut straight, and checked until Seidel finally took the bait on the turn and moved in, drawing dead with top pair. This sequence was shown not once but twice in the movie *Rounders,* and has become the poker equivalent of the guy crashing off the ski jump on the *Wide World of Sports* lead-in, a kind of cautionary reminder of how it can all go wrong.

Before you start feeling too sorry for Seidel, though, consider this: He is probably the most famous runner-up in poker history, more so even than the perennial bridesmaid T. J. Cloutier and the amateur fluke Kevin McBride. He has also managed to recover from the "humiliation" of finishing second in the world championship to capture six gold WSOP bracelets and numerous other tournament titles, winning millions of dollars along the way.

Curiously, I remember sitting next to Erik during a flight to Las Vegas in 1989. Back then he was still living in New York, and he was a little paranoid about the poker in Las Vegas because he had heard numerous stories about the cheating that went on. Apparently, he's gotten over it. Now, he makes his home in Vegas full-time with his wife Ruah and their two children. "I don't really worry much about cheating anymore," he says.

At this table, he's in the 10 seat behind a nice pile of chips. I unrack my chips and take up my position in the 6 seat.

"Hi, Erik."

"Hey, Peter."

I look around at the rest of the table, hoping my connection to a player of Seidel's caliber will alert the other players that they should not get out of line with me. That's when I see the other familiar face, a black man with a prominent scar on one cheek and scary-looking mirrored sunglasses. I can't remember his name, but he and I have a history. He's an Atlantic City guy, rumored to be in the drug trade, though that may just be on account of his look. The first time I played with him, six or seven years ago, during the U.S. Poker Championship, I immediately identified him as a horrendously bad player—and therefore dangerous. There's a rule of thumb when playing bad players and drunks that is both wise and difficult to adhere to: Don't try anything remotely tricky and don't even think about bluffing them. I told myself that the first time I played with Scarface, then proceeded to bluff off all my chips to him (he called my river all-in with only an ace high). I've played with Scarface a couple of times since, and though he is not as horrible a player as he once was, he seems to put some sort of unholy hex on me. Of course, that has not brought me into his consciousness. He has no idea that we've ever played together. It is part of what makes him my nemesis.

On the first hand I play at my table, Erik limps in for $150, and I raise it to $450 with 8-9 suited. Mucking his hand, Erik says, "We're not doing that at this table. We're friendly here."

"Sorry," I say. "I promise I won't do it again."

It's fascinating to watch the way most of the other players avoid getting involved in hands with Erik, meekly folding to his raises and reraises. He senses which of them are most afraid, picking on them without mercy, knowing that if they play back at him it'll be only with a huge hand.

Scarface, my nemesis, meanwhile, who is not one of them, soon gets involved in a big hand with an Asian guy in a San Francisco Giants cap. They both have well over $6,000 in chips, and there's a raise, a reraise, and a call pre-flop, creating a pot of over $1,400. The dealer spreads out three cards on the table, the K-10-3 with two diamonds, and the Asian guy says, "All in," and Scarface instantly calls. They both turn over their hands. Scarface has K-10 for top two pairs, and the Asian guy has pocket aces. The only problem is that this isn't no-limit, and the all-in bet wasn't a legal one, and therefore neither hand should have been exposed. What the hell to do now?

The dealer calls over a floor man, who makes a ruling: It's a $1,400 bet and call. And since nothing can be done about the fact that both hands were exposed, they'll just have to play the hand out with their cards faceup.

The turn card is the jack of diamonds, giving the pair of aces a straight flush draw. Scarface, holding top two pairs, now bets the pot, which is $4,200, nearly the rest of his chips. The Asian guy grimaces, faced with a quandary. He has nineteen outs to win the hand with one card to come. I can see him doing the math. He's certainly getting the right money odds to make a call, but there's also an almost 60 percent chance that he'll lose and be knocked out of the tournament. After a full minute, he sighs loudly and folds.

Erik shakes his head. "I've never seen that one before," he says. "Betting where the hands are turned up. No matter how long you play this game, it always throws something new at you."

Erik is right, but for me the hand is fascinating less for its novelty than for the philosophical divide it so vividly illustrates. I can think of a lot of players who might have called in that spot, including Stuey Ungar and a player whom many might consider his polar opposite, Dan Harrington. If the Asian player had, in fact, called, four out of ten times he would have increased his stack to over $12,000; and if he had called six out of ten times he would have busted out of the tournament. By folding, he was guaranteeing that he would survive the hand, albeit with a stack of only slightly more than $4,000 (which was still above average). So what is the best play? Are your chances to cash out best served by surviving 100 percent of the time or by surviving only four out of ten times but with triple the amount of chips?

Depending upon what stage of the tournament you're at, the answer might change. On the bubble, you might fold to ensure finishing in the money. But after making the money, you would certainly consider it worth your while to gamble, since tournament payouts are generally so top-heavy (significantly favoring the first few finishers).

This hand is in fact such a perfect illustration of the dialectic that it almost becomes a litmus test of character. When I describe it to Nicky later, he says, "If I were first to act [as the Asian player was] I would have moved in with the ace of diamonds, because there's always the chance that your opponent, even as a favorite, might be risk averse and fold. But I would always take the gamble in that spot because with $12,000 in chips at that stage I would have my full arsenal of weapons and really be able to dominate the table. It would be worth the risk to me."

Greg Raymer, the 2004 world champion, is even more adamant. "Once I do the math and see that my chip equity for calling is so much higher than it is for folding, I call without any further hesitation. To do anything else in this spot is a huge mistake. It would be one thing if his edge on this call were 5 percent or less. However, his edge here is about 75 percent. This is massive by any standards, even those of Phil Hellmuth [noted for his reluctance to risk all his chips unless he thinks he is getting way the best of it]. To fold here is simply a huge mistake. In fact, it is a huge mistake at probably *every* stage of the tournament, even on the bubble."

Since I am more from the Phil Hellmuth school than from Raymer's, my approach to tournaments, especially in hands against inferior players, is to build my stack gradually, risking all my chips only when I think I'm well ahead. For the next couple of hours, I manage to steal a few blinds and bob and weave, reaching the six p.m. dinner break having increased my stack slightly to $6,000. I'm still above par, though not by much, but I'm alive, along with 400 others.

I find Nicky, who's still plugging along, too, and we have a brief confab to decide on our dinner strategy. With only an hour and fifteen minutes, we decide the buffet is probably our best bet. It's a ten-minute hike just to get there, down the Rio Pavillion Center's crowded and endless carpeted hallways, the walls of which feature artwork by the likes of Richard Serra and Mary Warner. Along the way, I hear snatches of poker conversation all around me: "And then I made it five hundred to go, and he pushed and I had to give it up" and, "You have to just bet there. You can't give him a free card" and, "I just can't seem to get anything going."

There's a long line at the Carnival World Buffet that stretches and snakes around a series of railings. It's made up mostly of families and weekend tourists.

"This is nuts," I say. "There's gotta be some way to bypass this."

Shane and Tommy Duncker, another New York player, who is known as "Tall Tommy" because—love those clever poker nicknames—

he is six foot seven, show up with the same idea we had. We all stand there for a minute, trying to figure out what to do. I notice there's a VIP station. On a hunch, I go over and show them my WSOP food coupon, and voilà, Harrah's has actually done something right—we get to bypass the peon line. Of course, Harrah's being a heinous corporate money-making enterprise, we also have to pay the difference between our ten-dollar meal coupon and the twenty-three-dollar buffet price. Not enough that they're taking 7 percent out of the over $100 million prize pool from the six-week series of tournaments. Or that they and ESPN (but not the players) will reap enormous profits from the telecasts of these events; they can't even cover the price of an entire meal for us. It almost makes you want to, uh, unionize. Well, maybe not.

The Vegas hotel buffets are, of course, famous for their lavish over-abundance. The Rio's is supposedly one of the best in town, though to my knowledge nearly every Strip hotel makes that claim for its buffet, and I'm not even sure what "best" in this context means. The one most likely to result in coronary bypass surgery? Or the one that guarantees that you will keep eating until you puke?

The discipline that it takes not to overeat in a buffet is equivalent to the discipline required to fold in a game in which the chips have no monetary value. The point is that the food has already been paid for, regardless of how much you eat, so you're freerolling. And if there's anything poker players have a hard time turning down, it's a freeroll. After grabbing multiple plates, Shane, Tommy, Nicky, and I branch off in different directions and start loading up.

I make it back to the table at the same time that Shane does, but Nicky and Tommy are from the school where they have to scout out the entire spread before making their choices, so it takes them longer.

Shaniac busted out of the tournament just before the break, but the rest of us are on the clock, thirty-five minutes and counting by the time we're all sitting down. Believe me, there's nothing better than wolfing down obscene amounts of food in a hurry to promote peak brain function.

The thing is that no matter how much you'd suppose we'd want to take a short break from thinking about the game we've been playing for six straight hours, we can't. We're obsessed. All the poker players I've ever known have, during these rushed dinner hours, found the time to talk about poker: hands they won or lost or misplayed or played brilliantly or weren't involved in but found fascinating anyway. We are no different.

As we consume fresh Alaskan crab legs, shrimp, clams, oysters, sushi, teriyaki chicken, mashed potatoes, corn, broccoli, dumplings, chimichangas, tamales, chicken mole, Mandarin chicken, shrimp toast, beef stir-fry, creamed spinach, prime rib, roast pork, fried catfish, paella, lobster Newburg, barbecued ribs, macaroni and cheese, cheesecake, ice cream sundaes, cannoli, and crêpes suzette, we compare chip counts, discuss strategy, and add percentage points to our pieces of one another. We also gossip: "Is it true about Ben Affleck and Annie Duke?" "No way. The guy could get any babe in Hollywood." "Yeah, but could they help him improve his no-limit hold'em game?"

Tall Tommy and Nicky leave while Shane and I are still finishing our dessert and coffee. They're both short-stacked and worried about getting back late and being blinded off. I was on the button when we broke, so I'm slightly less concerned, but as soon as they leave, the possibility kicks my anxiety to a slightly higher level. It's not unheard of for players to get blinded off, even at crucial points in major events. In the 2004 Main Event, John Murphy, the eventual thirteenth-place finisher, overslept and missed the first hour of the final-two table, during which time his stack was docked $200,000 in blinds and antes. But that's nothing compared with Stuey Ungar OD'ing in his hotel room during the 1990 Main Event and missing the final two days of the competition while he was in the emergency room recovering. Even horizontal on a hospital gurney, he managed to finish ninth—that's how long it took for his chips to be anted and blinded away.

"I guess I'd better head back to the trenches," I say to Shane. "What are you gonna do?"

"I think I'll take a taxi to my apartment, smoke a spliff, and play online."

It kills me. Shaniac and his Internet compadres travel across the country to a poker tournament, then sit in their rented rooms playing against a computer screen. "Why don't you play in a live game?" I say.

"The competition's tougher."

"Oh," I say, as if that explains everything. And in the poker universe, in a way it does.

"You want to try getting in some tennis tomorrow?" he asks me.

I pat my distended belly. "Yeah, if I don't last till tomorrow in the tournament, I think that would be a very good idea."

"Right on."

Near the end of the walk back to the Amazon Room, a check of my watch shows that I'm running late, so I wind up jogging the last few hundred yards. I get to table 89 out of breath, but having missed only one hand. Twenty minutes after we resume, Scarface, who is now the big stack at the table with about $8,500, makes it $400 under the gun. I'm sitting across from him, in middle position, and fire back a $1,000 raise at him, holding A-K suited.

It's folded back around to him, and he calls without hesitation. Even though I have position and in all likelihood the best hand, I hate Scarface's call. The guy has some kind of weird juju on me, and it's made worse by his not even knowing it. No matter how many times we play, no matter how many times he works his evil magic on me, the fact of my existence just doesn't seem to register with him.

This time, however, *this* time, I'm going to make him remember me.

The flop is so delicious that I have to blink away my disbelief. A-K-2 rainbow.

Yeah, baby. It's my time now.

Scarface checks.

I contemplate giving him a free card, but with a flop like that it would be suspicious after my reraise. Plus, he could easily be playing a hand like Q-J, Q-10, or J-10, and I don't want to give him a free draw to the straight. Instead, I make a probe bet of $1,200, as if I have a hand like pocket queens or pocket jacks and I'm afraid that he's playing an ace. This is not a bet I'd try against Erik. He'd see right through it and suspect a powerhouse. But against Scarface, it seems worth a shot. To my astonishment and delight, he not only calls but check-raises me the *pot,* which puts me all in, about another $3,000. I call immediately, certain I'm about to double up. I turn over my A-K, and Scarface triumphantly smacks his two cards faceup in front of him: two little deuces, that together with the one on board give him a set.

I'm so stunned that I barely register what comes on the turn and the river. I just know that I'm out. He's done it to me again. *My God,* I want to say, *how the hell did you call my pre-flop reraise with pocket deuces, out of position?*

But the answer is axiomatic. It's how he plays. It's what you're up against with Scarface. Myself, I would never make the initial raise from early position with pocket deuces. I would certainly never call a reraise. How can you? If you don't flop a set, you're in a hopeless situation, completely at the mercy of your opponent. Every card on the board is an overcard to your pair, and your only real option is to check-raise and hope your opponent folds, or bet on the turn if he checks the flop. Neither choice is very appealing.

I look up at the hanging video screen, which shows that there are only 241 players left out of the original 1,071. Actually, there are only 240, but my absence hasn't been officially noted yet. Once again I have outlasted more than 75 percent of the field, yet have nothing to show for it. Getting eliminated from a tournament is always a shock. One minute you're alive; the next you're dead. The suddenness of it, the finality of it, is almost impossible to metabolize. For the first few minutes, you're dazed, walking this way and that. The world of the tournament is still going on but you are no longer a part of it; the other world, the world beyond, is less alive, less engaging, less focused. You are in a kind of limbo.

It is natural to think about these events in terms of life and death. Freeze-out tournaments are by their very nature existential: All the losers die, and the eventual winner is the sole survivor. Death as a metaphor suffuses the language of tournament poker, which is also rich in references to medical conditions that could result in death: "crippled," "barely hanging on," "blinded to death," "anted to death," "crushed," "annihilated," "vaporized," "bleeding to death," "drawing dead," "on life support." There are an equal number of terms to describe those who have narrowly avoided death: "still breathing," "off the respirator," "still alive," "new life," "back from the dead." And as sex and death are so often connected, it should come as no surprise that a lot of the terminology also invokes sex. Phrases like "the nuts," "all-in," "giving action," "good position," or "coming over the top" suggest things more carnal than poker.

Since I am in the limbo between life and death and also between life and sex, I decide that it is probably a good time for me to register for my press credentials. Who could be more of an interloper between two worlds than a journalist, after all? With my press pass I will be able to circulate among the tournament tables and go inside the rails that cordon off the players from the casual spectators.

Especially in the early days, when the World Series was held at the Horseshoe, the press people were treated like royalty: A limo would pick you up at the airport, the rooms were free, and meals at the restaurants and the buffet were on the house. Jack Binion understood that good press was gold, and he did everything he could to make sure reporters were pampered. That changed somewhat over the years, as the Horseshoe hit hard times on Becky Behnen's watch and corners had to be cut. Here at Harrah's, print journalists are treated only slightly better than head lice. After all, what good can we really do them? Television is another matter, of course. I imagine Norman Chad and the rest of the ESPN crew get comped like high rollers. But the noncelebrity players and print wretches? No point.

Nevertheless, I am happy for even small favors. My media pass, a purple-bordered laminated card that identifies me as being from Atria Books, affords me entrée into the pressroom, where there is a cooler full of bottled water and soft drinks, and a desk where I can plug in my laptop. The pass also gives me (nearly) unimpeded access to events in the poker room. If I am not going to be inside the rails as a player, at least no one will be able to stop me from entering as an observer.

Back in the Amazon Room, I take advantage of the pass right away, trespassing into the cordoned-off area where the final twenty tables of the pot-limit tournament have been placed. I see Nicky's orange hat right away. He's still in it. Making my way over to his table, I put a hand on his shoulder, causing him to recoil slightly. I always forget. He's slightly phobic about being touched.

"Sorry," I say. "I got carried away. I'm just glad to see you're still here."

"Thanks."

Gavin Smith is in the seat next to him, raking in a big pot.

"He had six hundred dollars when he came to this table," Nicky says. "Then I doubled him up. And now look at him."

"Hiya, Gavin."

"Hey, Peter."

Gavin is a Canadian with a fondness for booze and poker, often at the same time. I've played with him for many years, mostly in tournaments at Foxwoods, and always considered him talented. But the booze, although it gave a nice edge to his sense of humor and made him the life of the party, also usually led him to play too recklessly. A year ago, though, he quit drinking and really dedicated himself to becoming a top player. The results have been incredible, especially of late: In April of 2005, he won $56,615 in the WPT Championship at the Bellagio; on May 16, he won $155,880 in a tournament at the Mirage; and then, just a week later, he won the WPT championship event there for $1,128,278. Not a bad way to come into the 2005 WSOP.

Nicky, however, starts critiquing the hand that Gavin just won, telling me what happened and how he would have played it, before adding tartly, "But then again, I didn't just win a million dollars."

Gavin laughs at the gibe. They have that kind of relationship.

Not too long ago, the WSOP was the only tournament to boast a million-dollar winner. It's still the biggest, but last year, over thirty $1 million prizes were awarded in tournaments around the world. That's a lot of new poker millionaires walking around. I've got to hand it to Gavin, though; he hasn't let winning go to his head. He's as friendly and humble as ever.

Over by the front of the room, an even bigger crowd is gathered around the final two tables of event 2, the $1,500 no-limit. I wander over to take a look and see what could have been. Heath Boutwell, the fellow whose pocket jacks cracked my pocket queens yesterday, and who, as a result of having survived that brush with mortality, now stands to make $725,425, is one of the eighteen players remaining. Not surprisingly, I imagine myself in his seat. It is impossible to look at him without thinking that it should be me. At the same time, as odd as it sounds, I'm glad that he's put his good fortune and my chips to worthwhile use. My poker death counted for something.

I watch Boutwell long enough to see him double up once, by which time they're down to the final twelve players. When I walk back over to the pot-limit tournament to check on Nicky, he's gone. Vaporized. "Yeah, first I beat him a hand," Gavin tells me, "and then he got unlucky."

I groan, suddenly weary, and in a profound way aware of the fact that I'm going to be here for nearly six more weeks and that I've already eaten too much buffet food and walked too many long, carpeted surfaces, and played and watched enough poker for one day.

On the marathon hike back to the Gold Coast, I take out my cell phone.

"Where are you?" Alice asks.

"Walking back to the room."

"What's all that noise?"

"They've got a rock band and people up on trapezes. It's crazy. It's the Rio. You know, Carnivale."

"Are you all right? You sound a little stressed out."

"I'm fine. How about you?"

"I just got back from the shower."

"Oh, fuck, that's right," I say. "Today was the shower."

I ask her how it went, guilty because I needed a prompt. She tells me that a dancing man appeared at the door in the middle of the festivities; stripped off his clothes to reveal a Wonder Woman costume underneath; and was then egged on by my mom's oldest friend, Rhoda, who kept chanting, "Take it off. Take it all off!"

"And did he?"

"No. But it turned out I knew him. He was dancing in front of me and suddenly he went, 'Alice?' and I said, 'Seth?' "

"You're kidding! You knew him? How'd you know him? This isn't somebody you slept with, is it?"

"No," she says with a huffy growl of indignation. "Nothing like that."

"Are you sure?"

"Hey, you're in *Vegas*," she says.

"So?"

"So you're not allowed to be jealous." Even as she says this, I know that she doesn't entirely mean it, that she's actually secretly pleased that

I might be jealous. It's an indication that I care and that I know what I want, and that what I want is her. It is a sign that the biggest problem in our relationship all along, namely, my ambivalence, is not currently operational.

The thing about my ambivalence, though, is that it's never been anything but generic with her, a knee-jerk response to the prospect of real commitment. Alice's corresponding questions about me, on the other hand, are quite specific: I'm a writer, I don't make much money, I play poker, I'm selfish and immature. Not only that but for the longest time I couldn't even seem to make up my mind about her. These deficits, balanced against her own needs—late thirties, desire to start a family as well as have a career as a writer—suggest that she should have taken her business elsewhere long ago. Yet in an odd sort of reverse whammy, my ambivalence, the thing that actually should have been my most terrifying and off-putting deficiency, is actually the thing that has kept her sticking around or coming back.

I'm not going to pass judgment on that because, as I said earlier, historically, once the object of my desire started to get hinky on *me,* I was almost always hooked. And the truth is that when I first met Alice, despite my vow to myself not to get involved in any more destructive relationships, part of the attraction was my sense that it wasn't the greatest idea. She was married, for one thing. Not just married, but *recently* married.

I suppose at this point I should just tell the whole story.

It starts one evening about ten years ago when a friend who was a theater director invited me to go see a one-woman show about Emma Goldman that she was directing at a small venue in downtown Manhattan. The curtain went up and revealed, in spotlighted profile, a red-haired woman of stunning beauty. The absurdity of asking us to accept this luminous woman as the rather plain, matronly revolutionary, was trumped utterly by my pleasure in just watching her.

After the show, the director and I, along with a small group of others, went to a restaurant around the corner. I was seated across from the writer-star of the show, and she and I immediately struck up a conversation. I can't remember much of what was said now, but I do remember looking into her pale blue eyes and thinking, "I could be in real trouble here." A short while later my fantasies received a crushing blow, however: Her husband arrived, sliding into the chair next to her. The flirtation was effectively over, at least for the moment.

The next day, still obsessing, I called my director friend, desperately looking for a shred of hope. Maybe the marriage was rocky or on the way out? No, she said. They were virtually newlyweds.

I tried to absorb this disappointing news. I had just gotten my first book published and a movie deal on top of it. I was in a better place than I had been in for a long time, and I was trying to do things differently in my life. I commanded myself to put the ravishing Alice O'Neill out of my mind.

Two years went by. I went to see a show that my cousin, a performance artist, was doing. To my surprise, the evening's program also included a play written by one Alice O'Neill. She wasn't in it, but when the play was over, during an intermission, I turned around and there she was: pale skin, lovely delicate features, and a cascading halo of now blond curls. I began sweating instantly, talking nervously, a no-doubt goofy grin pasted beneath my goofy glasses. I had loved her play. "It reminds me of Beckett," I said. "Very Beckettian." She thanked me, blushing slightly.

The next day I queried my friend the director all over again. How was the marriage now? Were she and her husband still together? Were they perhaps having problems?

Still solid, she said.

"Never mind," I said. "Set up a dinner anyway. Just the three of us."

She told me I was being stupid, but did what I asked. On the appointed evening, I waited nervously with my friend in a Mexican restaurant in Chelsea. When Alice arrived, I sprang to my feet, but as soon as I did, I noticed a man trailing behind her. She'd brought *him*. The husband. It knocked the wind out of me.

Another two years passed.

Eight o'clock on a beautiful Saturday, the beginning of spring. I'd just played in a $5-$5 pot-limit game at the Diamond Club and won $1,000. On my way home, I stopped inside a gourmet market called the Garden of Eden on West Twenty-third Street in Manhattan. I'd bumped into several people already that day—it was one of those days when New York seems like a very small town. Now I looked up and saw her face, the face from my dreams, in the checkout line. I said hello. She instantly lit up, seeing it was me. The container of pasta she placed on the counter looked too small to feed two people. *Unless they were dieting. Or he didn't like pasta. Or . . . stop it. Don't do this to yourself.*

Outside the store, we continued to talk for another twenty minutes, standing on the sidewalk in the soft night air. I was headed off to L.A. in a few days. A producer at Paramount, after acquiring my book in turn-around from Castle Rock, had hired me to write the screenplay. I gave Alice my e-mail address and told her that if she had any plays coming up, she should let me know. I was dying to ask her if she were still married, but I couldn't bring myself to do it. It seemed inappropriate.

That night, however, I called my director friend with the perennial question. This time my friend didn't know what was going on with her. She and Alice had had a falling-out and hadn't talked in over a year. Last she knew, though, Alice was still married.

In L.A., I checked my e-mail one morning a few days later and my heart stopped. She had written to me. It was one line: "Hope wherever you are, the sun is shining on you." Innocuous enough, but all the encouragement I needed. I wrote back the following:

Dear Alice, it's always so—nice doesn't quite describe it—so warm seeing you, so full of some feeling that I've nearly forgotten about except that I felt it the first time I saw you and it's never gone away. I know I shouldn't be writing like this but I feel past caring about shoulds and shouldn'ts. Seeing you the other night came at the end of one of those extraordinary weeks that happen in New York sometimes, full of coincidences and chance meetings, where everything is full of promise and possibility and you feel lucky. Standing there on that corner talking to you, wanting to stay there talking to you, I thought maybe you were having one of those weeks, too, and maybe I was part of it, the way you were part of it for me, that we were both feeling lucky like that. I don't know, Alice, I keep waiting for you not to be married so that I can tell you these things, but maybe you never will be, so I'm telling you anyway. Maybe this kind of thing happens all the time, there are hundreds of men walking around New York in love with Alice O'Neill, waiting for her not to be married. If that's true, I'm jealous of them all but I don't blame them one little bit. I know so precious little about you, Alice, maybe if I knew more all this would go away—or if you told me that you were deliriously happy I would try to kill these feelings again the way I have before, the way I do every couple of years when I see you and you're still married. . . . Am I crazy? Dreaming? Or is my friend Matt right when he says that sometimes married people are just mean and fall in love with people for fifteen minutes on their way home from work? Oh hell, here you just wrote me a few friendly words and in return you get this. *I guess it's just more proof (as if one needed it) that New York is a dangerous place. . . .*

Six days went by while I was driving around L.A. going to meetings. I began to think that sending the e-mail had been a colossal mistake. She must think me insane or a stalker. Then on the seventh day came a response: "I'm sorry it's taken me so long to write back, but your e-mail kind of blew me away. You see, three days before I got it, I decided to leave my husband."

I caught my breath and read the words over again. Then read them once more. It was all I could do not to jump on a plane that minute.

The three months that followed my return to New York a few days later were as good in their way as this novelistic preamble, which is to say they were highly romantic, full of passionate sex, jealousy (it was during this period that she flew out to L.A. to have dinner with the rakish Irish movie star Gabriel Byrne, who was interested in her screenplay), and lots and lots of projection, at least on my part. The line in my e-mail "maybe if I knew more, all this would go away," was in some ways prophetic. But ironic, too, because as I did know more—came finally to line up the projection with the actual, like a piece of tracing paper over a drawing—I was stunned to discover that the real Alice was not the person I had imagined. She was not someone who was going to torture me or freak out or run back to her husband.

This was good—and at the same time not so good. The way I was wired, once I saw that she wasn't going to give me a hard time—I know how bad this is going to sound—I got bored. *Oh, so this is what a healthy relationship is like. Fuck.*

I'd painted myself into a corner. I wasn't going to be with someone who would make my life miserable, but I wasn't sure I could be with someone who wouldn't make my life miserable. So I did what any other normal neurotic New Yorker would do: I went back into therapy, back to the couch. I wanted to make this relationship work. I'd been with enough women to know that it wasn't them, it was me, and here was a good one: smart, beautiful and apparently capable of loving me. Why couldn't I be happy with her?

I'd like to tell you that I came up with answers, that a lightbulb went on one day. Mostly I just continued to vacillate. After several years of this, Alice finally decided that she'd had enough, that I wasn't ever going to come around, and she broke up with me for what was apparently the last time. I wasn't devastated. I didn't fall apart—even after I heard she was going out with other men. I starting going out on dates myself. But it was like watching a magic show after you'd found out how the tricks worked. There were no surprises left. I didn't believe the fairy tale anymore. I didn't believe that some new and different woman was going to come along and this time it would all fall into place. I was forty-nine, and fairly certain that whatever I thought I was looking for probably didn't exist.

Nine months went by. I had to move out of the Brooklyn Heights apartment I was living in, and I wound up taking a place two blocks away from Alice's apartment in Carroll Gardens, Brooklyn. Psychologists have a term for this kind of behavior: care solicitation. Whatever it was, proximity led to our talking again after a period of not talking. Then we started hanging out as "friends," going to movies, having dinner together. Both of us were wary, unsure of what exactly we were doing. Her anger kept boiling over. If only I could get past my issues, we could make this work. For my part, I felt misunderstood. I was who I was, and that was a guy ambivalent about being in a relationship.

"You're not the only one," she said one day in exasperation. "I'm ambivalent, too."

"No shit," I said. "Otherwise you never would have gotten involved with someone like me in the first place."

I knew I didn't want to lose her again, but I still couldn't seem to make the big gesture. Then came the baby stuff, her wanting to get pregnant, and I started to think, okay, that would be a reason to get married. But then that began to feel like a stupid way to go about things. She deserved better than that.

So it wasn't some dramatic breakthrough. I'm still afraid that if

I'm honest with her she won't understand, she'll get pissed at me, and the whole thing will fall apart.

"Are you there?" she says as I step outside from the cool darkness of the casino into the sultry night air of the desert.

"I'm here," I say.

"I thought I'd lost you for a moment."

"No, I'm here."

"You just got quiet, I guess."

"I guess that's what it must have been."

5

Something Bright and Shiny
and Worth the Pain

I open the door of my room and see Nicky lying in the bed that had formerly been my luggage stand, his head propped up by a bunch of pillows. He's reading my book, *One of a Kind*, although I pretend not to notice.

"I went back over to your table to see how you were doing," I say, "and you were gone."

He emits a sound of disgust, a *ppht*, shaking his head.

"Gavin said you got unlucky. What happened?"

"It doesn't matter," he says. "Nothing matters. The world has no meaning; it's all a black void and I don't care."

I can't suppress a laugh. This is vintage Nicky. He laughs along with me.

"Your book's pretty good, by the way," he says. "Better than I thought it would be."

"Thanks."

"I'm not saying I thought it would be bad. I just didn't think it would be this good."

"You can stop talking about it now. But thank you. I'm glad you're enjoying it."

"At least you have something to fall back on."

"Yeah, thank God I picked a lucrative profession like writing."

His turn to laugh. "So how'd *your* day go?"

"About as well as yours. I've decided I'm taking tomorrow off. I need to clear my head and not lose any more money. I'm gonna play tennis with Shane in the morning, hang out by the pool, and after that maybe type up some of my notes."

"Sounds like a plan."

"What are you going to do?"

"I was thinking about mainlining some heroin. Or possibly driving my car into oncoming traffic. Or maybe I'll just take the money that was earmarked for my daughter's education and play some more poker."

"Seriously."

"I'm being serious. I think I'm going to play in one of the tournaments they're having over at the Palms. They have two a day. One at noon and one at seven. They're unbelievably soft. I already played a couple before you got out here. I cashed for four thousand in one. It's the one positive result I've had here."

"What's the buy-in?"

"Two hundred and thirty with one optional rebuy. You start with a thousand in chips and ten and fifteen blinds, half-hour rounds. It's a good structure, and the players are unbelievably bad. First prize in the last one I played was twenty-four thousand."

"And there's one at seven at night?"

"I'm telling you, they're really soft," he says with an evil grin.

"Well," I say, already feeling temptation getting the best of me. "I'll see how I feel."

In the morning, I call Shane, who gives me directions to his apartment. He's reserved a court for us at the Flamingo Hilton. The apartment he and his Internet buddy, Ari Abramowitz, are renting is right off Flamingo. It has a radio-controlled front gate and a series of interlocking condo units arranged in a court, with roofed parking ports out front. The apartment itself has two bedrooms, white shag carpet, wide-slat vertical blinds, and soulless generic art hanging on the walls in unoffensive shades of pink and blue. Shane and Ari, who I think is twenty-one and looks it, are sitting in the dreary air-conditioned gloom in their boxers, with their laptops open, multitabling some online cash games. The air reeks of potent marijuana.

"Quite a scene you've got here," I say, aiming for somewhere between old bastard and sarcastic.

Ari grunts, staying focused on his screen, while Shane logs off, gets dressed, ties up his sneakers, mumbles something to Ari about seeing him later, and heads with me out the door.

On the drive across town, we pick up some sunscreen and some bottled water, and I start laying the groundwork. "Between the heat and jet lag, I don't know. I hope this doesn't kill me."

"Are we betting?" Shane asks.

"Maybe we shouldn't."

In Brooklyn, we've been playing once or twice a week since spring at the Prospect Park public courts. Even though I'm fifty and Shane is still in his twenties, I'm the stronger player. It's less a physical thing than it is mental. It reminds me of when I was in my twenties and playing against my father. I'd long since surpassed him in terms of skill, but I still had trouble beating him. It's the same way with young Shane. Even though his ground strokes and serve keep improving, when it comes to the mental aspects of the game, I've got him severely psyched out.

The Flamingo Hilton's tennis courts are located in the hotel's inner grounds, beyond the pool. To get to them we have to walk under a manmade waterfall and up a twisting set of stairs carved into the fake stone. We've reserved a court, but it wasn't really necessary. No one else is playing. Eleven a.m. on a Sunday in June in Las Vegas when the temperature on the court is about ninety five degrees. Go figure.

We begin to hit, and I'm spraying balls all over the place. Shane isn't doing much better. Between the glare, the heat, and the insta-sweat, it's a bit of an out-of-body experience. We hit balls for ten minutes without getting much better, and Shane finally says, "You wanna play?"

"Sure."

"You wanna put anything on it?"

"Up to you."

"A hundred bucks that I get three games in a set?"

"How about two hundred that you don't get more than two."

"Three *is* more than two."

"Right. So two is a push. Three is a win."

He grins, knowing that I'm fucking with him.

There is a delicate balance in this kind of negotiation. I'm not only trying to up the ante; I'm trying to get inside his head. Of course he could turn it around. If he were to say, "Okay, let's make it a thousand," then I might be the one psyched out.

Though on the surface, betting on a game of physical skill like tennis and betting on a game of deductive skill like poker would appear to be quite different, there is in fact a great deal of similarity. Essentially, in both, you are determining your odds of success, then betting money when you feel you have an edge. In poker, my opponent and I may interpret the relative strength of our hands differently, and then both bet thinking we are getting the best of it. Similarly, in tennis, my opponent and I, once a handicap has been established, may each feel that we are getting an edge. Obviously, in both situations, only one person can actually be getting the best of it, but that, as they say, is what makes horse races. When speculating about a future result (who will win and by how much, or, say, will the marriage last and for how long), there will almost always be divergent opinions, and therefore an opportunity for a wager.

Winning gamblers take great pride in their ability to sniff out an edge, or work an angle to give themselves an edge. As we well know, however, even a hustler can get hustled (think of that great and devastating scene in *The Color of Money* when Forest Whitaker hustles Paul Newman's "Fast" Eddie Felson). Whenever I've been hustled, it's been my ego that's done me in. It doesn't matter who's the better player; the thing that really separates two gamblers when they're negotiating a handicap is which one has a clearer view of reality. As I say, it's a delicate balance. Too cocky and you can build yourself a mountain that you'll never get over. Too meek and your opponent may get a dangerous psychological boost. I'm pretty sure I can skunk Shane if I put my mind to it, but I wouldn't want to bet on it. If I did make a bet like that, it would be pure ego.

"All right, two hundred," Shane says. "You're on."

Almost effortlessly, I jump out to a quick three-love lead, dropping maybe two points along the way. I'm not doing anything great, but Shane can't hit more than three balls in a row without missing. He gets to 40-40 in the fourth game, and I say, "Good. You were making it too easy." He promptly flubs the next two points and gives me a dirty look. At 5-0, during the changeover, I hand him the three green Wilson hardcourt balls, flashing him a little smile.

"You fucking hustled me again," he says.

"Hey, you want to get out of the bet? I'll let you out for a hundred and seventy-five."

"Very generous of you."

"I'll tell you what. If you win the next game, we'll call it even, but if I win, you owe me three hundred."

This is actually an intriguing proposition, and Shane considers it, drinking from a bottle of Poland Spring.

"Let's just keep it the way it is," he says.

"Okay."

Of course, what happens is that, after turning down my proposition, he actually wins the next game. I'm not going to say that I allow him to, because I don't. But to him it seems as if I'm taunting him, and it pisses him off. His anger seems to fuel him, because with me serving, up 5-1, he suddenly bunches a string of shots together and wins the next two points. At 0-30, we have another long exchange, and this one ends with me getting lucky on a net cord and winning a point that would have put me in a 0-40 hole. Unfazed, Shane rips a backhand winner on the next point, and suddenly he's a point away from a push.

I hit my first serve into the net, and now I can feel the tightness in my right arm and in my legs. I toss the ball, and for a moment, as it's suspended in air, silhouetted against the cloudless blue sky, I think about double-faulting. Usually, the next thing that happens will be exactly that: the thought made manifest. Instead, I somehow let go of the fear and just hit the ball. The serve spins in deep to his backhand. He tries to block it back, but the kick pops it off the face of his racket and it sails wide. Thirty-forty.

The tightness is gone now. I'm breathing and thinking only about hitting the ball. Shane gets my next serve back, and we exchange several shots. He hits a short ball, which I slam deep into the corner and follow to the net. He just barely gets it back, and I punch a volley into the open court for an easy winner. Serving at set point, I smash a flat serve that catches the center stripe, and he doesn't even bother to swing at it. He just looks at the spot it hit, shaking his head.

He walks up to the net, radiating disgust.

"Well, you made me sweat," I say, shaking his hand.

"I had you. That fucking net cord saved your ass."

"I got a little lucky," I admit. "Just like when you called my kings with your threes."

"You're still thinking about that hand? That was over a year ago."

"You always remember the bad beats. Double or nothing?"

"Nah. I'm wiped out."

I'm relieved. I could go another set, but it wouldn't be fun in this heat. Shane peels a couple of bills off his roll and hands them to me.

"I'll give you a chance to get 'em back," I say.

"Next time we'll make it that two games is a win for me."

"I don't know about that. You were coming on."

"I sucked."

"Hey, don't feel so bad," I say. "You just helped me book my first win of the trip. Now I'm only down half a million dollars."

Returning to the Gold Coast, after dropping Shaniac off at his front gate, I change into my swim trunks; put on a pair of flip-flops; glob on some more sunscreen; and grab my room key, notebook, cell phone, pen, and my copy of Harrington and Robertie, Volume 2, before heading back out to the elevators.

I'm feeling good, a combination of endorphins and the admittedly pathetic gratification of beating someone almost half my age in something physical. (*Yeah, I've still got it!*) I know it's goofy to derive so much emotional nourishment from this kind of temporal glory, but every little bit helps when you're in the hole.

The elevator door dings open, but before I can get on, Nicky steps off, looking glum. It seems that he decided to play in the noon tournament over at the Palms, and busted out before they even got to the break. "Another four hundred and thirty dollars down the tubes." He forces a wry smile. "What about you? How was tennis?"

"Good. I'm going down to the pool. You want to go?"

He sighs. "Nah."

"A swim might do you some good."

"I'm fine," he says. "I'm playing well, it's just . . . fuck, you know the story. Anyway, I'm probably going to take a crack at the seven o'clock tourney. You still taking the day off from poker?"

"The Palms is at seven? You might be able to twist my arm."

The elevator opens again, and this time I squeeze in next to two hefty men and a woman all wearing identical yellow T-shirts with a picture of a gray-haired, gray-bearded patriarch. Underneath the picture it says HENDERSON FAMILY REUNION.

"You seen Leon?" one of the men asks. "That nigger is drinking White Russians and losing all his money at the crap table."

"I told him to come back up to the room," the woman says. "He won't listen."

"Grandpa is gonna whup his behind when he finds out."

I can't help smiling at this, and one of the men, catching me, smiles back and says, "It's true. Ninety-seven years old today. But he will whup his behind."

For better or worse, ain't no one in Vegas who's gonna whup my behind. I'm on my own, totally without supervision. And so, four hours later, I find myself over at the Palms, buying into the $230 seven o'clock tournament. The room they're using for this tournament is the same space that they use as the set for *Celebrity Poker Showdown,* the truly awful but high-rated Bravo show that features a bunch of mostly clueless second-tier celebrities playing no-limit Texas Hold'em for charity. The tables we're using are straight off the set, and they're felted in dizzying, wild zigzag stripes, some of them in red and purple, others in green and blue. But Nicky was right: The competition is equivalent to what you'd find on the TV show. With a starting field of 200, and a full complement of rebuys, we're vying for a $24,000 first prize.

I manage to work my stack up to $6,000 by the break, from a starting stack of $1,000, at which point I get moved to perhaps the best tournament table I've ever played at. There are several happy-go-lucky Brits, who seem only to want to gamble at breakneck speed. Unfortunately, before I fully catch on to what they're about, I make an ill-advised bluff against one of them, who calls me down with bottom pair. This is nothing. Three of them are playing nearly every hand, calling pre-flop raises with any two cards, and moving in on any flop where they hit top pair, no matter the kicker. Once I get the lay of the land, I sit back patiently and wait for my opportunity to double up, which I know against this crew is only a matter of time. The problem is that I go totally card dead. By the time I'm down to $2,300, and the blinds have elevated to $200-$400, I can't afford to wait any longer. Finding an A-10 under the gun, I shove, only to have one of the suckers wake up with pocket kings. No lucky suckout for me, and I'm done.

I pass by Nicky's table on my way out the door, wishing him luck. We totally forgot to make a trade, so I don't have even a stake in him, though of course I'm pulling like hell for him to get a cash.

I look at my watch. It's not even ten o'clock. What the hell am I going to do now? Go back to my room? Get something to eat? I pass by the Palm's "high stakes" poker room. They've got a 2-5 no-limit game going. Sizing up the players at the table, most of whom look like vacationing, hip weekenders from L.A., I immediately pull out my roll. Time to play my first "live" poker of the trip.

There are two obnoxious drunks at the table. One of them resembles Vince Vaughn, whom he has clearly modeled himself after, right down to the open-necked white dress shirt and expensive vintage swinger suit. He keeps chatting up a curvy Asian princess, who sits down a minute after I do. She has a bare midriff, perfect breasts, and an expressionless face that is as icy as it is beautiful.

"What am I going to do?" Vince says to everyone else at the table. "She's so beautiful. I think I'm in love. Should I ask her for her phone number? Do you think she'd give it to me?" He keeps talking about her in this way, as if she isn't there, despite the fact that she never once smiles or gives any indication that she finds him amusing or charming. Meanwhile, Vince's buddy, a short, bald, muscular, bug-eyed little fucker, sucks on a dead cigar and keeps shouting obscenities. "Will you fucking make up your mind already? I could have gone out and gotten a lap dance in the time it's taking you to decide whether to call me." Though he's cautioned by the dealer and directed to a list of rules posted on the wall, one of which prohibits abusive language, he can't control himself. After the warning, every time a swear word escapes his lips, he chides himself, saying, "Shit, rule number ten; I keep forgetting!"

Everyone at the table quickly tires of their antics, which are amusing to them in inverse relation to how unamusing they are to us. After a seeming eternity, waiting for a situation where I can bust one of them, I finally lose my patience and stupidly bluff off $800 to the bug-eyed jerk, who, as he rakes in the pot, says, "What'd you think, I was gonna be afraid of your little bet there?"

I'm half an inch away from getting into something with him. Instead, I push back from the table, deciding it's not worth it, and take my leave, silently calculating my total investment for the trip so far, which now stands at a not-for-the-squeamish $13,675.

Before leaving the Palms, I check back in the tournament room. It's down to the final two tables, and Nicky is at one of them, very much alive. Eyeballing his stack, I put him third or fourth in chips.

I take up a post right behind him, and he obligingly lifts his hole cards a little higher so I can see. I can tell it means a lot to him that I'm there rooting for him. But the truth is that being able to watch him while being privy to his cards is so riveting and educational that I'd want to do it even if he weren't my friend.

One example: He's in late position; there's one middle position limper; and with A-Q, instead of raising, Nicky just limps. The flop has an ace in it, and the limper bets. Again, I'm thinking *raise*, and again Nicky just calls. Turn card is a blank, and the limper bets again. Is Nicky raising now? No. He just calls. The river is another blank. It doesn't fill any straights or flushes. The limper checks. It's a clear check-and-call move. He puts Nicky on a busted draw and wants to get a bluff out of him. He probably has ace rag suited, himself, and thinks his ace is good.

So when Nicky makes an almost pot-sized bet, the limper immediately calls with his ace rag. And he's stunned when shown the A-Q. Nicky played the hand in a totally unorthodox way that maximized his profit and left his opponent befuddled.

I keep watching until well past two in the morning. By then, they're down to four-handed, and the blinds are huge. Nicky becomes the short stack after absorbing a vicious beat, after which he tries to broker a deal that will give him $4,600 instead of the $2,800 he'd get if he finishes fourth. The deal-brokering process gets very contentious, and the tournament director, who is tired and wants to go home, winds up inserting himself into the negotiations.

Nicky tries to explain something, but the T.D. is an ex-army drill instructor and he doesn't like anyone interfering with him. Things quickly become tense.

Meanwhile, Chris Grigorian, a well-known tournament player whom Nicky knows from L.A. and who has the 5 percent of Nicky I should have had (they'd been sitting at the same table earlier and traded), swoops in and starts saying, "No deal. No deal," which doesn't help at all. Grigorian, the self-anointed "Armenian Express," of course wants Nicky to play it out and maybe get lucky and win the $24,000 because the difference between $4,600 and $2,800 to him is only $90 (he stands to make either $230 or $140), whereas if Nicky wins the thing outright, Chris will make $1,200.

While the tournament director tries to run the numbers through the computer, Nicky's frustration bubbles over. "It's so simple," he says. "If you'd just listen to me . . ." The stupidity of people is like an affront to him. The world would be so much better if he could just eliminate all the imbeciles who prevent things from functioning in sensible ways.

Myself, I'm tired as hell and just want to go back to the room and fall into bed, but I also want to be there for him, so I endure what turns into a thirty-minute imbroglio. Everyone is so beat and cranky that it seems as if a deal is impossible, but Nicky's persistence eventually pays off. He wears everyone down.

"Is it me?" he says, as he counts his $4,600 in winnings and pays off Grigorian. "Am I just an incredible asshole? Or is everyone else as stupid as I think?"

"It's probably a combination of the two," I say.

He looks at me for a moment, debating whether what I'm saying makes any sense or whether it just puts me into the offending camp. Then he lets it go.

"I hope you're hungry," he says, "because I'm fucking famished."

"You want to eat? *Now?*"

According to him the Chinese place in the Gold Coast, Ping Pang Pong, is a little-known Las Vegas treasure. I'm too tired to argue that sleep might serve me better at this point, so I go along with him. Once we get there, he orders wonton soup and moo shu chicken to go, and we bring it back to the room and sit there on the edge of our beds, eating with our hands and slurping the soup out of its container because Ping Pang Pong forgot to include plastic utensils.

We could be two prospectors at the end of a long day, back at our desert campsite, sitting by a fire eating our grub while the womenfolk are back home, keeping up the house, not knowing exactly how our time is being passed, but hopeful that someday we'll return, bringing them something bright and shiny and worth the pain.

6

The Heart Is a Lonely Hunter

I remember the first time I came to Las Vegas. It was 1974 and I was a freshman at Berkeley, suffering writer's block over a paper that was due on the American Revolution. Always resistant to doing anything that was assigned or required, I had been procrastinating in my usual ways, which included voracious consumption of any reading material that was not on my course lists. One of my recent purchases from Moe's used bookstore was a paperback copy of Hunter S. Thompson's *Fear and Loathing in Las Vegas*. After racing through it in one manic sitting, laughing as hard as I had ever laughed at anything, and feeling inspired by its spirit of anarchic lunacy, I said, "Fuck the paper," and headed straight to Vegas with a fellow literary adventurer and a healthy supply of pot, speed, and LSD. We didn't have a Red Shark convertible, but we did drive very fast through the desert while tripping, and we did go to Circus Circus among other places mentioned in the book. In retrospect, I count it as something of a minor miracle that we didn't die in a car wreck, get arrested, or suffer a psychotic breakdown. That I also managed while there to actually write the overdue paper ("Fear and Loathing in the American Revolution: A Dark Journey from the Birth of the American Dream to Its Death"), I consider nothing short of astonishing, although my professor gave it a D— and scrawled in red ink in the margin, "Do you think you're on television?"

His snide dismissal of my attempt to link Thompson's paranoid, comic novel with the American Revolution, as well as my central thesis that the spirit that formed this country and the impulses that led to the invention of a place like Las Vegas were essentially the same, did not spoil my enthusiasm for the conceit. From Columbus to the Pilgrims to the Founding Fathers to Bugsy Siegel, we were a nation grown out of the spirit of adventure, independence, and risk-taking. Vegas embodied all those things, albeit in their most hucksterish, P. T. Barnum form (it's no coincidence that Thompson lights on the Circus Circus casino, with its schizophrenic disconnect, as the flash point of everything gone wrong).

The thing that most impressed me about Thompson's gonzo adventure story was how he and his 300-pound Samoan attorney consumed massive quantities of drugs as if drugs were the most natural and obvious way to deal with a place like Las Vegas. Their heroic intake of uppers, downers, screamers, hallucinogens, and ether ("there is nothing more depraved than a man in the depths of an ether binge"), rather than serving as some form of insulation, instead turns the banality of their ersatz surroundings into a terrifying chamber of horrors in which "bad craziness" lurks around every corner. Searching for the American Dream in a town where you can walk up to a gambling table and walk away rich but where the very qualities of the American character that are most admirable seem to inevitably lead to grotesque and hideous excess, Thompson concludes that the Dream, at least for him, is dead. "You can see the high water mark in Las Vegas," he writes, "where the great wave of the '60s crested, and then the waters receded."

A child of that decade myself, I never felt the instinctive horror of Las Vegas that Thompson did. I loved the kitsch, the stuck-in-time corniness, the celebration of artifice. I loved the mobbed-up, bodies-buried-in the-desert history, the appeal to vice and sin. Vegas didn't pretend to be anything that it wasn't, and for me that made it okay. With a little bit of cash in my pocket, I could roll high and hard for as long as my luck lasted.

But maybe Thompson was right to be wary. He recognized the town as a place that hates losers—even as it depends on them. Talk about a microcosm of where things were going! Look at the world we live in now. It's all a big Ponzi scheme on the verge of collapse, built up on the sagging shoulders of the world's suckers, benefiting the clever few. Yet we all are so invested in seeing the possibilities for ourselves, in denying the very real likelihood that we might be the owners of those sagging shoulders, that we throw in with the side that tells us it's all good.

Vegas, like everything else, has succumbed to the corporate oligarchy; the mafia has mostly been squeezed out by the faceless, soulless, number-crunching conglomerates. As Terry Gilliam, the director of the movie version of *Fear and Loathing in Las Vegas,* has said: "Las Vegas is maybe the perfect reflection of America at this stage of its history. It's Disneyland, and everybody's becoming these mindless infants who wander around and don't do anything."

My fear is that I am one of them. What am I to make of my continuing attraction to this ever-more-tricked-out Xanadu? Or to poker (which, before its television-bred popularity, was getting squeezed out of casinos along with anything else that didn't serve the bottom line)? I like to think that there is something essential about both that has not been lost despite the obvious changes and the co-opting gravity of commerce and loyalty to stockholders. As I try to make sense of my life at this stage of my own history, I think about my relationships, my obsessions, my passions, my hopes; and I optimistically believe that as long as I can still look beneath the surface and see something pure, something real, something that hasn't yet lost all connection to what it was, then living will remain worthwhile. It may be pathetic that I dream about a big poker score the way some ghetto kid dreams about making it in the NBA. But you can't be a gambler unless you're an optimist.

Hunter S. Thompson went another route. In February 2005, three and a half months before I came out here, he shot himself. Fred Reed, the author of the wonderfully titled *Nekkid in Austin: Drop Your Inner Child Down a Well,* had this to say about Thompson's suicide in an Internet blog: "Then it was over. Everybody went into I-banking or something equally odious. We gave up drugs as boring. You can see why he ate his gun. Everything he hated has returned. Nixon is back in the White House, Rumsnamara risen from the dead, bombs falling on other peoples' suburbs. The Pentagon is lying again and democracy stalks yet another helpless country. This time the young are already dead and there will be no joyous anarchy. The press, housebroken, pees where it is told. But he gave it a hell of a try."

In the morning, after a breakfast of steak and eggs at the coffee shop, I talk Nicky into taking a drive downtown. I want to see what's going on at the Horseshoe now that the WSOP has moved on (yes, it's true, the final two days of the Main Event will be played at the 'Shoe, a farewell homage to the old place, but it's little more than the poker equivalent of "throwback jersey" night; a last nod to the past).

Nicky, off his nice little Palms cash, is in a much better frame of mind today than yesterday, although it would take a whole lot more than a $4,000 win to "shift the paradigm," as he says. Hearing Dylan's "Joker Man" on the car CD player, he's reminded that he "actually woke up with this song in my head, except it wasn't Joker Man, it was Poker Man."

I nod, only half listening, lost in my thoughts.

"Lighten up, dude. You look like you have the weight of the world on you."

I let out a sigh. "It's just that when I get back, I have to write a book about this shit."

"Oh, the book." He laughs.

"Don't laugh too hard. You're probably gonna be in it."

This makes him laugh harder. "I'm sorry," he says. "I just hope that you're going to put this whole thing into some kind of contextual framework."

"Yeah?"

"Because otherwise it's just going to be a book about poker."

"Well . . ." This is not the kind of thing I want to hear right now.

"You haven't thought about this?"

"I've thought about it. I just haven't gotten a . . . handle on it."

"How exactly did you get them to give you money for this?"

"I wrote a proposal."

"In which you said?"

"A bunch of shit that I've forgotten and that I'm not going to use anyway."

"Can you do that?"

"Sure."

"So you scammed them?"

"No, I didn't scam them. I just—"

"You scammed them," he says, and laughs again.

"Yeah, I'm making a real killing on this."

"I just hope you don't turn me into some loser," he says. "That's all I need, for my family to see me immortalized as some kind of self-deluded degenerate."

"What about me? How do you think I'm gonna come off?"

"I don't care about you."

With downtown coming into view around a bend in the freeway, my cell rings. It's Alice.

"Hey," I say, "I'm with Nicky. We're driving to the Horseshoe to see what's going on there. . . . No, nothing's going on. . . . That's why we're going. To see what that's like. . . . I know that doesn't make any sense. It's just—never mind, it's too complicated. . . . How are you? . . . What's been happening? It's hot there? Yeah, it's hot here, too. . . . No, things are okay. I'd be having a great time if I could win a few hands. . . . I mean, it hasn't reached the point where we have to cancel the wedding yet. . . ."

Suddenly the connection goes very quiet.

"Hello?" I say. "Are you there?"

"Yeah, I'm here."

"That was a joke."

"Uh-huh."

"Alice, it was a joke. I—" She cuts me off, saying that someone just came into her office and she has to go. She hangs up.

"I might have fucked that up," I say to Nicky, who just looks at me and shakes his head.

Our visit to the Horseshoe is a bit like returning many years later to a school that you went to as a child. Everything looks much smaller in reality than it did in memory. The casino floor is virtually gambler-free, a ghost town, in stark contrast to the crush of bankroll-toting rounders over at the Rio. The company that took over management of the Horseshoe property from Harrah's has done a decent job of tidying the place up, although it has cut overhead by eliminating a lot of the services that required staffing. There are new carpets, and the fixtures have been spiffed up and polished clean. Downstairs in the back of the Mint side, a permanent poker room has been installed, with about a dozen tables featuring small-stakes limit hold'em games and $1-$2 no-limit games. On the wall just past the snack bar, by the cage, is the famous Gallery of Champions, eight-by-ten framed pictures of every WSOP winner from Johnny Moss to last year's champ, Greg Raymer. It's anyone's guess what will happen to this wall next year.

The sports book is gone, as is the deli across from it, which makes me sad. I miss the always cheerful guys in toques who worked behind the counter there, serving great matzo ball soup and pastrami sandwiches, which I'd eat, along with a Dr. Brown's Cel-Ray, while watching a game on one of the sports book's numerous televisions.

Upstairs on the second floor, the Gee Joon Chinese restaurant is also shut down. I remember having dinner there with the British author Anthony Holden in the late 1980s while Stuey Ungar and Doyle Brunson sat at a neighboring table with Jack and Benny Binion, Benny wearing his trademark white Stetson. I was on my first assignment for a big national magazine at the time, trying to act as if I belonged, hoping I wouldn't be found out.

The gift shop, farther down the hall, across from what used to be the buffet and is now just a sitting area, has been shorn of all WSOP memorabilia. It probably has to do with some corporate restriction on WSOP logos enforced by Harrah's, but it's still odd that the birthplace of the World Series should be so cleansed of the connection to its past. It's like something they'd do in the old Soviet Union.

The tournament room, which had once been a bingo hall, is now called Benny's Bullpen and has been transformed into a theater featuring the Vinnie Favorito Show. Nicky and I try to open the closed door of the place, but it's locked. I walk around to the side door and give that a try. To my surprise, it opens. Inside the thirty-by-forty-foot room, there are tables and chairs scattered around, a small stage with a blue velvet backdrop, and some black-and-white photos on the walls, pictures of the Horseshoe back in the 1940s when Benny first bought it and it was called the Eldorado.

"It's hard to believe the World Series ever took place here," Nicky says, walking in behind me. Harder still to believe that in five weeks ESPN will be filming the final two tables right where we stand. It's like holding the NBA Finals in a high school gym.

After we cut out of the Horseshoe, we drive around looking for a place for Nicky to buy a set of electric clippers. He's decided that before he goes into battle again he wants to shave his mostly bald pate fully clean ("I just want to be stripped down and unencumbered by anything unessential like hair," he says), but since he left his clippers in L.A, he's going to have to spring for another set.

Downtown, the main boulevards are full of seedy-looking strip malls and used car lots, with residential one- and two-story painted stucco and cement boxes on the side streets. Despite the urban blight, the word is that real estate speculators have already been buying, and Nicky's convinced that nostalgia for Old Vegas is certain to kick in sometime in the next few years. He actually starts getting all worked up about it, in his manic, half-serious, half-ironic way, saying that it's a perfect place for artists, and he's going to look into buying something— except that his grandiosity takes him way beyond "Maybe I can get the money to buy a house" to "Maybe I can set up a meeting with someone like Steve Wynn and talk him into financing a mega arts complex." Besides reality there's one other wrinkle in this idea that he hasn't considered: Em has told him that the only way they're ever moving to Las Vegas is over her dead body.

It's a funny thing. My writer and artist friends are always coming up with get-rich-quick schemes, very few of which they ever follow up on. I think mostly it's a way to blow off some of the steam of having made a life choice that consigns one to near poverty.

The truth is that most people make the choice to become an artist when they are young and idealistic, when the consequences of that choice seem far away and abstract. We all believe that we are going to be the rare exception, whose books or paintings bring us fame and commercial success. But as the years go by, and we haven't become the next Julian Schnabel or Jonathan Franzen, such optimism or delusion becomes harder to sustain. So the schemes start. The pipe dreams. Mostly it's just talk. A way to escape. We've given up so much to be what we are that we can't help fantasizing about how nice it would be to be something else. But when it actually comes to *doing it*, to actually being something else, we can't pull the trigger. In fact, I can't think of any artist friends of mine who have ever launched a business unless they already had money or came from money. The ones who ultimately give up on the artist's life and move on to something else tend to get jobs in academia or publishing, or they go back to school and become psychotherapists. The closest most of us get to being entrepreneurs is dabbling in the stock market. Or, in my case, in Nicky's case, playing poker. But underneath, even in these, lies the paradox, the tug-of-war between the impulse to do something that will sustain our art and the impulse to leave it behind for something less taxing and more taxable.

Nicky pulls into the parking lot outside a drugstore. It's not one of the chain stores—far from it. When we walk through the door, out of the scorching, dazzling heat, we walk into another era. It seems quite possible, in fact, that this store has not received any new inventory since the 1970s. A random arrangement of display cases house a sparse dust-covered collection of tonics, shampoos, and obscure remedies and powders. Along the wall, there is an old-fashioned soda fountain with a Formica counter and swiveling stools. Nicky and I peruse the goods briefly, but there doesn't seem to be any point in inquiring about an electric clipper. A double-sided razor, maybe.

As we're on our way out, we notice an open door along one wall that connects for no apparent reason to the bar next door. Curiosity gets the best of us, and we look in: Two old men are sitting at the end of the carved mahogany bar, by the front window, their faces backlit by a slanting shaft of sunlight that suspends dust motes above them. Stuffed moose and deer heads hang from the walls.

"You want a drink?" Nicky asks.

"A drink? Are you serious? It's noon. We haven't even eaten lunch."

"We've got burgers and sandwiches," a barkeep pipes in, appearing from out of the gloom.

I look at him, a knobby-limbed fellow with gray, pockmarked skin; then I look at Nicky, who shrugs. "What the fuck, why not?" he says.

I can think of about ten reasons why not, but something, perhaps the spirit of Dr. Gonzo, overrides nine of them. We take a booth and order cheeseburgers and beers.

"What do you think the odds are that these burgers give us mad cow disease?" I say.

"As long as we're not eating the bodies of those heads on the wall, I think we're probably okay," Nicky says.

Halfway through the meal, Alice calls back. "I'm still with Nicky," I say, "Now we're having lunch."

"I need to talk to you."

"I can talk," I say, chewing a mouthful of burger.

"Look," she says, "I know you were joking earlier, but it scares me."

"Hey, we're not calling the wedding off. That was just me being a jerk."

"But when you make jokes like that, how do you think it makes me feel?"

"I'm sorry," I say. "I—"

"I just —sometimes I don't know what to think."

I could fumble this. I certainly have in the past. But somehow this time I don't. I say, "Think about how in a little over two weeks you'll be getting on a plane and flying out here and . . ." As I'm speaking I happen to glance over at the bar where the two geezers sit, necks twisted around, looking at me, grinning. "And then," I continue, "in a little over two months, we'll be in Provincetown, standing on a sandbar, in front of everybody we love, getting *freakin' married*. . . . Think about that."

The geezers raise their beer mugs and one of them gives me the high sign. Nicky cracks up.

Back at the Rio, the poker action rages on, oblivious of the existence of the Drugstore That Time Forgot or the Stuffed Animal Head Saloon.

If I find it somewhat comforting to be back among my brethren, it is also slightly disorienting, as if I've just returned home after being out of the country for several months.

In one corner of the room, by the entrance, tables 150 through 200 are running cash games, ranging in size from $2-$5 no-limit to $100-$200 no-limit to $3,000-$6,000 limit. The other side of the room is all about today's tournament, the $1,000 no-limit with rebuys. A thousand dollars is the least expensive buy-in at this WSOP, with the exception of the Ladies and the Seniors events. But prudence prevented me from taking a shot. Rebuy tournaments are quite a bit different from non-rebuy events. If you're not prepared to fire more than a single bullet, you're putting yourself at a huge disadvantage relative to your opponents, just as you would be if you sat down in a cash game with too little money. In many ways, a rebuy tournament is like a cash game that becomes a tournament after the rebuy period is over. Shane mentioned to me the other day that he was planning to play in it, so as I walk among the tables, I'm looking for him. There are plenty of big names still left, with the tournament down to the last ten tables and near the money. I see Barry Greenstein, Phil Gordon, David Williams, and Scott Fischman, among others, all with decent stacks. Scanning chip stacks quickly to see who the leaders are, I spy a mountainous pile at one table, and looking up to see who it belongs to, I do a double take. Holy fuck! It's Shaniac. I walk over, stunned and giddy. "*Shan-i-ac!*"

He nods, not wanting to grin too much, but clearly pleased with his situation.

"Six more players and we're in the money," he says.

I do a quick count of his chips. He has six towers of black $100 chips, each sixty chips tall; four towers of pink $500 chips forty-five chips tall; and one tower of yellow $1,000 chips forty-five chips tall. That's easily $160,000. "How many rebuys?"

"I'm in for four thousand."

"Not bad."

It's actually probably around the average. Most players have some sort of mental cutoff for how much they'll put into a rebuy tournament. Obviously, the less you put in, the better your equity. But just as in a cash game, as long as the game feels as if it's good and as if you've got an edge, you can and probably should keep playing. Last year in this event, Daniel Negreanu, a thirty-year-old Canadian pro, carried that theory to absurd lengths, setting a record with twenty-seven rebuys. What this means is that he had to finish in the top six just to break even. Not a very good strategy, but Daniel made it pay off by finishing third and collecting $100,940.

Coincidentally, Daniel is sitting in the 7 seat at Shaniac's table. He's not the only big name, either. Shane also has to contend with Stevie Zee and Meng La, as well as a couple of other tough players I recognize by face but not my name.

Negreanu and I have played together many times, including once at a final table in Foxwoods, at a tournament which he won and in which I finished fourth. I've always liked and admired him, not only as a player but as a thoughtful and articulate ambassador for the game. For a while, a few years ago, before the recent poker explosion, we struck up an e-mail correspondence. I was interested in doing a piece on him for a national magazine, and so we tossed the idea back and forth for a while, discussing hand strategy, as well as some of the finer points of tells.* I can't recall why I didn't wind up doing the piece, but it was a tougher sell back then, as was poker in general, and

---

* I wish I'd kept or printed out that correspondence. My computer's hard drive crashed and all the e-mails were wiped out. I remember that he teased me with one tell that he had recently picked up that had to do with what a player would do with his betting hand when he was bluffing, something about the way he'd be afraid to retract the hand after putting his chips in. He wouldn't get more specific, but it's a tell that I've used ever since nonetheless.

I may have thought that it needed some kind of topical peg that it didn't have.

As poker has ascended, however, so has Negreanu. In 2004, he was Player of the Year, earning a mind-boggling $4.5 million in tournaments alone. He also began playing regularly in the largest cash game in the world at the Bellagio with the likes of Doyle Brunson, Chip Reese, Barry Greenstein, Jennifer Harman, Howard Lederer, and Phil Ivey. That changed this year when he signed an exclusive contract with Steve Wynn to promote the new Wynn Hotel, which prevented him from playing the big game at the Bellagio. Negreanu's other poker-related side ventures include a Web site and blog, fullcontactpoker.com, which receives 100,000 visitors per month and is an affiliate of the online poker site EmpirePoker; a video game called Stacked; a poker-chip set; and a bobble-head doll in his likeness. He also signed a deal to endorse Clear Edge, an adrenaline blocker popular with NASCAR drivers.

Unlike many of the top players, who employ professional writers to assist them in putting together articles and books, Negreanu is an accomplished wordsmith who writes a monthly column for *CardPlayer* magazine and is finishing up a poker how-to book. He is slight of build, with Hollywood–blond highlights in his George Clooney–style hairdo, and his poker wardrobe alternates between expensive tailored suits and hockey jerseys.

I walk over and say hello and pat him on the shoulder, and we start to talk; but he's the big blind, and when I notice, I'm embarrassed that I wasn't paying closer attention. "Sorry," I say. "Play the hand."

He calls a $1,200 raise from Meng La, and I watch as the flop comes 6-8-10, and Daniel checks. Meng La bets $2,800 and Daniel calls. I can see his hand, a J-10 off. The turn is a jack.

At this point I'm thinking Daniel's just hit a bingo card and I'm wondering how he's going to play it. To my surprise, he checks. Maybe he's going to check-raise, I think. But when La bets $9,000, not only does

Daniel not raise; he starts talking: "You got a big hand," he says to La, "don't you?"

La says nothing. There isn't a flicker of change in his expression. If I had to guess, though, I'd say he doesn't want a call.

Daniel spends a long time staring him down. He's got about $24,000 left. Finally, he counts out $9,000 and slides it toward the pot.

On the river, a deuce comes, apparently changing nothing.

Daniel checks again, and La moves all in.

Daniel stands up. He picks up all of his belongings, zips them into his knapsack, and slings it onto his back. "I call," he says.

La turns up 7-9. He flopped the straight. Daniel nods, thumbs his J-10 in amusement, and mucks it. I feel as if I should apologize to him, as if somehow I've brought him bad luck, but he just shrugs, then walks away to applause. The damnedest thing about the hand is that he *knew*—or at least was 90 percent certain—that he was beat. He just couldn't get away from the hand.

A few minutes later, as I go back to sweating Shaniac, Stevie Zee moves in for $15,000 after Shane opens the betting, and Shane quickly calls him. Zee looks as if he's going to be one more notch in Shaniac's belt, but his A-10 sucks out against Shane's A-K, taking a bite out of Shane's tall yellow-chip tower. The good news is that everyone is now in the money.

In an event that started with over 800 runners, the professionals are dominating. Looking around I see (in addition to Zee, Greenstein, Gordon, Williams, and Fischman) David Pham, Hoyt Corkins, Jennifer Harman, Annie Duke, Tony Cousineau, Ram Vaswani, and Robert Williamson.

Despite this all-star cast, by the time the field is whittled to forty-two players, who's the chip leader with nearly $350,000 and a sixth of the entire amount in play? My main man the Shane Man. He slips a little as the day stretches on; but when they break for the night, down to the final twenty-seven, he's still the tournament leader with $250,300.

Predictably, he doesn't sleep well. When I see him the next morning, he's jangly and a little bleary-eyed. I give him a shoulder rub and a pep talk.

"Today's your day. You played beautifully yesterday, and I want you to just keep doing what you've been doing."

"Yes, coach."

"I can't believe I don't have a fucking piece of you in this."

"You didn't play. How were we gonna trade?"

In fact, Shane is being backed in this and a number of the other events by two guys from New York: one who goes online by the name of Sheets and whom I know slightly; and another whom I don't know at all, whose Internet name is Johnny Bax. They've got half of him.

Let me lay this out another way:

Shane: 50 percent
Backers: 50 percent
Me: 0 percent

However, as a journalist and his friend, I am selfishly rooting for him anyway.

On the first hand of the day, with both the small and the big blind not yet having arrived, Shane goes for a steal from the cutoff. Meng La, on the button, says, "I don't think so," and comes over the top for a serious raise.

Okay.

A few hands later, Shane raises $10,000 under the gun, and this time the player in seat 2 moves in. Shane has to muck again.

Is it going to be one of those days for him? Sometimes you sit down and in the first couple of minutes you just know how the whole day is going to go. You don't know what you did or whom you offended, but the poker gods are pissed. In a cash game, when this happens, you might think about getting up. You might say, "I can see it's going to be one of those days," and just leave. Of course you never actually do. To leave would be to admit that you believe in the supernatural—and your whole ethos, your pride in your ability at this game, is based on a rational approach and understanding of what is important. Feelings are important, but only in so far as they relate to the other players and their motivations. I *feel* he's weak, for example. But never in terms of the supernatural—I *feel* a jack is coming on the next card. No, that way lies madness and disaster. So you leave those kinds of feelings to the suckers. And yet . . .

In a tournament, of course, all this is academic. You can't leave the game, at least not on your own terms. The tournament dictates the terms by which you leave: that is, with no chips or all the chips. So your relationship to the supernatural is more fatalistic. Still, the feeling continues to plague me when Shane bets $10,000 with pocket jacks and true to the current of the day is reraised all-in for another $26,000. The money odds dictate a call, which is what Shane does. Still, it's hard not to think that the other guy will turn up pocket queens or kings because it's feeling so much like one of those days. To my surprise, and to Shane's, his opponent flips up a J-9.

In a perverse way, however, this is potentially even worse: a hand to truly test the gods' intentions. Lose here, and there is no other interpretation possible: Doom is the decree.

But the jacks, an 88 percent favorite, hold up.

Shane is healthy again, up to about $260,000, with the average stack at $90,000, and all the mental gyrations around the supernatural now seem silly. Not too long after the jacks, he wins a big pot when he flops a set of sevens, putting him over $300,000 with nineteen players remaining. Then, with fifteen players left, he loses a sizable pot with top pair, top kicker, against middle set. And so it goes, up and down, as the eliminations continue, until they're down to the final ten, and just one more player needs to be eliminated to reach the final table.

It's at this point that Shane makes an ill-advised preflop call with J-10, and dumps a bundle when he turns two pairs and Phil Gordon turns a straight. What it means is that when Eli Elezra moves in with pocket eights and gets busted by 10-9 suited to stop play for the night, Shane is down to $134,000.

But fuck all that neg-head shit. My boy is gonna be on television!

To celebrate we have dinner at Le Cirque in the Bellagio, along with Shane's roomie, Ari Abramowitz; and another friend of his, Matt Kirisits, a chemist from Buffalo. We try to get Nicky to join us, but he's playing the tournament at the Palms again, so it's just the four of us. Outside the Rio, the sky is streaked with red, and the air temperature is perfect. We run into Daniel Negreanu, who's on his way back inside to play in the stud tournament after a break, and he offers us a warm "East Coast Posse!" and asks Shane how the day ended up in the rebuy. It's hard not to love Vegas at moments like this. For Shaniac, it's his moment of having arrived. Acceptance from the big boys, a final table, and—oh, yeah—a guaranteed minimum score of $44,000.

I've never been to Le Cirque in Manhattan, but the Vegas version acquits itself nicely. The food is top-notch, and the decor—billowing silk in shades of burned yellow and red—is circusy and elegant. It doesn't seem to matter that we're dressed in grungy poker duds and that two of us are wearing sneakers. As long as you're waving money around (and it's definitely Shaniac's money tonight) nobody gives a shit.

"Check out Antonio," Shane says, nodding toward the other side of the room.

Antonio "the Magician" Esfandiari is sitting with a gorgeous girl, looking relaxed and sure of himself. It's amazing how these young poker studs emit the same kind of star power as professional athletes and young movie actors. Antonio is Omar Sharif circa *Funny Girl*. He has dark flashing eyes, thick black hair, and a neatly trimmed goatee. The truth is he had "it" long before he made a splash on the WPT. He started showing up in the New York clubs in the company of Phil "the Una-bomber" Laak several years ago, playing in the $5-$5 pot-limit hold'em game. I could see right away that he had talent. He was fearless and ag-gressive and he knew how to handle himself (he was funny, needling, and manipulative—all assets to have at a poker table). One night, I think it was the fourth or fifth time he'd come around, the game broke around three in the morning. I was up $3,000 and Antonio was about even. He asked me if I wanted to play head's up with him, and I said, "Sure." It was an ego thing for me, no question about it, the kind of thing I was usually too disciplined to get caught up in. But Antonio had such a swagger, even then, that I just wanted to knock him down a peg.

He played head's up super-aggressively, always putting me to the test. I got a little unlucky, flopping two pairs when he flopped a set, but worse than that, I didn't feel comfortable. His aggression forced me into the role of counterpuncher and trap-setter, and I didn't like it. It felt as if I were getting backed up to the edge of a cliff. After losing $1,100 of my profit, I parroted Nick the Greek's famous line to Johnny Moss, saying, "Antonio, my friend, I'm afraid I'm going to have to let you go."

I wasn't surprised when he subsequently won a WPT event and a gold bracelet at the 2004 WSOP.

Returning from a trip to the men's room, I run into him.

"Antonio."

"Peter, dude, what's going on?"

I catch him up a little, and then he says, "Man, I am so fucking stoned. Is it really obvious? Can you tell? We ate pot brownies earlier and holy shit!"

I laugh and tell him it's not apparent and that I won't tell anyone.

But of course the instant I get back to the table I immediately tell everyone.

The funniest thing about the dinner, though, is watching both Ari, who is twenty-two, and Matt try to get a handle on haute cuisine. The menu baffles them, so they settle on the prix fixe dinner. When the first course comes, and it's beef carpaccio, they both look at it as if it's something that the chef scraped off the bottom of his shoe.

"Do you want it?" Ari asks me. "I don't think I'm gonna eat it."

I contemplate trying to explain why he should give it a try, but in the end that seems simply patronizing, so I scoop it onto my plate. Shane does the same with Matt's.

In the morning, I call Alice and describe my latest adventures. She doesn't say it, but I can tell she's wondering why I'm so excited about Shane's good fortune when all I can do is lose. It's a good question. I try to explain that it's about the solidarity, about how when one of us does well, it lifts up the whole boat.

The truth is, despite my real and genuine happiness for Shane, a little something inside me, as Gore Vidal might say, is dying. I want to be at that final table. Shaniac's been playing, what, two or three years? Why is he at a final table? Why isn't it me? Or Nicky? For Christ's sake, Nicky. He's got a wife and a kid to support. He's ten times the player Shaniac is at this point. If there were any justice . . . But looking for justice in poker is like looking for virtue in a whorehouse.

I go down to a late breakfast, leaving Nick still asleep in the room. He didn't get in until very late, and I was afraid to ask him about his night. I could tell it didn't go well. I get to the Rio sometime past noon and check my e-mail in the media room. Alex Williams, a reporter for *The New York Times,* is flying out in a couple of days to interview me and Nolan for a feature he's writing about Stuey Ungar in the Sunday Styles section.

After writing back to my editor and publicist, assuring them that I'll try to be my most charming self with Alex Williams, I wander over to the tournament area about one o'clock. The television table is located in the back of the Amazon Room, up on a small raised platform with midnight blue curtains behind it, and little white lights twinkling like stars through pinholes. Combined with the Levitra flame logo emblazoned on the green felt of the table, the whole tableau is actually a weird visual echo of the roots of Texas Hold'em—when it was a game played by cowboys on the prairie, under the stars, by the light of a campfire. Now it's a game played under television lights and sponsored by an erectile dysfunction pill.

The ESPN camera crew dollies around, setting up shot angles and cues, while some of the players loiter inside the velvet ropes, behind which lie temporary aluminum bleachers on one side, and press row on the other. Beyond the fourth wall, today's other tournament, a $2,000 buy-in no-limit, is going on, along with the final day of yesterday's $1,500 buy-in seven-card stud.

After a few minutes, Shane wanders out from somewhere in the back production area. He's just finished doing his interview with ESPN. He's wearing a black leather jacket, and his curly hair is extra thick and lustrous under the lights. I imagine the producers must love his ass. And why not? He's young, quotable, and telegenic. If I were the producers, I'd be lighting candles, hoping that it'll come down to him and Phil Gordon at the end.

"How'd it go?" I say.

"Pretty good. I think I gave 'em some good stuff."

"You nervous?"

"A little. I had trouble sleeping again."

While we're standing there, Rich Korbin from PokerStars comes over and grabs Shane's elbow. "Can I talk to you for a minute?" he says.

"Sure," Shane says.

They step a few feet away, and I hear Korbin say, "We should talk if you're interested in a deal." There's some back-and-forth, and then I hear Korbin say, "Well, good luck, and I hope you finish first or second."

THE HEART IS A LONELY HUNTER

"What was that all about?" I ask as Korbin walks off.

"I'm not sure," Shane says. "It was a sort of typically opaque Rich Korbin conversation." The stipulation that ESPN has made concerning endorsement contracts this year is that they must be signed before the start of a tournament if a player is to wear the logo of the site or company sponsoring a player. For those players who do sign on, PokerStars is offering $10,000 to players to wear their logo at a televised table and $25,000 if they win. At FullTilt the deal is even sweeter: $10,000 if you are at the final table and $50,000 for a win. As near as Shane could tell, Korbin seemed to be saying that if Shane finished first or second, PokerStars might be interested in sponsoring him in the future. "But the thing is, he didn't actually offer me anything. Besides, I want to wear my own clothes. The whole point of playing poker is that you're a free agent, not beholden to anyone."

"So you'd turn down a deal to wear their shit no matter what?"

"No, I'd have to see. I mean, the thing is, I actually play on Poker-Stars, but unless it was a really sick deal, I think I'm better off not affiliating myself with anyone."

I try to think what I'd do. Would I really care whether I was wearing someone's goofy T-shirt and cap or not if a sponsor was willing to pay me thousands of dollars? Is there relativity in all this? Can I be a little bit of a whore? Could I say, "I'll wear the T-shirt but not the cap because I look stupid in caps?"

I know that when I see all the FullTilt guys walking around in their ridiculous red and black hockey jerseys and hats, I think, "No fucking way. I am not going to look like a goofball no matter how much they offer me." I mean, would I drive around in one of those Mini Coopers with a Red Bull can on top if they offered me the car free?

I guess it all goes back to the same thing. How do you keep the connection to what is pure and real? How do you live in this world without giving in? Why did you eat the gun, Hunter? And where are you now?

— 139 —

7

Seduction, Fantasy, and
Getting Lucky
(Not Necessarily in That Order)

Johnny Grooms, the WSOP director, announces that the action will begin momentarily, so I take a seat in the front row of the temporary aluminum bleachers along with all the other friends and family members of the nine final-table combatants. Shane steps down off the slightly raised stage and ambles over to where I'm sitting, greeting both me and a dark-haired suburban-dad-looking fellow next to me.

"Do you guys know each other?" he asks.

The suburban dad and I take a closer look at each other and shake our heads. Shane makes the introductions. It turns out I'm sitting next to Johnny Bax, the near-legendary online player, who in real life is known as Cliff Josephy.

"Tell Peter the story," Shane commands him.

I look at Josephy, who has newscaster-perfect hair and large, perfect white teeth. He shrugs. So Shane tells me instead: It seems Josephy flew out yesterday, bought into the stud tournament along with 473 others, and is now among the twenty-one survivors. That would be a nice accomplishment by any standards, but the punch line is that before yesterday Josephy had never played stud in his life.

"Wow. Not even in a home game?" I ask.

"Not even in a home game," Josephy says.

"That's unbelievable."

"It's beyond unbelievable," Shane says. "And the sickest part is that he's gonna win it."

"Hey, there's a long, long way to go," Josephy objects.

"I'm telling you," Shane says. "I've got a feeling."

Josephy is typical of the new breed of Internet-schooled players who have been able to learn in six months what it took me twenty years to pick up. A former hedge-fund trader, Josephy made a ton of dough in the market and basically retired a few years ago. Finding himself at home in Syosset, Long Island, with his wife and two kids and time on his hands, he took up Internet poker at the beginning of 2004 just as a diversion and discovered that he possessed a knack for it. It's not surprising really that with his background in finance he had developed well-tuned math skills and an understanding of and a tolerance for risk, but it also turned out that he was a bit of a genius at making decisions based on incomplete information. Playing under the name Johnny Bax, he has quickly ascended to the number one ranking online. In the past couple of months alone, he has won seven $10,000 WSOP seats, mostly in double-shootout tournaments.

His live tournament experience, however, is extremely limited and confined to hold'em. It's safe to describe his entry into the seven-card stud event as a lark. Arriving in Las Vegas two hours before the start of it, he solicited the advice of some of his Internet poker friends. Brett Jungblutt aka Gank, one of the original members of The Crew, advised him that the secret was "to just play tight." Scott Fischman, another member of the The Crew and a two-time WSOP bracelet winner at the tender age of twenty-four, said "play position, just like in hold'em."

Darrel Dicken aka Gigabet, another top online player, told him to "see who plays what kinds of hands," and act accordingly. Synthesizing their impromptu advice with his own instincts, Josephy made a flush on the first hand and kept doing what no one could teach him—catching cards—all the way to the final twenty-one. "Sheets," Shane's other backer, and a former client of Josephy's, was critical of him, Josephy says, for talking too much during hands and revealing his thought processes to his opponents. "But I haven't stopped doing it," he says. "I'm having too much fun."

Josephy can't wait around any longer for Shane's final table to get under way. Nicky is just arriving when Josephy gets up. He hears me wish him good luck.

"You know that guy?" Nicky asks as Josephy heads off.

I tell him the whole story. Not unexpectedly, this prompts a display of eye-rolling incredulity.

"You believe him? That he's never played before?" Nicky asks.

"I actually do."

All we can do is giggle about it, about the arbitrary, capricious logic of a game that so annoyingly defies the Horatio Alger paradigm. And then there's Shaniac. As we settle in to watch his big television debut, it is impossible, looking at him both in the flesh and on the TV monitor, not to consider what I know about his personal history: that eight years ago, in the fall of 1997, when he was twenty, he went mad.

It happened while he was in the city of Amsterdam, on vacation, and was triggered by the ingestion of some powerful psilocybin mushrooms. At the end of a trippy twenty-four-hour odyssey through the city, he returned to his hotel, mistakenly entered someone else's room, stripped down naked, took a bath, and got arrested for trespassing. The arrest was the least of his problems at that point. Far more serious was the fact that the hallucinations induced by the drugs did not go away and Shane entered that mysterious netherworld in which the separation between what is real and what is fantasy blurred. He spent the next five months of his life in and out of psycho wards.

Back home in America, the doctors characterized what was happening to him simply as a psychotic breakdown, neglecting to factor in the recreational drugs. The possible underlying disorders, they speculated, ranged from bipolar mania to schizophrenia; and they put him in psychiatric lockup, on a heavy diet of antipsychotic drugs like Haldol, which seemed only to exacerbate his problems.

Eventually a more suitable concoction brought him back to earth, but the side effects were miserable, and as soon as he felt confident that he could discontinue taking it without relapsing, he did so. "I sincerely believe," he wrote subsequently in an essay published in *The New York Press*, "that if I were ever to experience symptoms reminiscent of my psychosis I'd be able to handle them in a way more fruitful than simply checking into a psycho ward. You wouldn't take antibiotics every day and see your doctor every week for the rest of your life in case a cold comes back, and I've decided it's equally inappropriate to take Depakote and Zyprexa for the rest of my life lest I suffer another psychotic attack. . . . I just feel the business of keeping my head stable is best left to me."

Seven years later, he sits here under blue-filtered lights at a final table in the World Series of Poker and hears himself introduced as "a semiprofessional poker player from New York whose previous occupations include various ditch-digging jobs." Talk about cognitive dissonance!

As the cards are dealt at last and the cameras begin to roll, the final-table chip count looks like this:

Chuck Thompson:	549,000
C. T. Law:	516,000
David "the Dragon" Pham:	318,000

Shae Drobushevich:	248,000
Pascal Perrault:	225,000
Michael Gracz:	169,000
Shane Schleger:	134,000
Phil Gordon:	91,000
Meng La:	71,000

I'm nervous and excited for Shane, worried that he'll succumb to the TV jitters and do something foolish. But he looks calm and cool. His black leather jacket hangs on the back of his chair, and he's wearing a lavender dress shirt, the unbuttoned neck revealing his thick chest hair.

Early on, Phil Gordon doubles up against C. T. Law, who is a loosey-goosey Asian player.

"At least I won one hand, guys," he says, smiling and raking in the pot.

"We don't have to applaud when you double up, do we?" Shane says cuttingly. Gordon is definitely not a player anyone wants to see accumulating chips.

"Why are you picking on me?" Gordon says, mock-wounded. "I thought we were buddies."

"All I care about is the rock-paper-scissors championship," Shane says, needling Gordon about the charity event he's hosting, in which the top tournament poker players are contributing to his cancer charity by playing rock-paper-scissors, the children's game also known as Roshambo.

"You want to go for a thousand right now?" Gordon says, calling Shane's bluff.

"How about a hundred?" Shane offers meekly.

"Okay," Gordon says.

"Let's make it two out of three, though," Shane says, continuing to lose ground.

They shake their fists in the air, saying, "One, two, three, shoot. One, two, three, shoot," throwing out either a flat hand for paper, a two-finger V for scissors, or a fist for rock. If they both throw the same thing it's a push; otherwise scissors beats paper, rock beats scissors, and paper beats rock. It's a simple game with a strong component of psychology, perfect for poker players. Gordon wins the first round, Shane wins the second, and then Gordon takes the decisive third. A sheepish Shane has to toss the gloating Gordon a crumpled-up C-note on national TV.

As silly as this seems, it's the kind of gamesmanship that could easily put a guy on tilt—and Shane is susceptible, as I know full well from our tennis outings. To his credit, he doesn't let it get to him and stays disciplined, continuing to fold one hand after another. A little while later, after C. T. Law takes out the short-stacked Meng La, Phil Gordon gets all in pre-flop again, this time against David Pham. Gordon is one of the most visible players in the world, thanks to his announcing gig on Bravo; yet he's still never won a bracelet, and he desperately wants one. When he turns up pocket aces and Pham shows pocket tens, it looks as if he may finally be on his way. If the aces hold up (and he's a four-to-one favorite), Gordon will have gone from last to third in chips, with over $400,000.

Instead, rather shockingly, Gordon becomes the second casualty of the day when Pham hits a ten on the turn, making a set. The thirty-five-year-old millionaire takes the brutal beat with grace. But you know it stings. Had this hand gone the way it should have, he would have been in an excellent position to finally achieve his goal.

Michael Gracz, a twenty-four-year-old from North Carolina who won a WPT event and a million-dollar prize earlier in the year, shortly after graduating from college, has been similarly quiet at the final table. But when Shane opens a pot with an under-the-gun raise up to $36,000, it is Gracz, in the big blind, who stares him down.

Under the pressure of Gracz's gaze, Shane blows his opponent a kiss, then forces a little laugh and looks away. As I watch from the bleachers, it feels to me like weakness. But then I've played with Shane quite a bit. Gracz apparently senses it, too. He calls, following Mike Caro's dictum: "Figure out what your opponent wants you to do, then disappoint him by doing the opposite."

The flop is 8-3-7 rainbow, Gracz checks, and Shane checks back. When another seven comes on the turn, pairing the board, Gracz again checks. Shane is leaning on his elbow, his hand against his cheek. He says, "All in," and gestures casually at the pot with two fingers. As opposed to his pre-flop bet, his body language now radiates calmness and strength. Watching, I'm certain he's ahead.

Especially when he takes another look at his cards. Unless he's trying to give off a reverse tell, this is almost always a sign of strength.

Gracz seems less certain and again stares Shane down. He asks for a count. The dealer stacks Shane's chips, announcing that the bet is $121,000.

Gracz shuffles his chips over and over, fluidly, his fingers dancing.

At last, almost defiantly, he says, "I call."

"Good call," Shane says with a sigh, turning over his K-J suited. He's shocked, however, when Gracz flips up A-10. How the hell did he make the call? Even if Shane was on a bluff, of the most likely hands he might be holding, Gracz can beat fewer than half. Gracz is ahead of K-Q, K-10, Q-J, Q-10, J-10, A-9 or the hand Shane actually has; and he trails A-K, A-Q, A-J, or pocket twos, fours, fives, or sixes. Even if Gracz *is* right and he's ahead, Shane still has six cards in the deck to win.

Both players stand up as the dealer pauses dramatically, milking the tension. Shane walks over to where Nicky and I are seated and says, "What could I do?"

I shrug.

The dealer finally taps the table, burns a card, and reveals the river. It's an unhelpful ten. Shane quickly slings on his leather coat on and just as quickly says his good-byes. He's out.

It's a tough way to exit, but he still has $132,000 coming to him for his fifth-place finish. A hundred thirty-two thousand! Shit, that's my wedding plus a down payment on an apartment! While Shane's dealing with the paperwork, and then going to the cage, Nicky and I watch the rest of the action. David Pham remains my pick to win, but after he gets outplayed on a hand where he makes a $60,000 bluff against Gracz only to have the kid rebluff him with the same exact hand for $200,000 more, he falls apart, blowing off the rest of his chips to C. T. Law in a spot where Law has him drawing practically dead on the flop.

Down to three players: Chuck Thompson, a genial, white-bearded poker veteran, who came into the day as the chip leader, opens for a raise of $45,000 with A-J suited. C. T. Law folds, but Michael Gracz moves all-in for $450,000. Thompson correctly wonders aloud, "Why so much, Mike? Why so much?" It's a good question, and Gracz refuses to answer, staying uncomfortably mum. Thompson, unable to satisfactorily answer the question for himself, calls. Gracz turns up pocket eights, and they're off to the races. It's basically all over on the flop, as Thompson hits an ace, but Gracz makes a set.

Head's up with C. T. Law now, Gracz finds himself down more than 2-1 in chips, $732,000 to Law's $1,589,000. That he doesn't cripple himself on the ensuing hand is pretty much just pure luck: Law makes it $30,000 pre-flop with A-K, and Gracz calls with A-5 suited. So far, so bad. The flop comes A-2-8 rainbow. Things have just gotten worse. Gracz checks and Law bets $50,000. Gracz immediately calls. Things have gotten much worse. The turn is a 3. Gracz once again checks, and this time Law bets $130,000, which Gracz again calls instantly. Now he is courting disaster, having called off a third of his stack chasing a better hand. Unless he hits a five or a gutshot four on the river, he's pretty much committed himself to calling what will undoubtedly be a much larger river bet. And if he doesn't call, he'll have squandered a goodly chunk of his chips without even knowing what he folded to.

Unfortunately for C. T. Law, the river is the near-miracle four, completing Gracz's straight. Inexplicably at this point, Law, who has actually played the hand well to here, totally loses his mind. After Gracz checks the river, Law bets $200,000, a reasonable value bet perhaps, although it should at least occur to him to consider what Gracz might have. But when Gracz raises $230,000, instead of realizing that he must be beat, or at worst making a crying call, Law pushes in the rest of his chips!

Gracz of course happily calls with his straight.

With the chip count basically reversed, the two players proceed to play another wacky hand. This time, Gracz calls $15,000 from the button with pocket deuces (in head's up, the little blind is the button and acts first pre-flop; the big blind acts first after the flop), and Law with 8-7 off raises $50,000. Gracz calls.

The flop comes 5-6-5.

Law leads out with a bet of $100,000.

Now, if I'm Gracz in this spot, either I decide I'm ahead and move in, or I decide I'm behind and fold. He does neither, simply calling Law's bet.

The turn is a jack, which by its very randomness illustrates the difficulty that Gracz has created for himself, because when Law now moves in, Gracz has to contend with the fact that his opponent might have been playing a hand like K-J or J-10 and just hit his best card. To give Gracz credit here, though, Law's all-in move is somewhat suspect. Would he really move in if he had hit the jack? Wouldn't it make more sense that he'd want to trap Gracz? And if he had a six or a medium-sized overpair like sevens, eights, or nines, mightn't he be afraid that Gracz had hit the jack? On the other hand, after his brain-dead play of the previous hand, how could anyone accurately deduce *anything* he's thinking?

But Gracz, who will later say in an interview that "there's nothing that brings me more pleasure than bluffing," has some of Stuey Ungar's blood in him. He gets high from bluffing and making the big call, even if, as a result, he sometimes has to go home. "It'll hurt but I'll still feel like it was the right thing to do," he tells an ESPN interviewer afterward. Like Stuey, he's the kind of player who's going to generate a lot of "You wouldn't believe the call he made" stories, but you're not going to hear many big laydown stories. And the reason is simple: Big laydowns don't produce a rush. Most of the time, except when an event is televised and you get to see the cards later, you'll never even know if you did the right thing by folding. You'll be stuck wondering, and this kind of sucks. Make a big call or bluff, on the other hand, and when it works, everyone gets to see the results. *Yee haw!* Now that's what I'm talking about!

If Shane had fully understood this about Gracz, he might have played his key hand differently. He might have moved in on the flop. But who knows? Gracz might have called him anyway. It's tough to play someone who's capable of the big call. It makes you reluctant to bluff that player—and thus reduces your options. You raise pre-flop with two big cards and miss the flop and you might try a continuation bet with another kind of player; but with someone like Michael Gracz you're going to be afraid he'll call or raise you—because he cares less about going home than he cares about getting that rush.

It's not surprising, then, when Gracz calls C. T. Law with his pocket deuces in this spot. And what do you know, it's another great call. Although maybe not as great as it first appears. Law, with his open-end straight draw, also has a ton of other outs. Let's count them. To win the hand: four fours, four nines, three sevens, three eights, three jacks (to make jacks and fives with an eight kicker). To chop the hand: three sixes (which would make sixes and fives with a jack kicker). All of which means that Law has a 44 percent chance to win or chop the hand. That's the upside for Gracz. The downside, were he wrong, is that he would need to make a third deuce, which means *he* would be a 22-1 underdog at this point. I call that extremely marginal play. A near coin flip if you're right; prohibitive dog if you're wrong.

As it turns out, the hand is a wash. A six comes on the river and they chop. A few minutes later, Gracz raises $50,000 with Q-8 of spades, and Law calls with Q-J of diamonds. On an 8-5-J flop, Law checks his top pair, and Gracz bets $75,000 with middle pair. Law raises to $180,000, and once again Gracz makes an extremely questionable play, coming over the top for all his chips. Against a conservative player, a play like this might have a chance, but he has to know that Law is going to call him here with any kind of jack, which of course he does. For Gracz, it's even worse than he imagined, as his kicker isn't even live. No matter. He gets the last little bit of luck that he needs when he hits the 11-1-shot eight on the turn.

It's nice to be young, talented, and charmed—and not afraid to go home.

"What a luck box," Shane says, still fuming hours later as we sit at a table in the Mandalay Bay incarnation of Aureole, Charlie Palmer's famous New York restaurant. A magnificent, glossy space with a spectacular forty-foot-high Lucite-walled wine tower descending from a walkway down to the dining room and bar, Aureole is the kind of architectural dream possible only in a place like Las Vegas where space is not at a New York premium. Two lithe, shiny-haired girls in black cat suits rappel on steel wires and harnesses, *Mission Impossible*–style, up and down the tower in pursuit of a requested vintage.

"Listen, you won a shitload of money and you're gonna be on TV, so shut the fuck up and quit whining," I say to Shane. "Nicky and I are just trying to stop the bleeding here."

"I know, I know," Shane says, "It just pisses me off. How could he call there?"

I look at Nicky, trying to get some support, but he's perusing a computerized tablet, trying to select a wine. Eventually, he settles on a $350 bottle of Chassagne-Montrachet, then shows the tablet to Shane, who nods his approval. There's no holding back tonight. Tonight, we're living large! I start with gnocchi in sage butter, followed by Maine lobster and roasted porcini; Shane gets American white sturgeon caviar to begin and a caramelized Sonoma quail with foie gras truffle stuffing; and Nicky goes for seared Hudson Valley foie gras, followed by sauteed Atlantic salmon with Jerusalem artichokes puree, arugula, and pear tomatoes. I mean, if not now, when? Shaniac's got $66,000 burning a hole in his pocket (after paying off Josephy and Sheets), and Nicky and I are doing our *Entourage* bit, playing Turtle and Johnny "Drama" to Shane's Vince Chase.

The meal is fabulous and very expensive, especially after we order a second bottle of wine (economizing this time with a $250 bottle of Barolo), and the conversation is well-lubricated and animated. With a good buzz on, we try to figure out where to go next, but since we're all in committed relationships, it's a difficult decision. In the end, the gravity of the Rio and poker pulls us back. Shane wants to root for Josephy, who, he finds out after phoning his roomie Ari, is not only alive but the chip leader in the stud tourney with two tables to go. By the time we get over there, it's down to the final table and Josephy is still leading.

"He's going to win a bracelet," Shane proclaims, as we stand beyond a velvet rope that encircles the table. "Do you realize how incredible this is? The guy has never played stud before."

Given that this is the final table of a World Series event, it's amazing that there aren't more people watching, but it's all about no-limit hold'em these days. Stud is the equivalent of Boys Singles at the U.S. Open. The finals wind up taking place on a back court in the shadow of the stadium with very few people even knowing that they're going on.

As I watch Josephy play, I am amazed at his confidence and comfort level. Clearly he has learned the game at a rapid rate even as he has been playing. He uses his chips to perfection, squeezing the air out of the others, who are trying to move up the money ladder. Before long, it is down to him; Kiril Girisimov, a Russian wunderkind with a WPT win to his credit; and Mark Burtman, a poker writer and physician. Stud can turn around on a dime if the cards don't cooperate, but Josephy suffers not even a bump in the road as he polishes off his two opponents in short order.

A day after landing in Vegas, having never even played stud before, Josephy finds himself fastening a World Champion gold bracelet around his wrist and collecting $192,150 in prize money. No wonder poker-playing dreams have replaced screenwriting dreams on the nation's college campuses. As someone has said, poker is the last great American gold rush.

While Shane goes off to celebrate, this time on somebody else's nickel, Nicky and I decide to try our luck in a $5-$10 no-limit game. We sit down at a table with a bunch of kids I've never seen before. They're all wearing dress shirts and mousse, looking as if they just ditched their dates at Light or Ghost Bar. My question is, Where do they get the money? When I was their age I was playing $5-$10 *limit* and my heart was pounding like a clock hammer. There's probably $20,000 in play here, and not a single face that I've even seen before or that I wouldn't card if I were working a club door. Nicky's a little amped and aggressive from the wine (as am I), and these twenty-somethings have no idea how good or experienced we are. They only know that they feel young and invincible. And they look at us and think that *we're* the fish.

After bluffing Nicky out of one pot and showing him the hand, one of them, a skinny, good-looking Asian kid in a shiny red shirt, says, "We might as well warn you, we're Internet pros."

Nicky rolls his eyes, laughing out loud. "Do you believe this?" he asks me.

I shrug, not wanting things to escalate.

"It seems like everyone who plays on the Internet these days is a pro," Nicky says.

"Whatever that means," the kid says.

There are times when Nicky's attitude is good for putting people on tilt, and there are times when it is less good. If he could allow these kids their misconceptions about us, we might actually profit by it. But their display of arrogance is too galling to him.

A few hands later, he raises another one of the kids, whom I actually recognize as the on-air interviewer for *CardPlayer* magazine's video spots, and the kid immediately reraises him back. When Nicky mucks, this kid too shows a bluff. They're all laughing now, and the Asian kid tries to rub it in, saying, "We tried to warn you."

"Talk to the hand, Jumpstreet," Nicky says, holding up his open hand.

"What are you, from the eighties?" the *CardPlayer* kid says. "You must be what, sixty years old?"

"Yeah, I'm sixty," Nicky says.

"Nicky, Jesus, just play poker," I mutter under my breath.

But it's too late. The *CardPlayer* kid starts calling him an "orange donkey" because of Nicky's orange Index Five baseball cap, and from there it just gets worse. Since this is a poker table, the best way to shut people up is by taking their money; but Nicky isn't on his game here, and he tries to push things. He plays too many hands in an attempt to teach them all a lesson, and it backfires. Finally, after dropping $1,900 in an hour, he gets up. I feel terrible, as if I didn't do enough to prevent it.

After Nicky leaves, the *CardPlayer* kid and the others start talking about him and snickering.

"Look," I say, "I don't know you guys at all. But you're talking about a friend of mine and I'd appreciate it if you don't have anything good to say that you just shut up."

"You're his friend?" the *CardPlayer* kid says. "So what's his problem?"

"I just asked you once nicely," I say. "Let's leave it at that and play poker."

"Fair enough," the kid says.

I go back to the room about an hour later, and Nicky's in bed, reading *The New York Times*.

"How'd it go?" he asks.

"All right. I got some of your money back."

"It's not my money anymore."

"Listen, you can't take shit so personally," I say abruptly.

"Dude, don't tell me you're gonna defend that kid?"

"He's just a dumb kid. *You* should know better."

"Meaning?"

"If you act like a loser, you're gonna lose."

I'm lecturing him, being an asshole, but I can't stop myself. To my surprise, he laughs.

"You obviously haven't heard about the new 'loser chic,' " he says, grabbing for the arts section of the *Times* and leafing through it. "It's all about how America is ready to embrace its inner loser."

He hands me the article and I skim through it. "When loser chic works, as in TV shows like *The Office*, . . . the characters are not pathetic but poignant and likable.

"So there's hope for us," I say.

"You can laugh, but I'm letting you in on something here. If you use this properly you might make some money off your book." He grabs back the paper from me and reads: "The shrewdest way to turn a loser character into a box-office or ratings winner is to walk the ultimate tightrope and let viewers have it both ways. *Napoleon Dynamite* and *American Idol* have thrived by presenting characters that audiences can either identify with or make fun of.' "

"Which are they gonna be doing with us?"

He shrugs. "Neither. Because we're gonna turn things around before this is over."

I exhale. "I sure hope you're right."

As if it isn't already clear enough that we live in a world of haves and have-nots, winners and losers, when I call Alice the next morning from the Monterey Room during breakfast, I get to hear about her weekend with our friends Pam and Daniel at their new million-dollar house in Sag Harbor. Did I know that they've furnished it entirely with stuff from ABC Carpet? No, I didn't know, and I'm confused. A year ago Pam was saying Daniel had this huge debt from law school. Now they're buying million-dollar homes and shopping at ABC Carpet?

I'm watching Nicky eat his French toast. He stops chewing, hearing the tone of my voice, and shakes his fork at me. I ignore him.

"So what does this mean?" I ask Alice. "What are we to make of this? That they're both making a lot of money now? Or did they come into some kind of inheritance or something?"

There's more. It seems Pam was throwing a dinner party last night and she and Alice went shopping because she needed place mats. They went to this place Loaves and Fishes in Bridgehampton and "Pam wound up buying twelve place mats there for thirty-five dollars apiece!"

I do some quick calculations. "That's almost four hundred dollars!"

But wait, Alice says. It doesn't stop there. After that they went to another place because Pam needed chairs. Six chairs for $450 apiece. Pam just whipped out her plastic.

By the time I get off the phone, Nicky is just shaking his head. "You're in trouble, dude."

"I don't understand it. These people didn't used to be rich."

"Whether you understand it or not, just the fact that Alice is telling you about it is trouble."

"You think?"

"I don't care how grounded she is."

"But she knows we can't live like that."

"Intellectually maybe, but emotionally?"

His words hang in the air, reverberating in a way that I don't like.

Later in the day, after finishing up a more formal interview with Cliff Josephy at the American Grill in the Rio, I'm walking back toward the Amazon Room over the endless miles of plush carpet when a pretty blond girl in a low-cut blue sundress walks past from the opposite direction and smiles at me. I smile back, swiveling my head to take another look. Almost simultaneously, she glances back at me. We both laugh. Then an even stranger thing happens: She stops, walks back toward me, and says hi.

"Hi."

"What are you doing?" she asks. There are fine gold hairs on her arms, which are slightly goose-bumped in the air-conditioned air.

"Nothing," I say, feeling myself blush a little.

"You feel like hanging out?"

I laugh abruptly, realizing suddenly, stupidly, what's going on. I actually thought for a moment it was something else. She's so fresh-faced, with her slight overbite and pale blue eyes, that I got fooled.

"What's so funny?" Her eyes are dancing, playful.

"No, it's . . . nothing."

"Yeah?" She's flirty and full of questions. What's my name? Am I a poker player? All these poker players around. They can't all be winning, can they? What about me? Am I winning?

"Yes," I lie.

Hey, she's got an idea. What if she and I went to my room and hung out?

I'm outwardly calm, but I can feel a kind of heat rising in my face. An embarrassment of complex proportions. I am embarrassed to say no to her. But I am also embarrassed to say yes. I don't want to be forced to make a decision like this on the spot. I need more time to think about what it means. I tell her that I'm on my way to meet someone (which is partially true—Alex Williams from the *Times* just called me from the airport). Could I contact her later perhaps? I rip half a page out of my reporter's notebook and hand her a pen. She scribbles her name and number. I watch her walk away, the sight of her swiveling hips and tan skinny calves inspiring something like pain.

I'm still trying not to think about her when I meet up with Alex Williams in the media room an hour later. It's actually important that I focus on him and make sure that he gets what he needs. He's in his early thirties, with dark curly hair and glasses, and the kind of slightly detached self-assurance that characterizes almost every reporter from the *Times* I've ever met. I spend the rest of the afternoon squiring him around, introducing him to players, trying to assist him and smooth his way. This is not generosity on my part; it is blatant self-interest. He is, according to my publicists, committed to writing a piece for the front page of the Sunday Styles section about Stuey Ungar and about the biography Nolan and I have written on Stuey, *One of a Kind*. I don't know how the PR team at Atria Books pulled it off, but it's a coup, and I am fully aware that it can give us the running start the book needs. I'm also aware that Alex can decide at any moment that there's a better story right under his nose and decide to go in a different direction. There are about twenty other authors out here trying to launch their poker books, including my friends Michael Kaplan and Brad Reagan, authors of *Aces and Kings;* and Michael Craig, author of *The Professor, the Banker, and the Suicide King*. So I'm treading a fine line. It's a little like taking a date to a party, trying to make her feel comfortable by introducing her around, but at the same time being careful that you don't introduce her to anybody too interesting (in case he proves to be more interesting than you).

I try to get a sense from Alex of how he's going to approach the story, but I don't want to push too hard, and he doesn't volunteer much, except to say that he's interested in talking to some of the younger players. I introduce him to Shane, to Adam Schoenfeld, to Daniel Negreanu, and to anyone else I can think of who is both young and quotable. At one point, I see Scott Fischman, and though I don't really know him, I try introducing Alex to him anyway.

Fischman says, "If you want to interview me, you've going to have to call my manager and set something up."

I almost burst out laughing. Leading Alex away, I say, "Well, in case you were wondering what it means to be a top young player in poker today, that about says it all."

"Yeah," Alex says, "Somehow I don't think I'll be making that call."

Shaniac finds me a little while later at a $175 buy-in single-table satellite.

"So did you talk to that guy?" I ask him.

"We're meeting in a little while. He's talking to Schoenfeld now."

"Adam, that media whore. He must be getting wet talking to a *Times* reporter."

"He seemed pretty happy."

I muck my hand and turn in my seat, noticing that Shane's eyes are bleary and bloodshot.

"Somebody ran out of Visine."

"I got a little drunk and stupid last night," he says.

As stupid as I almost got earlier?

"I dropped five grand playing blackjack at the Bellagio."

"Five grand! Jesus Christ, Shane."

"Yeah, I know."

"What else did you do?"

"You don't want to know."

"Yes, I do."

He shakes his head.

"Just don't pull a Levi," I say, invoking the name of Levi Rothman, a kid we used to play with in New York, who won a tournament out here for $150,000, and then blew it all in the space of a week, the punch line to his tale being "and then I wound up playing head's up $50-$100 pot-limit hold'em with O'Neil Longson"—O'Neil Longson being one of the best pot-limit hold'em players in the world.

"Anyway, I moved out of that place on Tropicana," Shane says. "The Bellagio comped me to a room."

"They comped you? What do you have to do for that?"

"Play a few hours of blackjack per day."

I look at him. "Shaniac . . ."

"It's cool," he says.

I keep staring.

"Really, it's cool."

After he leaves, I manage to get head's up in the satellite, and chop it up, taking $620 for my efforts. I'm playing well. The rhythm of playing every day is helping me get sharper, more focused. I can feel things taking a turn. When I got here, my plan was to run the first event, the Senior's, and the Main Event. I've already exceeded that goal by playing in the $1,500 pot-limit, but I want to do more. I want to give myself as many chances as possible to make a score. But it's expensive, and I'm already in the hole. To give you some idea of how expensive it is, if you were to play in every event over the course of the six weeks of the World Series, it would cost you $116,000, not including rebuys. Obviously, I'm not going to play every event, but I do make a deal with myself: If I can get back half of what I'm losing on this trip in the next week—which is now, after my no-limit win last night and my little win right now, $11,800—I'll buy into at least one more event.

To celebrate this decision, I immediately jump into another $175 single table; and an hour and a half later, I'm chopping that up for another $600. My bankroll—i.e., the rubber-banded wad of hundreds in my pocket—is now up to $4,000. My mood is on the upswing, too. Yeah, yeah, I know. Classic symptom of a compulsive gambler, the flip side to question 4 in the Gambler's Anonymous list of Twenty Questions*— "Have you ever felt remorse after gambling?" But come on, people, I ask you honestly, doesn't everything that can make you feel good have the capacity to make you feel bad? Think about it. Sex? Chocolate? What about a midafternoon snooze? A flip remark? An impulse buy? *Can we just relax a little?* Winning at gambling makes me feel good. Losing makes me feel not so good, even remorseful at times.

Later in the afternoon, I find myself trying to get through a bottleneck of people in the hall outside the Amazon Room when I suddenly see the reason for the congestion: The current world champ, Greg "Fossilman" Raymer, is surrounded by a gaggle of admirers who want his autograph

---

* The Twenty Questions are as follows: (1) Did you ever lose time from work or school due to gambling? (2) Has gambling ever made your home life unhappy? (3) Did gambling affect your reputation?(4) Have you ever felt remorse after gambling?(5) Did you ever gamble to get money with which to pay debts or otherwise solve financial difficulties? (6) Did gambling cause a decrease in your ambition or efficiency? (7) After losing did you feel you must return as soon as possible and win back your losses? (8) After a win did you have a strong urge to return and win more? (9) Did you often gamble until your last dollar was gone? (10) Did you ever borrow to finance your gambling? (11) Have you ever sold anything to finance gambling? (12) Were you reluctant to use "gambling money" for normal expenditures? (13) Did gambling ever make you careless of the welfare of yourself or your family? (14) Did you ever gamble longer than you had planned? (15) Have you ever gambled to escape worry or trouble? (16) Have you ever

or just want to shake his hand and say hello. They're handing him playing cards and World Series programs to sign, and the redheaded,
chubby-cheeked former patent attorney patiently obliges. Since I'm not
on my way anywhere in particular, I decide to say hello. Edging closer, I
try to make eye contact with him. He sees me finally and smiles, excus-
ing himself so he can reach out and shake my hand. "I might be the current world champion," he says to the small crowd, "but I've never been
able to beat this guy."

"Not true," I say with a laugh. "I can remember at least one time you
beat me."

If modesty is less characteristic of the author than it is of the world
champ, Raymer is unusual in other ways for a man in his position.
Poker, of course, has created a number of unlikely celebrities in the past
few years, but even within that realm, Raymer seems something of an
oddity. Moneymaker has that name and the folksy everyman backstory;
Hellmuth is the poker brat, the guy you love to hate; Gus Hansen is one
of *People*'s Sexiest Men Alive; but what's Raymer's shtick? A pair of goofy
reptile glasses and a collection of fossils? He's the poker version
of that guy you sometimes see on the beach with a Geiger counter.

I don't mean that in a pejorative way, either. It's just who he is and

---

committed or considered committing an illegal act to finance gambling? (17) Did gambling ever cause you to have difficulty in sleeping? (18) Do arguments or disappoint-
ments or frustrations create within you an urge to gamble? (19) Did you ever have an
urge to celebrate any good fortune by a few hours of gambling? (20) Have you ever considered self-destruction or suicide as a result of your gambling?

According to G.A., if you answer yes to seven or more of these questions,
you are a compulsive gambler. In an informal poll taken in the Amazon Room, the
average score was 14. My own personal tally is 12 (for those of you interested, I an-
swered yes to questions 1, 2, 3, 4, 5, 7, 8, 9, 10, 14, 15, and 17. Question 16—Have
you ever considered an illegal act to finance gambling?—proved tricky, since I have
committed illegal acts involving gambling but never to actually *finance* it. So I an-
swered no.

has been from when I first met him at Foxwoods in the early '90s. Though I wouldn't call Greg a close friend, we have played a lot of poker together and even gone golfing once (during FARGO*). And I can tell you that the reptile glasses and the fossils aren't self-conscious affectations; they're sincere, and they're actually refreshing in this age of irony. Greg knows who he is and doesn't pretend to be anything else. He doesn't want to join a club that wouldn't have him as a member. He's a straight shooter, and he's been a good ambassador for poker during his reign.

If it's true that in the cash games at Foxwoods we were always happy when he showed up, and often moved from another table to get a shot at him, it is also true that he was an extremely tough tournament player, capable of acquiring a lot of chips in a hurry. I wasn't at all surprised when he got his hands on a bunch of chips in last year's final. Of course, you never expect someone you know and play with on a semi-regular basis to win the Big One. But it wasn't shocking to me. I didn't consider it a fluke (insofar as anyone outlasting 2,575 other competitors isn't a fluke). In fact, it gave me hope in a much more tangible way than did Moneymaker's win or Varkonyi's.

In some regards, though, the real long shot was that Greg got to play the Main Event at all. His wife, Cheryl, was never happy about his passion for poker, and she indulged it only on the condition that he never augment his initial stake of $1,000, a stipulation that forced him to get creative. I mean, that's a lot of pressure, not ever being able to lose your bankroll.

---

* Foxwoods Area Recreational Gambling Outing, an annual convocation of nerdy poker players who subscribe to rec.gambling.poker, or RGP, an online poker discussion forum that was once must-reading for those of us in the serious poker-playing community, though in recent years, unfortunately, it's devolved into a repository for spam, paranoid rants, name-calling, political diatribes, adolescent humor, and very little useful poker content—a seemingly inevitable fate for open and unmoderated forums, and yet more proof, as if we needed it, that the shits are killing us.

But then Greg had some unique and innovative theoretical ideas about the game in general (not all of which I agreed with). For the bankroll problem, he devised a plan the prime thrust of which was to acquire backing. But rather than solicit it in the usual way, through private entreaties to friends, Greg did it by posting his "offering" on the Internet, in effect taking himself "public" and selling company shares and issuing dividends. This invited a fair amount of ridicule from skeptics, but Greg took the virtual snickers in stride, and ultimately rewarded his faithful beyond their wildest dreams.

Not all of Greg's investors through the years, it should be noted, capitalized on his $5 million win. A banker friend of mine from New York, who knew Greg from playing with him and reading his Internet posts on RGP and then later on a site called Two Plus Two (an offshoot of the poker theorist Mason Malmuth's publishing company of the same name), became his biggest investor in 2003, with a 5 percent stake. Unfortunately my friend neglected to renew in 2004, "not because I didn't want to or was in any way unhappy with him, but because I forgot to." It turned out to be a costly oversight. "My return would have been two hundred and fifty thousand dollars," my banker friend says. Greg's other, less forgetful, investors wound up dividing a total of $2.4 million.

The dream of hitting a hot streak, or winning a big tournament, and being able to leave your former life behind, as Greg has done, is one that nearly all the amateurs who come to Vegas for the World Series of Poker bring with them—at least those who have other lives. For the pros, especially those living on the edge, like Nicky and Shane, it is the dream of leaving the edge behind forever, as someone like Gavin Smith has done.

Myself, I haven't dared fantasize about what I would do if I won. I've been keeping my goals more modest, like making enough money to pay for my wedding. Maybe that's a mistake. Phil Hellmuth, before he left Madison, Wisconsin, for the 1990 WSOP at the age of twenty-four, recorded an outgoing message on his answering machine saying, "Next time you talk to me, I'll be the world champion of poker." Maybe that's the kind of positive thinking that's necessary.

I want to find out from Greg Raymer what this year has been like for him, and if the change has been as radical as I imagine. He gives me his card and says to call him. Maybe before his wife and family arrive we'll get a chance to hang out and talk.

I wonder what his wife thinks about all this. Does she consider what their lives would be like had he hit a bad streak early on and been forced by her stipulation to quit playing? And do I really believe he would have stuck by his promise?

Me? I'm smart enough not to make promises like that. Just not smart enough to have won the WSOP.

Yet.

8

ALMOST ALL OF THEM ARE TOUGH

"Who's Mia?"

"What?"

"Mia." Nicky picks up the slip of paper from the night table. He's sitting on the edge of the bed in his boxers. I turn around in the chair by the desk, where I've been catching up on some e-mail. He looks at me, waving the slip of paper.

After considering a moment, I decide to tell him the story, which he listens to, poker-faced and impossible to read.

"So are you going to call her?" he asks finally.

"I don't know. I don't think so."

"You don't think so? Dude, what are you doing? How could you even be contemplating getting married if you're really considering this?"

"I'm not *really* considering it."

"But you have the phone number. You haven't thrown it away."

"True."

"I'm not judging you. It's okay with me. I just feel I have to ask you these questions."

He stands up and walks past me to the little sink outside the bath-room. He splashes some water on his face, then turns toward me, wiping his face dry.

"It's not a moral thing. I'm not standing in judgment here."

"Just explain to me how people do it. I see a beautiful woman, I want to sleep with her."

"Of course. Who doesn't?"

"So how do you just have sex with one person and one person alone . . . forever."

"It's definitely something to ponder before you say 'I do.' " He squeezes some toothpaste onto his toothbrush.

"Well, it's no accident that I've never said it."

He brushes his teeth, while I continue to sit at the desk. The truth is, I've never been the type to be unfaithful. When I get to that point I just break up with them. Or at least I used to. This commitment stuff makes it much more complicated.

"What if getting caught wasn't part of the equation?" I ask.

"But it is. It's a fundamental part of it. For some guys it's why they do it, however else they might try to rationalize it or think that no one will ever know. The danger is actually the real turn-on. It's the same reason that people like to bluff in poker. They might get caught. That's what's so thrilling."

"I'm assuming that you've had opportunities."

"I didn't say I've never considered it. It just comes down to not wanting to hurt my wife. Her feelings aside, there's no way I could rec-oncile the idea that I might jeopardize her health. What if Em got AIDS as a result of me having sex with someone else? I'd have to kill myself."

"If you put it that way."

Nicky spits and rinses. "Even if the chance was one in ten million, it wouldn't be worth the risk. Besides, knowing my luck, I'd be the guy who'd be the one in ten million."

"Spoken like someone who's truly running bad."

He spits in the sink again. "Dude, just do me a favor. If you do call her, don't tell me. I don't want to know about it."

For the next week plus I leave the phone number lying on the night table, unable to bring myself to throw it away. It is there when I go to sleep and it is there when I wake up, tangible proof that there is a decision involved, that fidelity is not a given and that it is not too late to change my mind.

Over the course of the next few days, I go on a single-table satellite tear, chopping or winning outright six of the nine that I play. Added to a few modest wins in the $5-$10 no-limit games, it helps me climb a bit closer to the lip of the hole I've dug myself, enough so that I feel okay about using three of the seven $500 lammer chips I've collected to buy myself into event 16, the No-Limit Hold'em Shootout. While my little universe has been confined to the nine other faces around whatever table I happen to be sitting at, elsewhere out there in the vast chip-shuffling deep space of the Amazon Room World Series bracelets are being won. The early story in 2005, like 2004, is the continuation of the youth trend: young, unknown Internet geniuses bursting full-blown on the scene and making names for themselves. When the twenty-one-year-old pro Eric Froelich, aka E-Fro, takes down event 4, the $1,500 Limit Hold'em, he becomes the youngest WSOP winner ever. And of course there is Shane's nemesis, twenty-four-year-old Michael Gracz, winning event 7.

But in the days that follow, the older established players let it be known that youth will not always be served. When Erik Seidel wins event 9, the $2,000 No-Limit Hold'em bracelet, his seventh overall, along with a sweet $611,795, I find it oddly gratifying, and not just because I like Erik. It also seems to signify that experience and wisdom still count for something. Several days later, Josh Arieh, who several years ago might have been considered young but is now a battle-tested veteran (and, by the way, the third-place finisher in the main event last year), adds some ballast to the idea that this game might favor experience by winning event 12, $2,000 Pot-Limit Omaha with rebuys, and taking down a first prize of $381,600. On his way to busting the final table, he has to get past Chris "Jesus" Ferguson, the 2000 WSOP champ, and that man Erik Seidel again.

Event 13 proves to be lucky for another legendary pro, T. J. Cloutier, who wins the $5,000 No-Limit Hold'em and a whopping $657,100. Cloutier's stellar final table includes another near legend, seventy-seven-year-old John Bonetti, a player Nolan Dalla describes as a "Brooklyn-born ballbuster" (just ask any dealer who's ever had the misfortune of dealing him cards that didn't meet his approval); Johnny "World" Hennigan, also sometimes known as "Flakes"; Todd Brunson, son of the poker god Doyle and a world-class player in his own right; Hieu "Tony" Ma, a former Player of the Year who's been rounding back into shape after a few lean years; and Gavin Smith, the newly sober Canadian clubber.

Cloutier, despite the five bracelets he already owns going into the day, and the fifty-seven major tournament victories he's collected over the past twenty years, is almost as famous for being a final-event bridesmaid as he is for his accomplishments. He's twice been runner-up in the Big One, and has finished in the top five spots five times, prompting many to call him "best player never to win." The cards have been especially cruel to him on several occasions when he seemed particularly close to breaking through. In this tournament, however, Cloutier finally catches a break in a big spot, hitting a six-outer on the river early on at the final table, in a hand that would have knocked him out, then riding his second life hard to the finish line. "It sure felt good to suck out on someone for a change," he tells Nolan Dalla later.

* * *

At noon on Thursday, June 15, I drive the PT Cruiser out to Henderson, Nevada, about half an hour from the Strip, to visit Greg Raymer at the house he's renting on a golf course by Lake Mead. It's a McMansion, really, with four bedrooms, a fireplace, an ultramodern kitchen, two big-screen plasma televisions, and a landscaped pool in back with a view of one of the elevated tees and the mountains beyond. Greg tells me that he found it on the Internet, then came out and took a look before renting it for a very reasonable $1,500 a week. He's here alone now, but his wife, Cheryl; his nine-year-old daughter, Sophie; and some other family members are flying out in the coming days.

We go outside under a shaded trellis by the pool, and Greg, casually dressed in a red Polo shirt, shorts, and sandals and white socks, grills up some chicken and potatoes (no vegetables or salad in sight). Despite the fact that in most respects we are about as different as two people can be—he's a midwesterner, a chemist with a law degree, who went to work for a big pharmaceutical company and got married and started a family while in his twenties—we did until a year ago share the same poker fantasy. Now that he's actually gone and realized that fantasy I guess I can't count us similar in even that narrow respect. Even so, I'm dying to know what it's been like for him.

Instead of gushing about how wonderful and exciting it's been, though, Greg is oddly low-key, saying just that it's been a busy year with a lot of travel. "You know," he says, "I never imagined myself winning the Main Event, not before it happened, and in a way not even after."

"But you're a poker player now. You were able to quit your job. That must have been something you dreamed about."

"The truth is, I had often considered becoming a full-time pro, and was convinced I could do it successfully. I just never became convinced until I won the Main Event that I could do it and reasonably expect to make a better living than I was making as a patent attorney. If I had been single, I would've gone for it a long time ago; but having a wife and child to take care of, it didn't seem right to quit a great job and take on a profession that likely would pay less and include a ton of risk.

"Obviously," he says, "after the World Series I could have just taken the money, and gone on with life as before. But when PokerStars offered me more money than Pfizer was paying me, it became a pretty easy decision in terms of quitting my job."

His deal with PokerStars is earning him somewhere in the neighborhood of $100,000 plus expenses (which include entries into most of the big-ticket tournaments). PokerStars also has the right to renew for another year. This means he's being paid to go around the world playing poker—a privilege for which the majority of pros still must cough up their own expenses. Not only that, but any money that Greg wins in these tournaments is his to keep, hardly the usual deal that backers cut their stake horses.

On the other hand, he's in large part a salesman now, marketing his Fossilman image both for PokerStars and for any other commercial enterprises he can swing.

"Is that in any way uncomfortable?"

"To put it bluntly," he says, "no. I'm gonna try and make all I can off this while I can. It's hard to know if it will last, but I actually think it will. Poker isn't just a fad. All these young kids that are taking up the game, most of them, or at least a lot of them, are going to stick with it for the rest of their lives, just like you and I have. The main difference for me is that I have a lot more independence now. I'm not living paycheck to paycheck. So my money concerns have become relatively insignificant."

As a golfer steps up to the tee down below and smacks his drive down the fairway, I ask Greg whether he's had time to pick up his sticks at all with everything that's been going on. He says he really hasn't, but it's funny I should ask because just recently he met the PGA Tour pro Rocco Mediate, and that they're going to do a poker-golf thing for PokerStars and the Golf Channel. Rocco's going to play in the World

Series after Greg gives him some tips (with PokerStars paying his entry fee), and in exchange Greg's going to get some golf tips from Rocco. That's not all. Rocco's also arranging for Calloway to fit Greg for a free set of custom clubs. Just one of the perks of fame and celebrity. "I'm hoping to play a little while I'm here," Greg says. "It depends on my schedule with the poker."

Since winning the championship, he's had a couple of decent cashes but nothing substantial, and he's philosophical about it. "Let's face it, it's getting tough," he says. "The fields for all the major tournaments are so big now. And there aren't many tight players out there anymore, so that makes it even harder. When I came in third at Foxwoods at the World Poker Finals in 2001, there were eighty-some players. That was one of the major events of the year. Now, there's eight hundred playing that event. And all of these $10,000 buy-in events have at least three hundred players. So even if you manage to play twenty of them a year and you're an extremely good player, you're still only supposed to win once every twelve years. People have talked to me about being washed up because I haven't won a tournament since the championship. They don't understand how difficult it is."

"It's true," I agree. "Most poker players and people who follow poker are too result-oriented. It's very annoying. Especially for those of us who don't have the results to show we're as good as we think we are."

Greg laughs. "I was talking to Chip Jett," he says. "He was at the top of the Player of the Year list, but that was right before the boom, and now it's been a while and he's saying, 'Man, I need to get another result here soon.' He's worried because he had his breakout year a year too early."

Greg unwraps the aluminum foil envelope that he's used to grill the chicken and potatoes. Hot steam escapes. He hands me a serving spoon, which I use to shovel food onto my plate.

"If you want respect in this game," Greg says, "you have to show results. The more sophisticated people might be able to see past your results, but they're definitely in the minority."

It's to Greg's credit that he doesn't put too much stock in his world championship. He hasn't bought into his own press clippings. On the other hand, he's never lacked confidence in his own ability. "I've just learned to be social about it, and not in people's faces." He's aware that being underestimated can, and often does, work to his advantage, so perhaps the self-depreciation is something of an angle. He's a much, much better player than the top pros give him credit for being.

"The thing is we all have our good and bad days," he says. "I got a nice compliment from Phil Gordon on day two of the World Series last year. I got moved to his table and just started running it over, and he said, 'Greg, I didn't know you could play this well.' He had played with me in Foxwoods six months earlier and I had played like crap. I was just way off that day, making stupid mistakes, and I said, 'Yeah, that's because I played like crap the last time we sat at a table together.' But on this day, I was just in the zone. One of those days when you're seeing and understanding everything on a different level. You know how much to bet to get them to pay you off, and you also know how much to bet to get them to fold. I played a hand where my bet on the turn was an amount that I knew the guy would call. I was bluffing, but I did it because I wanted to win more of his money, and I was confident I knew exactly how much to bet on the river to take him off his hand. That's when you know you're zoned in and playing on another level."

Before last year's World Series, Greg was playing online nearly every day. He'd get home from work, eat dinner, do family stuff, play with his daughter, and then go to his home office, check his e-mail, take a look at Two Plus Two (where he often posts essays on poker theory), all the while playing Internet poker. He won his $10,000 seat in a $160 double shootout, the same type I tried playing at Shane's before coming out here.

Obviously, to win a tournament with over 2,500 players, in addition to playing well, you need to have a lot of things go right for you. "The way I accumulated most of my chips early on last year was by seeing flops," Greg says. "People just play so badly after the flop. So I'd call a couple of hundred, then hit the nuts, and a guy would just give me his chips. The first time I doubled up, I had about $13,000; the other guy had a little more. He bet, I called with pocket eights, and the flop came four-eight-jack. He bet, I raised, he moved in, and I called. If he had a set of jacks, I was going home. But he had kings, so I doubled up and he was all but eliminated. He put in $300 when he was a favorite, and he put in over $12,000 when he was a mile behind. There were a number of hands like that. And that's how I built up my stack."

Part of the luck factor in poker is situational. You flop a set when someone flops two pairs, that's good luck. You flop a set when nobody has anything, that could be considered bad luck. Of course, even in a good situation you still have to know what to do to maximize your winnings. Similarly, in a bad situation, knowing what to do can help minimize the damage. Greg tells me about a bad situation he got himself into that had nothing to do with poker. Well, not quite nothing.

It happened this past year, several months after the WSOP, during the Bellagio Five-Diamond tournament. Greg was returning to his room with several hundred thousand dollars in high-denomination chips in his pocket, chips he had withdrawn from the casino cage because he was checking out early the next morning and was planning to take them to another casino.

"I got off the elevator on the twentieth floor," he says. "And when I turned the corner, there was a guy walking down the hall about thirty or forty feet ahead of me."

Greg's room was almost the last door on left, and the guy just kept walking and walking ahead of him, finally stopping at the door next to Greg's, sticking his hand in his pocket as if for a key. Coming up empty, he started pounding on the door, yelling, "Helen, wake up! I forgot my key!" When Greg walked past on his way to his own door, he took note of the fact that the guy was dressed in a track suit and Gilligan-style hat, and had a shopping bag in one hand from one of the gift shops. Nothing extraordinary. Greg stuck his card key in his door. All of a sudden someone grabbed him from behind, another guy, who must have been waiting in the stairwell with the door cracked. It occurred to Greg later that the pounding on the door might have been the signal that he was approaching.

At any rate, while the one guy was grabbing him and trying to push him into his room, Greg started yelling for help. Meanwhile the other guy came up and began trying to help push him into the room.

"Somehow," Greg says, "I managed to knock them away from me, and I turned around." Now he was facing them. At this point, the guy who'd been knocking on the other door earlier reached into the white plastic bag and pulled out a big, shiny silver gun. It momentarily caused Greg to shut up. Then, seeing that two guys were still glancing at the open door of his room, and "realizing that their plan is to get me in there and tie me up, but that since I've seen both of their faces, the likelihood is that if I let them get me in the room, there's a good chance they'll decide to kill me," Greg started screaming for help again. "I mean, if they shoot me in the hall, it's gonna suck, but most gunshot victims survive. So I made a snap decision that staying out of the room was my best chance of surviving."

With Greg screaming for help again, the bigger of the two guys tried grabbing him once more, but Greg gave him a shove, using the full heft of his rather large body. It sent the guy to the ground. When he turned to deal with the smaller man, "he was running away down the hall. He'd given up." Deserted by his partner, the bigger guy now dragged himself to his feet and limped off down the hall, too.

Later, the police, using the Bellagio's surveillance videos, were able to track the two down and arrest them.

"Thank God these two guys were incompetent," Greg says. "Otherwise, I might be dead. I was lucky."

On my drive back through the desert after our lunch, I think about Greg and the nature of luck. Poker players, especially when they're running very hot or very cold, tend to think of luck only as it relates to occurrences at the card table. But it's always good to put things in perspective. Winning a million dollars, or five million, doesn't do you a hell of a lot of good if you're shot dead in a hotel room. By the same token, when you're in the midst of a horrible run, the stars might be smiling on you in ways you don't even realize. Luck isn't always so obvious.

I make a note to point this out to Nicky.

I also remember something else Greg said when I'd asked him what he was feeling like going into this year's championship. "I'd like to make a good showing," he said. "It would make a lot of people understand that as lucky as I was to win last year, it wasn't just a fluke. And that would feel good. But realistically I know the odds. In fact, it wouldn't be shocking to me at all if this year there was no one at the final table I'd ever heard of. I mean, I expect there to be one or two, but it wouldn't shock me if there weren't any. The other thing you need to understand is that even if they're not guys we've ever heard of, they're still going to be tough players. Almost all of them will be tough."

When I get back to Las Vegas, I spend the rest of the afternoon running errands. I drop off a load of laundry at the Wash-n-Spin; go to a Borders to see if the book on Stuey Ungar has come in yet (it hasn't); find a health food store so I can replenish my supply of Green Magma; and drop by a Staples to buy a few new pens and some other crap that makes me feel more like a professional writer and less like a degenerate gambler and reluctant groom. Around six o'clock, I head over to the Rio to see what's going on. It's amazing—if I'm away from the action for a day, I actually start to feel that I'm losing the pulse. Of course, once I walk into the Amazon Room, it looks exactly the same as it did the day before: a bunch of sick puppies feverishly indulging their addiction. I do run into Mike May, who's wandering around, wearing a Hawaiian shirt (good to see him back in the old Mike May uniform), looking slightly bemused and amused as he always does. We decide to get dinner and call Nicky to see if he wants to join us. It turns out he's already sitting down at Antonia's, the mediocre Italian restaurant in the Rio, by himself. Why don't we join him?

We go over and find him sitting in a corner booth, wearing a gray watch cap that makes him looks a bit like an aging white hip-hop kid.

"I needed some comfort food," he says, dipping a piece of bread into a plate of olive oil.

It's clear he's in a bad and vulnerable place, so we don't talk about it, at least to begin with. Eventually, though, Mike can't resist asking lightly: "So how was your day?"

Nicky nods, flashing his gallows smile, as if the last candle in an otherwise dark room has just been blown out. "I was hoping you would ask that," he says caustically. "I lost $2,200 today. I'm taking my last $1,500 and putting it in tomorrow's shootout tournament. If that doesn't work out, I'm going home. In fact, I may have to borrow a hundred to pay for gas."

His raw, wry angst makes it almost impossible to respond. We sit there, literally speechless.

"All right, well," he says, "I can see by the silence that you guys are worried about the hundred. It's okay. I'll get it from someplace else."

"Nicky, no, come on."

"No, it's okay. I understand."

We both reach into our pockets, but he shakes his head. "I was just giving you guys shit. I've already got it covered."

After dinner, by prearrangement, he meets up with Adam Schoenfeld, who lends him $1,000 (it should be noted that Adam backed Nicky for a while and did quite nicely, including taking half of a $90,000 score Nicky made in Tunica). We then head over to the satellite area to play some single tables.

Nicky busts out of his first one right away, and immediately buys into a $525, which, he argues correctly, has a much better structure than the lower buy-in structure. My feeling is that it's prudent money management to give up a little edge on the structure and spread out the risk by playing more of the lower buy-in ones. Also, the players in the $175 tend to be weaker.

As if to prove my thesis, I chop up my $175, taking $1,180 out of it, after which I walk over to Nicky's table and sweat him. Almost immediately, with the table five-handed, he gets all in with A-K versus A-Q and jacks. It's a chance for him to triple up, just about knock out two guys (he has one covered, the other almost covered), and pretty much lock up at least a chop of the $5,000 in lammers plus cash. So what happens? A queen hits, giving the guy with the worst hand the whole pot and sending Nicky to the rail.

"Of course," Nicky says. "Why should I expect anything different?"

As we leave the misery behind, headed back to the Gold Coast, he mutters over and over, "I can't win . . . I can't win . . . I can't win."

"It just goes like that sometimes. We've all been there."

He's numb.

"I'm going to have to find something else to do," he says. "I just have no idea what. What am I going to tell my father-in-law? That I went away for two weeks and came back with twelve thousand less than I left with?"

The $1,500 shootout the next day is like Custer's Last Stand for Nicky. For me, it's nowhere near as desperate. I've turned things around. I'm playing well. I'm confident. Especially in this format, which is like a series of single-table satellites, one winner emerging from each table and getting to move on to the next round, at which point he's in the money.*

Before Nicky and I head off to find our tables, we agree to our usual 2 percent trade.

"Be positive," I say. "One good day changes everything."

"Even a semi-good day would help a lot," he says.

I find my table, number 119, seat 7, and size it up. Not too bad. A couple of tough players, including Full Tilter Andy Bloch, but no one who really scares me. I start off playing exactly the same way I've been playing all the single-table satellites, patiently folding my way down to about $1,100 from a starting stack of $1,500. It's fine to lay back, especially with one-hour rounds, but I don't want to dip too much below where I am, and as a result I get a little impatient. With the blinds still at $25-$25, I make a questionable choice to come in for a standard three-times-the-blind raise with A-J off from early position, the kind of hand I hate to play up front. As punishment, I draw one caller from behind, a guy whose name, I think, is Daniel Alaei. A solid player.

On a K-10-3 flop, I make a continuation bet of $150, which he also calls. At this point, I'm disgusted with myself. But the worst part is that I don't think he has much; mostly he just wants to see if I'll slow down. If I do, then he'll try to take the hand away from me. The other possibility is that maybe he's got a monster, and he's decided to let me bluff off all my chips. Either way I'm not happy. I've gotten myself into the exact sit-

---

* For example, if you begin the tournament with 1,000 players, that would be 100 tables of ten players each, and the winners would move on to ten ten-handed tables. The winners of those tables would then move on to a single ten-handed final table. Since each time a new shootout begins, every player starts with the same number of chips, no one at the final table would begin with an advantage, as is the case in the traditional tournament format.

uation I try to avoid, particularly in these one-table situations, caught between two unhappy choices: weak play (checking and folding the turn) or bad play (bluffing without a strong read).

When another rag falls on the turn, I choose the latter course, since I can't see any other way to win the hand. I'm going to take one more valiant or stupid crack at it. To this juncture, I've invested $225 in this pot, and I've got only $875 left. The problem is that I need to bet enough to push him out, but not so much that I'll be hopelessly crippled if he calls or reraises and I end up having to fold. I push out $300 as casually as I can, trying to look as if it's not killing me. Once again, he reaches for his chips and calls. The only bright spot is that he doesn't raise. He lets me see the river.

I'm still silently cursing my horrible play when a funny thing happens. The river produces a miracle. The gutshot queen that makes my straight.

Holy shit.

Now, the only question is, How do I get his money? I decide that if I move in, it will seem like such a patently desperate ploy that he'll call me. So I push.

He's good, though. He knows something's fishy. "That card helped you, didn't it?" he says, counting off $575 and watching for a reaction. He feints a couple of times, then finally puts it in the pot. I flip over my cards, and he rears back, his face contorted in disbelief. I realize he must have flopped a monster. Top two or even a set. Wow. Still, it's hard to feel too sorry for him. He could have taken me off the hand at any point and didn't. He got greedy, especially just calling the turn.

A few hands later, I take out an Asian girl when she moves in her short stack with pocket threes and I call with pockets nines. That takes me up to over $3,000. Then I bust Andy Bloch after I limp under the gun with nines again, reraise his $150 raise up to $450, and am forced to call his all-in re-reraise up to $1,100 strictly on the basis of pot odds, even though I'm not thrilled about it. Bloch surprises me by turning over a mere A-Q, a strange play from a top player. My limp reraise from the first spot should have set off alarms in him, making him think he was behind and quite possibly dominated, so why not just fold?

Unfortunately for me, the Q-Q-rag flop seems to reward his odd play. That is, until I catch a miracle nine on the turn to send him packing.

The key hand of the tournament for me, though, the one that really puts me over the top, is the one that happens next. The player on the button, a bearded guy in his thirties with a nerdy academic bearing, raises my small blind to $200. I look down and find pocket tens. I reraise to $700, and he quickly moves in for $2,000 more. If I call and lose, I'll have under $1,500. It's tough because I haven't seen him get out of line. But again, it's a pot-odds situation. I'm getting the right price unless he has aces, kings, queens, or jacks. Without a good read, I'm forced to make the call. He shows . . . pocket threes.

From there, it's smooth sailing. When we get three-handed, I've got about half the chips. And when the kid in the Cincinnati Reds cap who might give me a tough time is eliminated, I have about a three-to-two edge over my remaining opponent, a friendly older gent in a white Bellagio cap and transition lenses who realizes he's overmatched and seems happy just to have lasted this long. At this point, Nicky, my one-man cheering section, shows up, having just busted out from his table. Buoyed by the support, I dominate, bullying my opponent, until he finally reraises me all in on a stone bluff and I make an easy call with top pair. I'm in the money.

Since every table has to be completed before the event can go on to the next round, and since there's no way to determine how long it will take, when you win your table, you go to the tournament director and give your cell number so he or she can call you and give you fair warning that the next round is about to begin. We started with 780 players at seventy-eight tables, which means that after this round is completed, there will be seventy-eight players left, and according to the director, these will then be divided up into thirteen six-handed tables. The winners of those thirteen tables will advance to the final two six-and-seven-handed tables, combining, after a total of three players are eliminated, to play a ten-handed final table.

Nicky says, "Come on, let's get out of here. We'll take a drive. You've got at least a couple of hours and it'll be good for you to get away."

I'm feeling great, the adrenaline still coursing through me. "I'm on a freeroll now. This is fucking awesome."

"You can win this thing," Nicky says. "You're playing good."

We take a drive over to the new Wynn Hotel. We'd been over there once before to check out the cash games in the poker room and found it oddly disappointing. Unlike the Bellagio, the Wynn didn't seem to have much of a buzz, but that may have just been our mood that night. Tonight, there's more energy in the place. And it does have that Steve Wynn touch—what passes for class in this town—glossy marble floors, colorful arrangements of flowers and blown glass, an air of posh opulence.

We eat at an Italian place on the main level, Corsa Cucina, which is decorated in expensive Ferrari red leather, clearly part of the Wynn-Ferrari synergy that is most visible in the Wynn Penske Ferrari Maserati Dealership situated right in the casino. (They actually charge admission to look at the cars!) I'm not crazy about all the red, but my fusilli with short ribs is *magnifico*.

It's hard for Nicky. I'm up, and he's down. And that isn't made any easier by what happened to him at his table, where he was chip leader with four players left and got into a pissing match with John Myung, a guy we both know from the Diamond Club who a little over a year ago won $1 million in a tournament in Atlantic City. "He'd been raising a lot, and I decided I needed to put a stop to that," Nicky says, "so I reraised him with 9-7 off, and he went into a long think and finally called. I knew he was weak at that point. I decided that no matter what came on the flop, I was moving in. It came J-10-rag, and boom, I closed my eyes and pushed. I actually had a gutshot draw. Anyway, he starts thinking again, and I'm looking at him, and I see this look pass over his face. I know the look. It's like, as soon as they make one score some guys get this mind-set that they won't be moved off a hand. It doesn't matter to them. John's one of those guys. Anyway, he had K-Q, and he called. And it came rag-rag. His king high was good. I had a few chips left, but that was basically that."

After I pick up the check, we drive back to the Rio in the Lexus. I get to my seat seconds before the resumption of play.

On the second hand, under the gun, I look down and find a pair of jacks. We've begun this next round with $15,000 in chips and the blinds at $200 and $300. Thirty M on the Harrington scale. A nice amount of play. There are five players at my table, none of whom I recognize, and a sixth, conspicuously absent, getting blinded off. I toss in a bet of $900. The player to my immediate left, prematurely gray and wearing a white button-down dress shirt, makes it $2,500. Sizing him up, after everyone else folds, I get a vibe that he's a guy who's reckless with money. Still, it's decision time. Raise, call, or fold? Jacks are tricky, especially out of position like this. I decide the best course of action is to see a flop, and take things from there. I call.

The dealer burns and turns a 6-7-8 offsuit.

If I bet and he raises I'm not going to have any idea where I'm at. He could have aces, kings, queens, a set—or nothing, ace-king. If I check, on the other hand, I can maybe get some kind of read on him, and if I sense weakness, I can check-raise him.

Without hesitation, he bets right out, strong. Five thousand.

Shit. What am I going to do now? I have nothing on this guy, except that my instinct for some reason tells me I've got him beat. The problem is that it's the second hand. It would really suck to get knocked out this quickly. A nice dinner, back for thirty seconds, and then wham! To hell with my instinct. I want to stick around. Later, I'll regret this fold, but at the time it feels like the sensible move.

A round later, the missing player shows up. It's John Myung, Nicky's nemesis. How fitting is that? I turn around and see Nicky and Mike May and Adam Schoenfeld all talking behind the rail. I want to say something but they're too far away.

Almost immediately I take a couple of thousand off Myung when I turn a straight. I check to try and trap him, but he doesn't bite, and he mucks when I bet the river. Still, after the hand, he's the low man at the table with around $8,000.

The guy in seat 10—a brutish-looking thug wearing a leather baseball cap—and the guy in the white dress shirt to my left in seat 3 keep getting into raising wars with hands that, when they turn them over, make everyone else at the table gasp because they're so weak. It becomes abundantly clear to me that I made a huge mistake dumping my jacks earlier. Hindsight and all that.

Eventually, the guy in seat 3 gives all his chips to Leatherhead, which is unfortunate because of the two of them, I now realize that I actually have a better read on the maniac in the white shirt. Not only that, but armed with over $40,000 in chips now, Leatherhead is running over the table.

Somehow, despite this, I manage to build my stack back up a little over the $15,000 we started with. It's not easy. Leatherhead, who's the button when I'm the big blind, is raising me every time. I'm waiting for a hand to play back at him with, but I keep looking at 9-3s and 10-5s, meekly folding while my testosterone level dips ever lower. Eventually I get up and walk over to the ropes where my homeboys are stationed.

"This guy is a pain in the ass," I say. "It's really starting to get on my nerves."

"He looks like a real monkey," Nicky says.

"Yeah, well, the next time he raises my blind, I'm playing back at him no matter what I have."

"There's the spirit," Mike May says.

Sure enough, the next time it's folded around to him, Leatherhead again raises my $600 big blind, making it $2,000 to go. As promised, I repop him to $6,500.

Without even flinching, he says, "I'm all in," and moves a couple of stacks forward toward the pot.

I'm stunned. This motherfucker. As if my raise means nothing. I've already seen him do this with the guy in the white shirt. It's just pure macho. *Oh, yeah. You think so? How's this?* The problem is I have shit. King-nine off. Am I really going to put my tournament on the line with that?

With pain, I finally flick my cards into the muck, reprimanding myself silently—*no balls, no balls*—while Leatherhead rakes in my chips, his face a blank mask of entitlement. I'm down to under $9,000.

On the following hand, we lose another player, my new nemesis once again doing the honors. He has well over half the chips on the table now. He's like a knockoff of Michael "The Grinder" Mizrachi, who is poker's version of Jake LaMotta, intimidating as much by virtue of his thuggish demeanor as by his superior skills. On my next big blind, Leatherhead again (naturally) makes it $2,000 to go. I look down and find K-Q suited. Given the circumstances: that we're down to four-handed, that I'm short-stacked, that this is the biggest hand I've seen in a while, it's a no-brainer.

"I'm all in," I say.

The "in" barely has time to reach the receptors in Leatherhead's eardrums before he says, "Call," and disdainfully flips up an A-3.

I'm only a 57 percent to 43 percent underdog to win the hand, but it feels as if I have no chance, as if the dealer and the very cards themselves are overwhelmed by Leatherhead's brutish will.

We both draw air through the flop, the turn, and the river, and his ace high takes me out in forty-third place, good for $4,305.

My posse, such as they are, console and congratulate me, as I mumble about what might have been if I could've gotten lucky the last hand.

The hand I really wish I could play again, though, is the pocket jacks against the maniac in the white shirt. If I'd taken a stand and doubled up there, then maybe Leatherhead wouldn't be in my nightmares tonight.

Before thoughts of sleep, however, there is the obligatory wild celebration with my homeys at Ping Pang Pong, during which I down double shots of hot tea and get crazy on pot stickers and moo shu chicken. I'm still semi-wired when Nicky and I get back to the room, and I want to take stock, so I go in the shitter, close the door, and pull out my bankroll. It's swelled to nearly $8,000. Add in the $2,000 in satellite lammers, and I've got almost 10K not including my already-paid-for seat in the Big One. I close my eyes for a second, fingering the money, imagin-

The author (on phone) and Nicky Dileo post-play chowing at Ping Pang Pong in the Gold Coast.

ing what it would be like to embrace a whole tableful à la Chris Ferguson in 2001.

When I head back out to the room, Nicky's got his suitcase opened on the bed and he's folding clothes.

"Dude, you're really cutting out?"

"I don't know what else to do," he says. "I really don't. I can't win and I've been away from Em and the baby for too long."

"I understand. You'll play some cash games in L.A. and build your bankroll back up."

"Yeah."

In the morning I open my eyes and he's already dressed, stuffing a few last things in the zippered pockets of his bag. I get out of bed and we say our good-byes, standing in the narrow space between the beds and the TV. I want to give him a parting gift, some bit of wisdom that will help make bearable what I suspect is going to be a very long drive. But I can't think of anything.

"Hey, uh, what about the 2 percent from yesterday?" he says.

"Oh, yeah, I forgot completely." I dig into my pocket and peel a hundred off my roll and hand it to him. "I think it's eighty something, but keep it."

We stand there a moment longer, and then I move to hug him, remembering just before I actually make contact that he's got his little weirdness about being touched. I end up just squeezing his upper arms. He turns and wheels his bag to the door, which when he lets it go slams shut behind him.

Suddenly I'm alone for what feels like the first time in a while. The room is less cluttered but somehow more claustrophobic. I quickly fish my cell from the pocket of my jeans, which are draped over a chair.

"Hi, I can't really talk," Alice says. "I'm about to go into a meeting."

"Oh."

"Are you okay?" she asks. I guess she hears something in my voice.

"Yeah, yeah, I'm good." Last night on the way to the Wynn, I'd called to tell her I'd made the money, but it had been too late to call back afterwards, and besides it would have been anticlimactic. "I wound up forty-third," I say.

"Is that good?"

"It's okay."

"You sound down."

"I do?"

"A little."

I tell her about Nicky leaving.

"So you're lonely," she says.

"Maybe that's it."

"Well, I got my ticket yesterday," she says.

"Really?"

"I'll be there in less than a week."

"Holy shit, that's amazing."

"So you're glad?"

I look over at the night table, catching sight of the little slip of paper with Mia's phone number.

"Yeah, of course I'm glad," I say, crumpling it up and looking for someplace to throw it.

9

STRANGERS WHEN WE MEET

With Nicky gone, I decide I'll track down Shaniac, who has been MIA the past few days. I have to wait a few hours, since it's against the code to call anyone before noon except for an absolute emergency. So I spend some time in the media room at the Rio catching up on e-mail and the latest WSOP gossip courtesy of Nolan Dalla, Amy Calistri, Mike Paulle, and some of the other press hounds hanging around drinking all the free Poland Spring and Diet Coke they can swig. For all of my money issues and Nicky's (and Shane's, for that matter), when the top pros run into trouble, which they do from time to time (or in some cases all the time), it tends to be on a slightly larger, more dramatic scale. Today, for example, there is a debate as to how much prize money T. J. Cloutier was able to keep out of the $657,000 he theoretically collected along with his sixth gold bracelet earlier in the week. The consensus is that after he paid out his backer's cut and the makeup* money, there was probably not much left to feed T.J.'s notorious alleged craps habit.

---

* The amount that has to be paid back to the backer for previous outlays before profits can once again be shared.

Also much discussed is the series of ten $500,000 head's up matches in different forms of poker that Daniel Negreanu and Barry Greenstein are playing over at the Wynn during breaks between WSOP tournaments. Amy has written in her blog that there is "whispered concern about Negreanu" with "some comparing it to Gus Hansen taking on the big-game players like Doyle and Chip and Greenstein during last year's Series over at the Nugget," a move that "many speculate led to his current situation."

The current situation is that Hansen, one of the biggest World Poker Tour winners, is rumored to be not just broke but over $1 million in debt. No one has seen him yet at this year's World Series to confirm or deny.

Personally, I'm not that concerned about Negreanu, who is being paid handsomely to promote the Wynn's poker room, although I suppose if he were to lose all ten matches and $5 million to Greenstein,* that might present some problems for him. But he seems to have the resources, beyond what happens at the table, to recover from a loss like that. He certainly would have no shortage of offers from people wanting to back him if he ever went broke.

A little after twelve, having digested all the gossip I can handle for one day, I go to check on the action in the poker room. While there, I bump into yet another esteemed colleague, Jim McManus, who's just flown in from Chicago. He's here under the same pretext as most of us

---

* Shane actually shares a cab with Greenstein one night, on his way back to the Rio from the Wynn; and Greenstein, Shane says, starts talking a lot of shit about Daniel. He says Daniel isn't a fully developed player yet, that he got lucky in the big game last year, and that he would have gone broke if he'd continued playing in it. Greenstein also says that he thinks part of the reason Daniel took the job at the Wynn was to avoid having to play in the big game.

I ask Shane if he thinks Greenstein really means the shit he's saying, or if there's something else going on there, and Shane says he thinks Greenstein's mostly just talking smack, that it's all part of the psych involved. But who knows?

PETER ALSON

poker-playing scribes, i.e., he's got a writing gig as a cover for his real purpose, which is to play as much poker as he possibly can. Jim and I first met back at the 2000 World Series of Poker, which was the scene of his triumphant fifth-place finish in the Main Event and his subsequent best-selling account of it, *Positively Fifth Street*.

My first reaction to Jim back then was jealous antipathy, which began from the moment we met on the first day of the Main Event. He was sitting down playing, while I was standing up, notebook in hand, reporting. That was bad enough. Worse, I was out there on assignment for a magazine called *Unlimited* that was produced by Hachette Filipacchi in association with Philip Morris, while he was out there to write a piece for *Harper's*. But the thing that really sent me over the edge was that he wound up making it to the final table while I was reduced to jostling the crowd to try and get a glimpse of the action. For that, McManus had to be killed.

My assumption at the time was that I was both a better writer and a better poker player and therefore more deserving of the lucky breaks that the universe was bestowing on him. This premise took a serious blow, however, after I read *Positively Fifth Street*. Okay, so the guy was a hell of a writer. I had to give him that. But I knew—*knew*—I could clean his clock at the poker table.

The long-awaited chance came during a cash game at Foxwoods in 2001. Unfortunately, it turned out he wasn't as bad as I thought. Do you need me to get more specific? Is the image of racks of chips in front of him and me walking away from the table unencumbered sufficient? But really, all of these other things aside, how was I ever going to hold a grudge against a guy who described me in print as being about his size "but twenty years younger." Twenty years! That would make me thirty-two! I mean, how can I do anything but love a man like that?

I'll tell you how: by finding out about his latest writing gig. The bastard has been hired by the freakin' *New York Times* to write a weekly column on poker. That's what he tells me when I see him now.

The Times!

Of course, I congratulate him, tell him how pleased I am for him. But a weekly column! For *The Times!*

Yes, it's some consolation when he tells me the pittance they're paying him. I express my outrage that a money machine like that would lowball writers just because it can. And the pressure. Who needs the pressure? I mean, really, who the hell wants to write a weekly column, when it comes down to it? Not me.

I'm actually lucky *The Times* didn't offer it to me. I would have had to turn it down.

McManus further mollifies me by buying me lunch at the Rio's seafood joint (or rather *The Times* buys me lunch), where we catch each other up on our various other projects and life developments. In particular, I am interested in what he has to say about the virtues and difficulties of marriage, since we are clearly made of the same tortured cloth. We agree that picking the right woman to go all-in with is crucial—but even with aces it is possible to get unlucky. At any rate, I tell him, I am anxious for him to meet Alice when she arrives.

"I'm looking forward to it," he says.

Midway through my bowl of fish chowder, my cell rings. It's Shane. I excuse myself for a minute.

"Where have you been hiding?" I say. "I was going to call you."

"I'm in the Rio poker room," Shane says. "Over in the satellite area, playing a one-table. Where are you?"

"Having lunch on the other side of the casino. I'll come find you when I'm done."

Half an hour later, I locate Shane at a table in the back of the room. He's sitting behind a healthy stack of gray and purple chips, facing down four remaining opponents.

"Yo," he says, seeing me approach.

"I was getting a little worried that I hadn't heard anything for a few days, but look at you. You got a haircut, new clothes, a tan." I finger the sweater he's wearing, a blue-gray zip-up cashmere. "How much did this set you back?"

"It was my one real indulgence."

"What, like five hundred?"

He jabs his thumb in an upward motion.

"Seven hundred?"

"Sixteen," he says.

"Get the fuck out of here!" My jaw is hanging. "Sixteen hundred? Shane . . ."

"I know. I got a little carried away."

"For a sweater?"

The other players at the table are eyeing him, checking out the merchandise. When I notice them looking, I say, "I'd be afraid of a man who spends sixteen hundred dollars on a sweater. Either he has little regard for money or he's crazy. Maybe both."

They laugh.

In the main tournament area across the room, the final table of yesterday's shootout is about to start. I glance over wistfully as Johnny Grooms begins introducing the players on the public address system.

"I didn't get to congratulate you for making the money in that event," Shane says, mucking his hand and turning to look at me.

"Yeah, a couple more cashes and maybe I'll be able to afford to dress like you."

"All right, all right. You made your point. Where's Nicky?"

"He drove back to L.A. this morning."

"For real? Is he coming back?"

"Doubtful."

"Wow, that sucks."

STRANGERS WHEN WE MEET

"Yes, it does."

I can hear the names of Phil Gordon, Erick Lindgren, and Young Phan being announced, followed by the sound of applause. "I'm gonna go over and check it out," I say. "See what I'm missing."

"Right on."

"Maybe we'll hang later?"

"Sure."

"And stop peddling the nuts with these guys. Loosen up a little."

The other players look at me and laugh again. I imagine Shane has shown down some funky hands in building up his stack.

I weave my way across the room in between satellite tables. A bored dealer in a white shirt and black string tie sits alone at one table, waiting for customers. There are ten stacks of chips lined up in front of him and ten red seat buttons turned facedown. I can feel the inexorable pull, the temptation to grab a button and a seat. But I keep walking, pulling my laminated press card out of my shirt pocket and hanging the chain around my neck.

As I duck under the rail that surrounds the final table, a security guard impedes my progress with the flat of his hand, moving out of the way only when I lift my pass up and away from my chest. I stand on the inner periphery of the rail for about twenty minutes watching the action, feeling an odd mix of emotions about Leatherhead having made it this far. When I used to play tennis tournaments, if a guy beat me, I'd root for him to win. That way I could say I lost to the eventual champion. At the same time, it would piss me off if he did win because then I'd think that if I'd played a little better it could have been me. What amazes me is that even against this star-studded final ten, Leatherhead manages to maintain his all-out aggression.

After a while, I begin casting furtive glances back at the satellite area, half a football field away. Despite the fact that I feel some curiosity about the outcome of this tournament, the impulse to go and play is stronger.

You'd think that after playing for two straight weeks, I'd be burned-out or bored. The opposite is true. My desire to play has actually increased the more hours I've logged. I try to equate this to other activities in my life. When I was a teenager, I'd play basketball until I was shooting at a rim I could barely see in the darkness and my fingers were black with dirt and rubbed raw from the pavement-scuffed ball. Summers on the Cape, I'd hang around the tennis courts all day, waiting for a game, hitting for five minutes with someone whose playing partner was late showing up, never quite able to get enough. Were these addictions? I suppose. I was addicted to playing and competing. I loved the feeling of being good at something. Probably more than anything, I loved the rhythm, the flow of being completely in the moment, in a place where the past and future, time itself, disappeared.

I've been able to find some of the same pleasures in writing. Sex, too. Though never for long enough. Someone once said, "Sex is good, but poker lasts longer."

The "itch for play," as L. J. Ludovici calls it in his book of the same name, ultimately proves more powerful than my journalistic fealty. I head back over to the satellite area. Shane has accumulated a mountain of chips, and they're down to three players. A few tables away, they need one more player for a $525 buy-in single table. I walk over and check it out. It doesn't look like too tough a table; there's nobody I recognize, at least.

As I stand there vacillating, a guy with bleached blond hair and an earring says to me, "Why not? The water's warm."

He's right. Why not? If Shane can play a $1,050, I can play a $525. I pick up the last red seat button. The dealer yells, "Sold out! Table one-fourteen," and a few minutes later someone comes around and collects our money. Shane walks over, a little while after, counting $100 bills. He's chopped up his satellite three ways, taking $4,200 out of it, almost what I made in the shootout yesterday. He sweats me for a couple of minutes, then heads off to who knows where, our casual plans subject to the vagaries of whatever action we're involved in at the time.

I'm in such a groove in this one-table format that getting down to three- or four-handed feels as if it's a given, like something inevitable. In this instance, it takes us a long time to get there, however, and as a result, things get hairy. With the blinds prohibitively high, you've got to make moves, and fortunes can swing in a hurry. But my luck is running good, and understanding the dynamics helps.

My three opponents are an old, frail guy in a snap-brim cap, who keeps chewing an imaginary cud whenever he has to think; a young kid, who turns out to be the pro Dewey Tomko's kid; and a dark-haired, puffy-faced Englishman with thick black horn-rims. The oldster is easy to read, still here only because the deck hit him in the head early. Tomko's kid, by contrast, didn't play a hand for the first couple of rounds, but when the blinds went up, he kicked into a higher gear. Dewey has obviously schooled him well. Fortunately, he gets knocked out in a race with the Englishman, which leaves us with three. It's at this point that Mike May comes wandering by. When he sees me, he says, "Do these people know who they're playing with?"

"Are you somebody famous?" the old guy asks.

"You don't know the famous fish, Peter Alson?" Mike asks.

"This is my press agent," I say.

Mike sticks around watching, as the clueless oldster basically lets himself be blinded off waiting for a hand. Head's up, just me and the Englishman. I say, "Why don't we just chop it?"

I have played enough of these single tables now to understand that a deal is almost obligatory head's up with the blinds this large and the chips nearly equal. We've been playing a couple of hours here. We can lock in $2,600. There's very little to think about. Sure, there have been a few single tables when I've gotten head's up quickly and the blinds were still reasonable and it made sense to keep playing. But in a spot like this, not making a deal is basically opting to flip a coin, all or nothing, for five grand plus.

The Englishman says, "I think I'd like to play."

It catches me off balance. "You want to gamble for five thousand dollars?"

"Come on, chop it up," Mike chimes in. "Peter's a very nice guy. And he's getting married in a few weeks. It's good karma."

"Nothing personal," the Englishman says. "I'd just rather play."

I look at Mike, who shrugs. It shouldn't matter but it gets under my skin. A coin flip for five gees. Everyone else I've played with has acted reasonably.

"All right," I say. "Fine. You want to spend two and a half hours of time and hard work and then walk away with nothing. That's your prerogative." I can feel myself steaming. This motherfucker. It definitely feels personal.

The very first hand, he raises my $1,000 blind to $3,000. I'm sitting on $9,000 minus the blind. I've got K-7 suited. Fuck him. He wants to play, we'll play. "All in," I say. "Call," he says almost as quickly, tabling pocket sevens.

I look at Mike, shaking my head. If there's any kind of karmic justice here, I'll spike a king or make a flush.

Apparently karma takes longer to kick in.

I study the board after the cards have been dealt and I've lost, trying to understand how I went, in a matter of minutes, from being certain that I'd locked up $2,600 to walking away empty-handed.

I stalk off from the table with Mike at my side, but I keep casting over-the-shoulder glances back at that Elvis Costello–glasses-wearing motherfucker, muttering every imaginable obscenity I can think of. "Fuck, that fuckin' prick just took twenty-six hundred dollars out of my pocket" and so on. Mike, with his usual equanimity, pats my shoulder and says, "Forget it, Jake, it's Chinatown." But the car horn keeps blaring.

We meet up with Shane and decide to grab a bite at the All-American Bar & Grille. But I can't let go of my anger.

"There's no rule that he has to chop it," Shane says.

"It's unspoken."

"He felt like gambling," Mike says. "There are a bunch of sick people in this place. I thought you knew that."

"I do know that. It just . . . threw me."

"There's that, too."

"It's true," Shane says. "Some guys, especially if they see that you're eager to make a deal, will refuse just to put you on tilt. It gives them the edge they need."

"But it's still stupid."

"He's got the five grand. You don't."

"I could just as easily have had king-eight, in which case I'd have the five grand because an eight hit."

"You can't let shit like that put you on tilt," Shane says.

I look at Mike, hoping for some support.

"I think Shane's right," he says. "You can't assume that a deal is inevitable. You have to approach it assuming that the guy won't chop it."

I draw in my lips, nodding grudgingly. They're both right, and I know it. *But that motherfucker . . .*

On our way back to the Amazon Room after chowing on burgers and fries, we're walking down the hall and I see him—I see the British guy—coming from the opposite direction with one of the members of the Hendon Mob, the older Brit version of The Crew.

"That's him," I hiss at Shane. "That's the motherfucker who took my money." I turn and hiss "prick" in his wake.

It's at this point that both Shane and Mike advise me that perhaps I should take the rest of the night off from playing.

As if I weren't already tilted enough, when I wander back over to the final table of the shootout, I'm stunned into an even higher level of tilt,

what I'll call tilt by association: Leatherhead, whose actual name is Anthony Reategui, is sitting on more than 85 percent of the chips with
three players left! In Nolan Dalla's account of the final table the next day,
he will write that "the tournament was effectively over"—less than an
hour into play—"when Reategui and the other chip leader, Allen Goldstein, went to war." Clearly Goldstein had become annoyed by Reategui's
bludgeoning style by then, and so, when Reategui, whom Dalla dubs
"the Demolition Man," raises under the gun, Goldstein, with pocket
nines, moves in on the button. This is precisely the kind of suicidal over-
bet that a player like Reategui inspires. His superaggressiveness leads
people to believe that he never has anything, and because of that they
want to beat him so badly they'll take a stand when they don't need to. In
this case, Reategui actually has a hand, pocket queens, and calls instantly, gobbling up Goldstein's whole stack.

In all, on his way to the bracelet and the $269,100 first prize,
Reategui, a twenty-nine-year-old pro from Arizona, single-handedly
knocks out seven of his nine opponents, a true one-man wrecking crew
if there ever was one.

I leave the Rio in the still-withering twilight heat and head back to my
hotel, calling Alice along the way. I've decided that walking is more
convenient, enjoyable, and healthy for me than the hassle of driving
back and forth every day. It takes about twenty minutes to get from
my room to the Rio poker room and vice versa: twelve minutes indoors
and another six or seven minutes outdoors. Some days, my circum-
navigation of the Gold Coast's three-story parking garage and crossing
of the wide boulevard between the two casinos constitutes the only fresh
air I get.

"Can you call me back from your room?" Alice says.

"Sure. What's the matter?"

"Nothing's the matter. It's just that it always feels like you're doing something else when you call me."

This is true, and though there is no real defense for it, I find myself trying to explain, anyway. The reason I call her from the media room, from restaurants, from my car, from the poker room, is that I am rarely actually in my room, and when I am it is usually too late at night.

"It just feels like you're squeezing me in, and I don't like it," she says.

"Okay."

"Okay, what?"

"I understand what you're saying."

"So can you call me from there now?"

"Yes. I can call you from there now. I'll call you in a few minutes."

Sheesh. What was that all about? She's coming out here in three days, why is she giving me a hard time? Is she feeling nervous? Insecure? What?

"Sweetie," I say, when I call her back, "I'm totally psyched that you're coming out. We're going to have a blast." I'm lying on the bed, propped up on a few pillows. I kick off my brownish-gold Ecco sneakers.

"Are you sure? You're not just saying that? You don't have *SportsCenter* on with the sound off right now?"

"No, of course not!" I say, grateful that I don't but wondering how it is that she knows that I might.

"I just get worried that you're out there having a great time, and now I'm gonna come out and gum up the works and break your rhythm and—"

"Cut it out. Don't even say that. I've cleared the decks here, no pun intended, and I've got some fun stuff planned for us."

"You do?"

"Yeah, I do."

"I'm sorry. I hate being like this. It's just—I'm here in the city and it's the summer and nobody's around and I have to go in to my stupid job, and meanwhile—"

"I know. I understand."

"Do you? I mean, if you want to play poker while I'm there or work on your book, it's perfectly fine."

"I'm playing my last tournament on Wednesday and I'll be there to pick you up at the airport on Thursday."

"What if you're still in it?"

"That would be a nice problem to have. But let's not worry about that."

"I love you."

"I love you, too."

What kind of woman, I wonder, after hanging up, would marry someone like me? I don't consider Alice to be significantly more masochistic than the average playwright-and-sometimes-actress-living-in-New-York-without-a-trust-fund-or-some-other-form-of-independent-wealth, but what exactly possesses someone of apparently sound mind to hitch her wagon to a gambler and writer (as if either alone would not be bad enough)? Let's face it, I'm off in Vegas playing poker and God knows what else. Even if the fiction is that this is my best shot at being able to pay for the wedding, does that really put a significantly better spin on things than the reality that I am merely making a declaration that I yam what I yam and will be till death do us part?

Sunday, I get a call from Nicky. He's back in Vegas. He had a phenomenal few sessions in the cash games at Hollywood Park and took down close to twenty grand. So yesterday he decided to come back and give it one more shot. He drove Em and the baby here and got them all a suite at the Bellagio. "This time I'm doing it right," he says. He realized that he was expending too much energy worrying about them. Now he's brought his base along with him. Obviously, the sensible thing would have been just to stay in L.A. for the week before they head back East to the house they rented for three weeks on Cape Cod, but it was driving him crazy knowing that we were all here and the World Series was still going on. "And I just needed to give it one more crack," he says.

If this were a movie or I were the kind of memoir writer who makes shit up, Nicky's return would wind up triumphant. He would at the very least make it to a final table, or if that was too obvious, I'd have his wife drop a quarter in a slot machine and hit a million-dollar jackpot. But this isn't a movie, I'm not a fake memoirist, and none of that comes to pass. He plays a few megas and some cash games, loses a small chunk of that twenty grand, and finally gives up. I see him at the Rio just before he takes off. "If I'd gotten in the Main Event," he says, "I'd come back for it, obviously. But, for whatever reason, I just can't seem to win here. I just can't."

Wednesday, I buy into event 22, $1,500 No-Limit Hold'em. There are over 2,000 entrants, but I'm feeling good, confident again. My little tilt from the incident with the Englishman is history. In the past three days, I cashed in four out of six single tables and took down another $3,400. I'm optimistic but also realistic about my chances today. As Barry Greenstein says in his book *Ace on the River,* an advance copy of which I've been able to get a peek at, courtesy of Adam Schoenfeld, "Poker tournaments are like lotteries, but with much better odds and an element of skill thrown in." Or as Doyle Brunson puts it, "It's a lottery, but some of us have more tickets than others." I certainly don't have as many tickets as Doyle, but I like to think I have more than some other players.

The best news is that even after I pony up $1,500 in cash, my bankroll is still a healthy $11,900. Not counting the $10,000 that I've laid out for the Main Event, I'm ahead nearly $7,000 for the trip. Unfortunately, that $10,000 counts.

As usual, I bide my time through the early rounds while the blinds are low. This is the time, according to Greenstein, when it is good to build up a conservative image so that you can "run some risky bluffs" later. In these big fields, the speed with which players fall by the wayside is astonishing. Less than four hours after beginning, we're down to 1,390 players, and I'm sitting on a slightly above average stack of $2,700, looking around at a table of unfamiliar faces. That's the good news. The bad news is that I recently got moved to this table and it's tough to make cold reads.

Still, with the blinds at $100-$200, I find myself in a good spot after it's folded around to the player on the button and he moves in for his last $800. I'm the small blind, with ace-king off, and I'm happy to move in on top of him for all my chips, $2,700, trying to win the $1,000 already in the pot without risking much of my stack. To my surprise, however, a blond woman in designer shades whom I barely cover makes a big over-call from the large blind. I'm expecting to see her flip up a hand like kings or queens, possibly jacks or tens. Incredibly, though, she tables the 8-9 of spades.

"Wow," I say, hardly able to believe it. This is what can happen, though, in these tournaments with thousands of entries. Maybe the 8-9 of spades is her lucky hand. Or maybe she believes that the big blind must be defended at all costs. What it means for me, as one player from one of my old college games was fond of saying, is that I'm "either in poker heaven or in poker hell."

An ace on the flop makes it seem like heaven. But a second spade hits the board on the turn, and I'm on the brink of hell. Lucifer gets the pearly gate slammed in his face on the river, though, and I've just bumped up my stack to over $6,000, busting two players in the process.

A few hours later, having methodically worked my stack up to $9,000, I get moved to a much tougher table with the backgammon legend and tongue-wagging weirdo Paul Magriel and the former attorney

Mark Seif, a wild, colorful player, whose WPT confrontations with the equally wild Hon Le rank among the best televised poker action ever. Seif has accumulated a mammoth chip lead, his towers of chips approaching the $150,000 level, which is terrible for everyone else, since he is probably one of the most fearsome big-stack players in the game. Fortunately for me, he is sitting three seats to my right, so I usually get to see him act first before deciding what I want to do.

My tournament swings on one key hand. The blinds at this point are $150-$300. There are 400 players remaining, and the top 200 will make the money. Seif raises in early position, as he has been doing frequently. A guy with shoulder-length blond hair calls the $1,000 from middle position, and it comes to me on the button. I've got pocket nines. Limping wouldn't be a terrible play, but I decide that moving in is worth the risk. Seif probably doesn't have much. I don't give the blond guy a big hand either, since he didn't raise. There's nearly $3,000 in the pot, which certainly makes it worth my while to pick it up.

"All in," I say.

As I figured, Seif quickly mucks. But the blond guy goes into the tank. He and I are roughly equal in chips. He's got me covered by a little bit, but he'll certainly be putting his tournament on the line with a call. He shakes his head after a while, saying, "I just hate going out of the tournament with jacks. That's how I went out of the last one." Some guys would be saying something like this to get a reaction out of me, but this guy means it literally. Christ, he's got jacks! What do I do now? How do I get him to fold? If he calls, I'm 80 percent sure to be history. I want to say something, but I'm afraid it'll backfire. Amarillo Slim and guys like him live for these situations, where they can talk the best hand into folding. Not me. I look down at the felt, avoiding his eyes. When he flashes his two black jacks and throws them into the muck, my relief is immense.

Two hours later, eleven hours after the day got under way, we're down to 202 players, two away from the money. I haven't seen a hand in two rounds and I've been blinded down to $8,000. But unless I get unlucky or do something foolish, I'll make the money—at which point I'll start gambling. Sure enough, two short stacks finally get eliminated, much to the delight of everyone left, but especially one young kid at our table, who has nursed a short stack through the last forty minutes and has only one black $100 chip left when we hit the money. It's his first-ever WSOP event, and the thrill he experiences outlasting more than 1,800 players and getting to cash leads me to pat him on the back and share in his uncomplicated joy.

I'm happy to make the money, too, but even happier to be able to shift out of bubble mode and try and get some traction. It doesn't go particularly well, however, as I move my last $6,500 into the pot in a race situation and come up short, finishing 179th. Mark Seif, who only six days earlier won his first WSOP bracelet in the $1,500 Limit Hold'em Shootout, rides his big stack to another victory and a $611,145 payday. His formidable final-table opponents include Minh Nguyen; Bill Gazes; Webber Kang; David Ulliott; and the Fossilman, Greg Raymer, who, had he not lost two coin-flips might have been able to add a second bracelet to his collection but still manages to walk away with $119,450 and some hard-earned respect.

Thursday morning, before leaving to pick up Alice, I go to the Robert Cromeans Salon at Mandalay Bay. For sixty bucks (half the New York price), I get the royal treatment: a twenty-minute scalp and shoulder massage, followed by an hour-long coiffure from a statuesque, braided blond haircutter in a tight midriff-baring halter top. Never mind that I'm doing this so I can look good for my baby, I still can't stop myself from having a little salon-chair fantasy. Thank God I'm not running for political office. Remember what happened to Jimmy Carter when he told *Playboy* that he had lusted in his heart? Does the phrase one-term president bring it back?

Shorn of some hair if not the tangles that lie underneath, I drive to the airport, park the PT Cruiser in the short-term lot, and head into the terminal. I actually start to get excited, my heart rate picking up, as I hike over to the security checkpoint and take up a spot outside Gate B. A steady stream of people make their way out from the gates toward baggage claim and transportation.

Twenty minutes later, she comes into view, wearing a short green piqué dress, pink T-shirt, and slutty heels, wheeling the same model Victorinox bag she bought for me. She's slightly tan, I guess from her weekend in Sag Harbor, and I notice I'm not the only one checking her out. I move down the slightly ramped walkway toward her and now she catches sight of me. The tilt of her face, the way the light catches her golden ringlets, takes my breath away. Whatever distance or uncertainty I've felt at times during these past three weeks vanishes. Grinning big silly-assed grins, we throw our arms around each other and squeeze tight.

"Hey, you."

"Hi. I was sort of hoping you were going to call and tell me that you couldn't get here because you were at the final table."

We kiss and I say, "This seems like a pretty good trade-off," taking the handle of her bag and turning toward the escalator. "The car's across the street."

We're sweet and nervous with each other, chattering about the flight, the latest New York gossip, the latest Vegas gossip, and what's on our agenda for the day. Earlier, I checked out of the Gold Coast, leaving a bunch of stuff in Mike May's room—books, a suit, my tennis racket, pretty much everything that I didn't feel like hauling back to New York with me.

I've booked a room at the Mandalay Bay on the poker rate (which requires that I play a certain number of hours—something I know I'm not going to do, but am hoping maybe I'll get away with not doing). When we get to the hotel, the lobby, with its gleaming marble floors, arching vaulted ceiling, and palm fronds, is as crowded as the marketplace in Casablanca, with long, headache-inducing check-in lines. Looking around, trying to figure out how we can beat the system, I see a sign that says V.I.P. services. "Wait here," I tell Alice. "I'm gonna try something."

I walk into the V.I.P. office, which has no line at all. To my surprise, as soon as I tell the woman working the desk there that I booked my accommodations through the poker room, the red carpet is rolled out. It's "Yes, Mr. Alson," "Anything we can do, Mr. Alson," and "We hope you have a nice stay, Mr. Alson." Not five minutes later, I'm walking back over to the check-in line, which has barely moved, waving a couple of room keys.

"Wow," Alice says. "You're *good*."

Need I tell you where this ends up? After six years of being a couple, three weeks apart are a strong aphrodisiac, turning the familiar into the strange. If what takes place on the king-sized hotel bed is not quite a clothes-ripping, Michael Douglas–Jeanne Tripplehorn *Basic Instinct* crazy animal thing, it's not Doris Day–Rock Hudson, either. Afterward, we pad around naked on the carpeted floor, the large, gold one-way mirrored windows offering a high-up view of the Strip in all its daylight glory. We stand there, unself-consciously naked, and Alice leans back into my arms. Her hair smells sweet and her skin is warm against me and not a single tortured thought assaults my brain.

Later, down by the pool, we order tropical drinks, then go for a float along the lazy river, a man-made moving stream that snakes around the vast acreage of pool and sunning areas. In the evening, we meet up with Shane and his girlfriend, Sheila, who is also in town, for dinner at Aureole. We get nicely buzzed on two great bottles of wine, and at one point, while Alice is off in the powder room, Sheila says, "So what's your fucking problem, dude? Your girlfriend is awesome—and she's hot!" And all I can do is duck my head and mumble in shame, "You mean my fiancée."

The next day, there's more pool time and a trip over to the Rio, where the $2,500 No-Limit Hold'em tournament is under way. I introduce Alice to various of my colleagues, although I can't find anyone who's seen Jim McManus for the past couple of days. Oh, well. I finish out my role as tour guide, leading Alice by the hand through the gauntlet of green-felt tables, saying, "There's Daniel Negreanu, there's Hellmuth, there's Doyle," none of which seems to impress her much, until we come to one table and she exclaims, "Isn't that Jennifer Tilly?"

At which point I discontinue the tour.

The afternoon is spent shopping at the Fashion Show Mall. Alice needs a bathing suit, and I need a shirt for our wedding. In Neiman Marcus, we're walking past a jewelry counter and one of the rings catches my eye. I stop. It's a thick, gold cable-banded ring with a large green gem, very similar to a ring we'd looked at in a store in Soho. Alice, whose tastes run counter to the classic diamond solitaire, had fallen in love with that ring. But at a cost of eight grand, it seemed to dictate that we make a Sophie-like choice between it and our Cape Cod wedding. I'd been thinking that if I had a really good World Series of Poker, maybe we could still swing both, but here was another possibility.

"What do you think?" I say, nodding at the case.

"I like it."

I catch the eye of the saleswoman behind the counter, who comes sailing over, smiling brightly.

"We'd like to see this ring," I say.

"Yes, of course."

She extracts the ring from the case and hands it to Alice.

"It's a David Yurman design," the saleswoman says. "The band is eighteen-carat yellow gold and the stone is peridot."

I have only a vague idea of what she's talking about, but it seems to mean something to Alice, who looks at the ring for a few moments and then slips it on her finger. The band is a little too large, but otherwise it strikes me as nearly perfect.

Alice extends her arm, cocking her wrist back, as she stares at it.

"Do you like it?" I ask.

She looks at me and nods.

"Do you really like it?"

She scrunches up her face, giving me the quizzical *What kind of game are you running on me here?* look.

"How much is it?" I ask the saleswoman.

"Let's see," she says, consulting a price list, "that one is nine hundred plus tax."

I'm floored. We are in Neiman Marcus, after all. I'd been expecting a figure three times that.

"Give us a moment," I say.

"Of course."

I turn to Alice. "So?" We're both smiling. Her eyes are as blue and alive as they've ever been. "Just tell me what you really think."

"What I really think is that I love it," she says.

"Then what the hell?" I turn back to the saleswoman. "We'll take it," I say.

"Peter, are you sure?" Alice asks.

"I just want to know if you're sure."

She nods, suddenly on the verge of tears.

"Okay, then."

I pull my roll out of my front pocket and count off ten bills. The ring has to be sized, which will take a couple of weeks, but I'll be able to pick it up when I get back from New York. A kind of giddiness sets in as we walk away across the store, and though we never do manage to find a shirt or a bathing suit to our liking, the drive back to the Mandalay Bay is a hand-holding, smooch-at-every-red-light testament to a shopping trip that turned out well.

The next day and a half is a blur of spa visits, lazy river floats, dinner at Daniel Boulud, and breakfast in bed. In the taxi to the airport, I begin to realize that after the five days in New York, I'll get back here and there'll be a bunch of book stuff and the Senior's and a few days after that the start of the Main Event.

"What's the matter, baby?" Alice says, seeing my face cloud.

"It's just that it's going by so fast," I said. "When I got out here I was wondering how I was going to make it through six weeks, and now it feels like it's almost over and I only just arrived."

She squeezes my hand. "Don't you know, that's what always happens when things are good?"

10

A Senior Moment

Maybe it's a Jewish thing, never wanting to talk about something good until it's actually happened. And even then . . . it's like tempting fate.

Quintessential Jewish phrase: *Don't count your chickens before they've hatched.* Likewise, it's bad luck to name a thing. You might incite the evil eye. In fact, religious Jews (not that I am one; I've just inherited the temperament) won't name their children before they're born or have baby showers until after the mother gives birth.

So it makes me a little edgy when Alice says what she says about things being good. I want to shush her. *Don't say it so loud. Someone will hear.*

Despite this, my little roll of good fortune continues in New York. I'm back for five days, most of them spent on location with the cast and crew of the television pilot I wrote, *Nicky's Game,* the filming of which is a dream come true. The first time I meet John Ventimiglia, the actor who has been cast in the title role, I do a double take. Probably best known for his role as Artie Bucco, the chef on *The Sopranos,* Ventimiglia looks eerily like Nicky Dileo, my inspiration for the title character.

Most of the scenes are filmed in an actual underground club, the Satellite, on West Thirty-eighth Street, one of the survivors of what is an ongoing and concerted effort by the city to rid itself of illegal poker. Only a month ago, the two biggest clubs, PlayStation and the Player's Club, were raided and shut down. The irony that New York is doing its damnedest to squash the game at the height of its nationwide popularity would be amusing if this weren't such a preposterously misplaced use of the taxpayers' money. Then again, if poker were ever legalized in the city, it would probably lose its charm and romance.

My main function on the set is to make sure that everything looks and feels authentic. Matt Strauss, the producer, and I agree that making this show look and sound real is crucial. The movie *Rounders* gave a good glimpse into the underground poker world, but its emphasis on cheating and mob-connected tough-guy stuff seemed more a concession to the exigencies of the box office than to what actually goes on in the clubs. The essence of New York poker is really to be found in its humorous and colorful characters, and in the rivalries, jealousies, gossip, and petty grudges.

It's for that reason that I have written a part into the pilot for a character based on Robert Hanley, the brother of John and Billy Hanley, the two Irish brothers who ran the legendary Diamond Club on West Twentieth Street before it was shut down several years ago. John Hanley himself was a larger-than-life character, who gave poker in New York a good portion of its salty-edged romance. But it was Robert, who once did a stretch in the slam for attempted manslaughter, whom I found the most entertaining of the three brothers. Particularly after he decided to become the world's toughest card-playing, ex-con, gay stand-up comedian. With Matt Strauss's encouragement, I wrote a little part for him that I thought would make use of his thoroughly original qualities. Unfortunately, his audition, which took place while I was in Vegas, did not go well. The director didn't feel comfortable with him, and it fell on

Matt to break the news to Robert that the decision had been made to go with a more experienced actor.

Since Robert is six-foot-three, with prison muscles and a kind of De Niro in *Cape Fear* thing going on, telling him was an unenviable task. I felt terrible, personally, because I like Robert and think he has talent, however unpolished it is, and because he had been led to believe the audition was a formality. When Matt broke the bad news, Robert, not surprisingly, was disappointed. Still, he seemed to be somewhat mollified when offered a featured nonspeaking role as a dealer.

On Thursday, my last day in New York, and the second-to-last day of production, filming goes well, but as is typical, there are numerous delays caused by retakes, lighting setups, and so on. Robert, who was making jokes and cracking on people through most of the afternoon, starts getting cranky, especially when he sees the actor who's been cast to play the role that I originally wrote for him. "This is fucking bullshit, Peter. Look at that guy. He's a boring piece of shit."

"Yeah, I know. It sucks," I commiserate. "I wish it had been my decision. But it wasn't."

"You know the only reason I'm sticking around is because you're my friend," he says.

"Just hang in there. You'll get some screen time. Have fun with it."

Everything seems to be fine when I leave for the airport. But just as I'm about to board my plane, my cell phone rings. It's Matt Strauss.

"We've got a problem," he says. "Robert Hanley just stormed off the set."

"What?" I laugh. "I thought only stars could storm off a set."

"I know. It's very funny. But if he doesn't change his mind we're going to have continuity problems tomorrow."

"I'm sure he'll cool down."

"I don't know. He really went off. He got in my face and kept saying, 'You fucked me like I fuck you,' over and over. 'You fucked me like

I fuck you.' I thought he might even get physical, but in the end he just stalked off."

"Listen, they're calling my flight. I'm sure you'll work it out or think of a solution. If you want, I'll call Robert when I get to Vegas."

"Would you?"

"Sure."

Matt's phone call is a reminder to me that I live in an odd and precarious world, full of the gently and not-so-gently mad, and that at any moment things can go tilt. Perhaps I shouldn't be surprised, then, when other things begin to go wrong. For starters, my seat is in the middle of a row, where I am squeezed between two 300-pound behemoths, one of whose carry-on is a fat sack of fragrant McDonald's burgers. Then the plane is delayed on the runway for forty-five minutes while I breathe in *eau de* Big Mac. Once we get off the ground, we hit serious turbulence, and at McCarran, my luggage is among the last down the chute.

It gets worse. There is a long line at the car rental and no upgrade this time, no PT Cruiser. When I drive over to the Gold Coast in my stylin' Geo Metro, the only room available is facing a wall. Before checking out a week ago, I had requested that I be given, upon my return, a room similar, in terms of location, to the room I was vacating. The news that this request hasn't been honored provokes a small temper tantrum. It's late, I'm tired, and I shouldn't have to deal with this shit.

"I'm sorry, sir," the desk clerk says. "There's just nothing else available."

"That's unacceptable. I'm giving you five weeks of my business; you should be able to accommodate a simple request. Let me talk to a manager."

There is something to be said for being a prick: You sometimes get what you want. The psychic price you pay for it, however, is that you are a prick.

My new room is on the sixth floor, all the way at the end, on the side facing the sky (if there were sky to see at this hour). It is as long and lonely a walk down that hall as I imagine Greg Raymer had to make at the Bellagio the night he was assaulted. Unlike him, I am not carrying several hundred thousand dollars with me, only several thousand. If this were an SAT question, you might accurately answer *Greg Raymer is to the Bellagio as Peter Alson is to the Gold Coast.*

I'm so tired that I don't even bother unpacking. I do, however, muster the energy to call Robert Hanley. It is a delicate call. Robert is still angry, and trying to reason with him or make him understand that if he wants a career in show business he needs to act like a professional does not seem to penetrate. Eventually I give up and make a quick call to Matt, telling him I was unsuccessful. He assures me that he'll figure out a way around the problem, and that's that. I get into bed and pass out.

In the morning, I take my time reestablishing my little home away from home. I set up my computer, check my e-mail, and call Matt Strauss to see if the issue was resolved. He says not to worry; they've figured out a way to get around the continuity problems. Good. I need to focus on things here.

After eating a room-service breakfast, I take a walk over to the Rio. It is obscenely, stupidly hot outside. One hundred seven degrees. The kind of heat that rises off the pavement in visible, tree-warping waves. The air is actually hard to breathe, stinging the way it stings when you inhale smoke from a fire.

When I walk into the casino it is, by contrast, like the death chill of a vampire's embrace, an unholy relation to the inferno outside. The long hike to the Amazon Room affords me plenty of time to reflect on the strangeness of being back, and the fact that things seem different—or, rather, *feel* different. The wind has shifted—and not in a good direction.

The enormous convention hall next door to the Amazon Room, which had previously been hosting a Caterpillar Machinery confab, is empty now, the doors open to reveal workmen inside its vastness, setting up booths for the next event. I bump into PokerPages blogger Mike Paulle, smoking a fat stogie in the hallway outside the poker room. He has no idea that I've been gone, but when I ask him to fill me in on what I missed, he tells me how Jennifer Tilly and Phil Laak, girlfriend and boyfriend, nearly lived out a dream date for the ages. She was playing the final table of the Ladies Championship while he was playing the final table of the $2,500 Pot-Limit Hold'em, both events unfolding at the same time, and they came oh-so-close to the ever-elusive simultaneous climax. The Unabomber ultimately finished second to a record-setting Johnny Chan, who scored his tenth gold bracelet, while Tilly, dubbed "the Unabombshell," punked the critics of Celebrity Poker Showdown by crushing the Ladies' field and winning her first bracelet.

"Other than that," says Paulle, "you didn't really miss much. Oh, yeah, Phil Ivey won his fifth bracelet and six hundred and thirty grand in the Five Thousand Pot-Limit."

"It's amazing how even with these big fields the cream's been rising to the top."

"Isn't it? You should see who's at the final two tables of the Five Thousand Short-Handed No-Limit. Doyle, Scotty, Layne, Men 'the Master,' Jesus . . ."

"It almost makes you think that skill counts for something in this game."

I finally make my way into the poker room, and it really is as if I'd never left, hundreds upon hundreds of men and a few women, slouched over green tables, passing chips and cards back and forth, back and forth. I watch the short-handed event for a while, then wander over to the satellite area, fingering the lammers in my pocket, nodding at familiar faces, none of whom know that I was gone or that I've just come back. There's a single table about to get off, but it looks like a tough field and I'm just not feeling it. Maybe it's that I don't want to find out that I've lost whatever magic I had before I left. I decide instead to try my luck in a cash game. There's an open seat in a $5-$10 no-limit game, and I sit down and almost immediately drop $1,000. I buy in for another $2,000, but after one hand, I realize that I'm not in a good space, so I get up, leaving my chips on the table.

The short-handed tournament is down to the final six. What a table it is! Doyle Brunson, Scotty Nguyen, Minh Ly, Layne Flack, Jason Lester. Holy shit! No lucky amateurs here. I watch for a while. It's sort of like watching great tennis players from close up. You can't help absorbing the grace and beauty of the way they move. When I go back to my cash game, I've got the rhythm of their play in my head. I feel confident and fearless.

And I lose another $1,200.

"Baby, maybe you should just lie low for a couple of days instead of trying to force things," Alice tells me when I update her on my unhappy return.

I'm sitting with the phone pressed to my ear in the Rio's Starbucks, nursing a stiff iced latte. Melissa Hayden and Allen Cunningham come in and glance over at me. I nod at them, then look away. "I'm not trying to force things," I say quietly into the phone. "I was just playing. It's why I'm here."

"You're the one who told me that you need to trust your instincts."

"I really hate it when you quote my own stupid shit back to me."

"It's not stupid."

"No, but it makes it impossible to disagree with you." I swirl the stirrer around in the ice at the bottom of my latte. "Anyway, I'm probably not going to play again until the Senior's the day after tomorrow."

Alice restrains her laughter, then says, "You really qualify for that?"

"Why? Does that scare you? That you're marrying an old geezer?"

"I'm just trying to figure it out, how you scored here, buddy. Do you even understand how lucky you are?"

I reflect on that luck, as I eat dinner by myself at the Rio's Carnival World Buffet the next night, while watching two 300-plus-pound ladies head back to their table carrying three dessert plates apiece. The bleakness of this life, this poker life, if I thought this was all there was, would almost be more than I could bear. It may be that this place is finally getting to me. Nicky's not around; Shaniac's off on his high-rolling Bellagio trip; Mike May is ever-elusive; Adam Schoenfeld is hanging out with Evelyn Ng again; and what I heard from someone yesterday is that Jim McManus got on a plane and flew back home to Chicago.

In a way I find this last bit of news even harder to digest than the absurd array of food on my plate. It is both incomprehensible and disturbing. *The Times* just hired the guy to write a freakin' poker column. How could he leave in the middle of the World Series? It makes no sense.

Nevertheless, he is gone. Out of here.

I am told that he was losing a lot of money and he missed his wife. This was an actual quote according to the person to whom I talked.

Because of my own issues, because of my fears of what marriage will actually mean for me, what I extrapolate from this is that his wife ordered him home.

But, honey, what about my column?

I don't give a goddamn about your fucking column, buster. Get your self-deluded ass on a plane home this minute and find something to write about that doesn't involve losing our money!

But what will I tell The Times? *What will I tell my readers?*

Tell them that you're married!

I actually call Jim in Chicago to find out the truth. He assures me that he just found himself getting lonely and missing his family. It doesn't sound so far-fetched the way he says it, but I still can't help wondering. Is he running a bluff on me? Tell me the truth now, Jimbo, while it's not too late. For my sake.

Saturday at noon, I sit down at table 41, seat 4, for the start of the Senior's $1,000 No-Limit Hold'em event. Looking around the table, it's all I can do to keep a straight face. Why, for God's sake, am I sitting here with all these old bastards? There are 824 of them seated at eighty-three tables, and I'm pretty sure every single one of them is older than me. Come to think of it, it's not so bad being the youngest one at the ball for a change.

The guy to my left, whose gnarled hands shake as he counts his chips, leans toward me and croaks, "Are you a senior?"

I assure him that I am.

He squints at me skeptically. "You look mighty young."

"I've got my driver's license," I say, "if you want proof."

"Truth?"

"No!" another guy shouts at him. "He said *proof*. If you want *proof*!"

"I know what he said. I'm not deaf."

"Hey, there's James Woods over there! You see him?" a third guy says. (Is that a hospital I.D. band around his wrist?)

"I remember back in the day when Telly Savalas used to play," says someone else.

"He's passed now," says Hospital Band. "He's betting and raising up in the big poker room in the sky."

As the cards are dealt, there's a lot of fingering of glasses and neck craning and "What's that card?" and "I can't see" going on.

But the most amazing thing about this event is how little restraint anyone has. You'd expect that age would have taught these seniors the virtues of patience, but they're all as eager to shoot off their loads as young bucks. Maybe it's just that they've decided they'd better use up their chips while they can.

For me, it works out well. I get a few early gifts and increase my stack from the $1,000 we started with to over $5,000. The quality of play, at least at this first table, is astonishingly poor. You forget what a huge edge that is because in most of the open events even the poorer players are much tougher than they used to be. In the early stages of this tournament, I'm actually reminded of the Sunday tournaments we used to play at the Diamond Club when they first began running them there in the old days. No-limit hold'em was still so foreign to everyone then that I, with my fairly extensive experience, made it into the money nearly every week. But after a while, as people improved, my edge decreased and my results declined. By the time the Diamond Club was raided and shut down, the Sunday tournament's fast structure and the much higher general level of play had made it a virtual crapshoot. From that experience, I was able to extrapolate that the edge that the Daniel Negreanus and Howard Lederers must hold over the average player in a major tournament, based on their rate of success, is nearly equivalent to the edge that I, as a veteran player, held over the neophytes in those Sunday tournaments at the beginning.

So to say that my table in this event reminds me of those days gives some idea of what a good spot this is for me. Unfortunately, the guy with the hand tremor twice sucks out against me when I have him in for all his chips. The first time, I make a flush on the turn and he makes a higher flush on the river. The second time, he hits runner-runner for a chop. I stay cool, though; I don't let it tilt me. After two hours, I'm still the chip leader at my table with $4,000.

During the break, I call my mom. When I tell her that I'm playing in the Senior's, she starts howling with laughter. Thanks, Mom.

The second hand after the break, a guy in early position raises to

$400 with the blinds at $75-$150. I reraise him, making it $1,600, with A-K suited. He moves in for $700 more.

This is how badly some of these guys play.

There's no chance he can get me off the hand with his final raise. So what is his objective?

With pocket threes, which is what he shows, it's pretty hard to say.

I'm tired and I feel like going home and taking my nap? Maybe. At any rate, I call, his threes hold up, and I'm down to $2,300. A few hands later, I again get A-K, but this time I bust a guy and I'm back up to $4,300.

About an hour later, I suck all the chips out of a raiser when I flop the nut flush and let him bet into me, taking another peek at my cards before calling his bet, really Hollywooding. It works, too, because he moves in on the turn so he can prevent me from making the flush I already have. I'm up to $7,500.

At this point, Charlie Shoten is moved into the empty seat next to me. I recognize him because he's a tournament regular with some good cashes, who appeared on one of the early WPT broadcasts, finishing second for a $200,000-plus payday. Nicknamed "Scotty Warbucks," I'm guessing on account of his totally bald pate and the fact that he looks something like the character Daddy Warbucks, from the comic strip *Little Orphan Annie,* he's also the author of a self-published poker and self-help book called *No-Limit Life* that is being sold in Trinket Alley, the hallway concession area outside the Amazon Room. I had been curious about it and about him and was going to pick up a copy of it until I was confronted by the slim paperback's $30 price tag. Later, when I mentioned my curiosity to Nicky, his reaction was scornful. "Oh, that guy. He's a strange little man. I've played with him a number of times. He portrays himself as enlightened and joyous, but he mostly seems bitter and unhappy."

Wanting to find out for myself, I introduce myself, telling Shoten that I wrote the book about Stuey Ungar. He immediately peppers me with all sorts of questions about publishing, most having to do with how he can find a mainstream publisher for his book. Then he reaches into a zippered airline bag he's got with him and gives me two copies, one for me and one to pass on to my editor.

I thank him, leafing through it quickly in between hands. The message of *No-Limit Life* seems simple enough. We all have what Shoten calls "Thought Terrorists," specific negative thoughts that prevent us from being fully who we are. The most dangerous of these Thought Terrorists, or TT's, as Shoten calls them, are phrases like "Hard to do" and "I'm trying." These are self-defeating thoughts that do terrible destruction to us. "If you are TRYING," Shoten writes, "you can never succeed. Letting go of TRYING and HARD TO DO brings you into a world where all of your deepest hopes and dreams can come true. All of your future actions (without those two Thought Terrorists) can be DOING. Because you are not attached to the outcome anymore, you will be happy and at peace with your efforts and will embrace and find a prize in any outcome."

I find little to take exception to in these ideas, although they do seem mostly to be a rehash of Zen and other Buddhist philosophy, with a little Marianne Williamson and Anthony Robbins mixed in. I am not surprised to find *The Celestine Prophecy* among Shoten's list of "personal milestone books" in the back of the book.

Apparently, however, the principles he espouses are not as easy to apply as he makes out. In fact, the author himself, at least from my vantage point, could seem to profit from rereading his own book. For the several hours that I sit next to him, until he's gradually blinded down and busted, he complains pretty much continuously about shitty cards and about how badly he's been running lately. The only time I actually see him wearing the radiant contagious smile that his book describes is when I look at the picture of him on its cover. It's a shame, really. For many players, myself included, the lessons of his book are relevant. One just shouldn't count on turning to the author himself for inspiration.

An hour before the dinner break, with over 150 players still left, I get moved to a new table. I was one of the chips leaders at my old table, with $11,000, but here at the new one my little stacks are dwarfed by big towers of chips everywhere I look. "I think I liked my old neighborhood better," I say. To compound matters, I go absolutely card dead. Thankfully, the dinner break comes in time to stop me from doing something stupid. I've still got a decent stack of $10,000. I just need to readjust to my new surroundings and station in life. The TT's are really bringing me down. "Imagine the thousands of situations that would make your current concerns seem minor," reads a passage in *No-Limit Life.* "Accept yourself and your current situation. It is what it is. Your old perception is what upsets you. Replace your old perception with your new one." If only I could read these words without considering the source. But perhaps that's part of the point.

Nicky calls while I'm eating a burger at the All-American Bar & Grille. He's at the house they rented on Cape Cod, sitting out on the porch with Em and the baby. He sounds great, light-years away from the past few weeks. "It's beautiful here," he says. "The sun set about half an hour ago; the sky is a dark, dark blue; and fireworks are shooting over the bay. It's just beautiful."

He asks me how things are going, and I tell him good, that I've made it pretty deep into another tournament.

"That's actually why I'm calling," he says. "I want to send you a check for five hundred bucks for five percent of your action in the Main Event."

"You're kidding?"

"Nope. Em and I discussed it. She wants to do it, too. I told her how well you're playing. We both decided it would help you to know we're behind you."

"Wow. I'm blown away."

"Give me your address. I'll send you a check."

"Just give me the money when you see me."

"No, no. You should always get the money beforehand. You don't want to have to go and ask for money after you've been knocked out of a tournament. That's no fun at all, believe me. I learned that the hard way."

"All right." I give him my room number at the Gold Coast and tell him to send it there.

"I'll call you in a few days," he says. "Meanwhile, say hello to everyone for me. Mike May, Adam, Shane, whoever else you see."

"I will. Thanks, dude. You just made me feel really good."

After the dinner break, my mood and outlook buoyed, I go on a blind-stealing, bluffing mission, making something out of nothing. From 7:30 until 10:50 p.m., I see one small card and one big card nearly every hand, but picking my spots, I manage not only to maintain my stack but to increase it. We reach the money at seventy-two players. Down to forty-five players at five tables, I've got $16,000, which is just slightly below average. I get moved for the fourth time. My new table is a little more to my liking than the last one. Nobody I recognize or fear, but a few good, solid players. One of them is a guy named Bob Hume, whose nickname is the "Human Calculator"—get it, Hume-Man Calculator? He looks to be not much older than I am, with an angular face, blondish crew cut, and glasses. Apparently, he's won five $10,000 Megas during the past four weeks; this puts him five up on me. But right now his more immediate concern is that the blinds have just escalated to $600-$1,200, with $200 antes, so it's costing a steep $3,400 a round.

Hume only has $6,900 left, and I can see the gears of his built-in calculator smoking. When he moves all in, it smells of desperation. Holding A-Q, I have a pretty easy call from the big blind. Sure enough, he's on a move with J-9. But he snags a jack, and just like that I'm knocked down to $9,000. Even more galling in a way is that I get moved again on the very next hand.

After paying my next big blind and the antes, I find myself down to $7,000. A cheery Frenchman with loads of chips moves one of his towers forward from the cutoff. I'm only too happy to call all-in from my small blind when I find a couple of fours in the hole. There are just thirty-seven players left and there's a $500 pay jump at thirty-six, but I'm trying to win this thing, not make an extra five bills. The Frenchman has A-Q, which is a real hand but almost beside the point. I figured to be up against two overcards. My play is very simple here. Double up to about $18,000 and have a real chance, or go home. I'm a 55 percent favorite, awaiting the verdict.

The flop is clean.

So is the turn.

Now I'm 89 percent.

The river is an ace.

I want to somehow reverse time and put that damn card back in the deck. Deal it again. But I haven't developed those powers yet. So I stand up and say, "Good hand," looking at that ace one last time to see if it's changed.

One table over, Bob Hume, the Human Calculator, suddenly has an enormous castle of black, pink, and yellow chips.

"Wow," I say. "What the hell happened?"

"I went on a little rush," he says.

On the brink of elimination, he instead winds up as chip leader at the final table when they break for the night.

The next day, I watch the final table play out. As the bit players fall by the wayside, Hume winds up facing off against an eighty-year-old West Virginian, Paul McKinney, a strong, silent John Wayne type who just chews on his big dead stogie and plays a mean game of poker. I find myself rooting for McKinney, and not just out of spite (not that I really begrudge Hume his good luck). I'm standing by the rail next to one of McKinney's grandsons, who looks like a younger version of him, with pouchy mournful brown eyes and the same stoic indomitability. "Yeah, he's a tough old bird," says his grandson. "Granddad never gets tired. Never. He can play poker all night long and not get tired."

Eventually, the indefatigable McKinney wears Hume down, taking the first prize of $202,725, and in the process becoming the oldest player to ever win the Senior's Event. The Human Calculator has to settle for $106,230, which by my calculations is $104,055 more than I make.

11

THE PERFECT PATH

On the Fourth of July, I tag along with Shane to a barbecue at the house that Brett Jungblut, a former member of The Crew, is renting with his girlfriend and a few other people. Actually, "tag along," is the wrong way of putting it, since we drive in my Geo Metro. Shane just takes taxis wherever he goes.

The house is out in the middle of nowhere, in some development plopped down randomly on the desert sand. We drive around for a while before we find it, Shane needing to call Brett for updated directions because all the houses out here look the same.

It's still a million degrees out, just the kind of day you want to barbecue, but I'm happy to have been invited somewhere, happy to be away from the Rio for a few hours. In a way this is like the last pit stop and refueling before the end of the race. It's T minus three days to the Main Event and counting, and you can actually feel the excitement and anticipation beginning to mount in the Rio poker room as the ranks swell with players flying in from all over the world.

We park across the street, and Brett comes out of the door of a small two-story white stucco house, still holding the phone he was using to talk to Shane. He's tall, broad-shouldered, and good-looking. Up until a couple of days ago he'd had a mop of white-boy dreads and a scragged-out beard. Now he's clean-shaven and motocross handsome because ESPN decided it would be fun to do a makeover on him to air during the broadcast of the 2005 WSOP in September. Turns out Brett's a former model but kind of hated the whole pretty-boy thing. So this look is less a new thing for him than a return to an old thing.

We go in the house, and there are three young and beautiful women in the kitchen area, making dip and cutting vegetables. They introduce themselves and offer us drinks, while Bret heads back outside to a little patio to get the grill going. Shane and I sit on stools by the kitchen island and talk to the ladies for a while. They're all in for the weekend from L.A., where they're involved in production and development in the film industry. A joint is lit up and passed around. I notice a big bag of buds on a desk next to one of the several computers. More people arrive: a guy named Jon Eaton who edits a Web site started by Brett called Poker-Trails.Com, and some other young poker players and their girlfriends. It's interesting to me the way that poker is so much more acceptable among this generation. It's just another cool profession, like filmmaker or rock musician.

After a while, I go outside and talk to Brett, as he grills up burgers and dogs, joint in hand. He offers me a hit, but I decline. The heat from the grill added to the heat from the desert sun forces me to keep my distance, but Jungblut seems not to be bothered as he puffs on the joint.

"If I didn't smoke weed I'd be throwing chairs through windows," he tells me. "I've got ADHD* and it's the only thing that works to control it."

I tell him that I think he knows my friend, the writer Ivan Solotaroff.

"Sure," he says. "I talked to Ivan a lot for the *Rolling Stone* article."

---

* A kind of turbo-charged attention deficit disorder with hyperactivity thrown in.

"I haven't read it yet," I say. "But I'm really curious about it from what he's told me."

"I've got a copy of it inside. I'll find it for you."

Ivan's article is about The Crew, the group of Gen Poker twenty-somethings which Dutch Boyd assembled during the 2003 WSOP to "take over the poker world" and of which Brett, who is also known as Gank, and Scott Fischman, were a part. I know that Brett is no longer a part of the group, but I'm curious to know what really happened.

"We just went our separate ways," he says. "It wasn't what I thought it was going to be. People got involved in ego trips and other bullshit, and you know the whole thing from the start was just about Dutch and his talent for marketing. As far as that goes, you have to give him credit. ESPN ate it up."

Brett again offers me the joint, and this time, to be polite, I take a tiny puff. My serious pot-smoking days are long behind me, and with good reason. You know that scene in *Jackie Brown* when Samuel L. Jackson finds Bridget Fonda toking up in front of the tube one morning and says, "You gettin' high already? That shit gonna rob you of your ambition," and Fonda replies, "Not if your ambition is to get high and watch TV"? Well, that was pretty much how I spent my early twenties. Brett doesn't seem similarly weed-handicapped. He's smart and ambitious, and his conception of the possibilities in poker ranges way beyond just playing. Among his various poker-related business ventures, he's purchased Internet domain names by the dozens, has a couple of sites up and running already besides PokerTrails, and has accumulated one of the largest collections of vintage clay poker chips in the world.

As day turns to night and more booze and pot and burgers and Jell-O shots get passed around, Brett organizes a little no-limit hold'em tournament with a $50 buy-in that we play in two flights on the dining room table. I crap out about midway through, and rather than hang out and watch, I ask Shane, who's still in it, if he can get a ride back to town from someone else. Not surprisingly, given the trouble we had getting here, I get lost on my way back, but the fireworks are pretty to watch as they rocket through the night sky, and the neon glow of the gambling capital is always there as a guide during my slightly melancholy, zigzaggy trip back home.

Tuesday morning, T minus three and counting. I decide the time has come to embark on an exercise regimen to prepare myself for the rigors of what I hope will be (for me) a poker marathon. The Main Event this year will be contested over the course of ten days, with the first three of them all being different flights of Day 1; in other words, the field will be divided up into three parts, which will, after being winnowed down, combine to play Day 2 on the actual fourth day of action. Those unlucky enough to draw Day 1C will have to play eight straight days to make it to the final table (although by then, presumably, they will no longer care about that hardship).

I have drawn Day 1B, myself, which, by general consensus, is the best day (a little bit like Goldilocks's porridge, not too hot, not too cold, but just right). No matter which day you draw, however, endurance will be an enormous factor, and my belated attempts to whip myself into fighting shape are in recognition of that. I don't kid myself that I can actually get *into* shape in the next two days, but I want to get my blood flowing and my endorphins activated, and since it is impossible to play tennis in this heat, the Gold Coast's gym will have to do.

Located in a small windowed outdoor room just past the equally unglamorous pool, the gym consists of about eight machines, only five of which actually work, and an incline bench along with a few free weights. On my one previous trip here, I had the run of the place. This time, there is one other person taking advantage of it, an older, gray-haired man, wearing a tight white tank top and shorts, walking at a swift pace on one of the two treadmills.

I do some sit-ups on the incline bench, a few curls with a fifteen-pound dumbbell, and two sets of twenty-five push-ups, and then I get on the second treadmill, setting the device for a speed of four mph. I glance over at the gray-haired man's settings and see that he's been on his treadmill for twenty-five minutes already, at a 4.5 mph pace.

Jesus.

I glance at him again, taking a better look this time, and realize that it's Jay Heimowitz, one of the legendary players from the Mayfair Club back in its heyday, and the winner of six (!) WSOP gold bracelets, not to mention two Main Event final-table cashes.

He nods at me without recognition, through we have actually met on several occasions, then stops his treadmill, having reached the half-hour mark, collects his things, and walks over to the water cooler, filling up a cup. Jay must be in his seventies but he's built like an ex-athlete—I imagine he was some kind of handball or squash champion—and he carries himself with that confidence. He drains his water, throws out the cup, and takes his leave.

I punch up the treadmill to 4.7 and keep going on it past twenty-five minutes, past thirty, all the way up to thirty-five minutes. I'm exhausted and bored and I feel it in my legs, but I'm not going to let a guy in his seventies outdo me no matter how many bracelets he's won.

After I shower and get dressed back in the room, I decide I'd better call Alice before leaving for the day. Even though it's quiet in the room and distraction-free, we have a strange, disconnected conversation. She's at work, and not happy about it. She gets cranky when I tell her about the barbecue. Turns out she spent the Fourth alone. I tell her that sucks, that I wish she had been with me, but it doesn't help. She's moody and pissed off.

"And then there's your book. It makes me nervous. I'm afraid you're going to portray me as some kind of harridan," she says.

"Don't be ridiculous."

"Well, you'd better not."

I spend most of the afternoon playing in a $5-$10 no-limit game at the Rio, booking a $500 win. Afterward, I hook up with my editor at Atria, Wendy; and her boyfriend, Warren, who are in town on a working vacation. They both seem nearly as excited about the start of the Main Event as I am, and when they hear about Nicky giving me $500, they decide it's such a good idea that they're going to give me $100 for 1 percent.

In case there was any doubt about whether poker has entered the mainstream of American life, it officially ends on Wednesday morning, July 6, 2005, when the doors to the convention hall next door to the Amazon Room open, and the First Annual Poker Lifestyle Show begins. Since I am actually part of the madness, having agreed, along with Nolan and Madeline and Stefanie Ungar, to sign copies of *One of a Kind* at a booth set up by the local Borders bookstore, I will at this juncture defer to a more objective observer to put things in perspective. Here's what Mike May wrote about the Poker Lifestyle Show in his online blog*:

> Imagine sneaking up behind Jules Verne, clocking him with a lead pipe and stuffing him in a freezer. Then thaw him out almost two hundred years in the future and show him videos explaining the fax machine, the atom bomb and Paris Hilton. Now look at the expression of slack jawed, bewildered disbelief on his face. That was the expression I wore for about 43 minutes the day before the final event of the World Series started. That

---

* Mikemay.Blogspot.com

was when I first laid eyes on the Poker Lifestyle Show, a convention full of vendors that you had to walk through to get to the tournament area in the Rio.

Perhaps my initial reaction to all this poker marketing will seem very dated shortly, but for me, the Poker Lifestyle gig is a little disorienting. Sure, there has always been a "poker lifestyle," but it just wasn't something you really wanted decent folk to see, much less ask them to buy. Not very long ago, the poker lifestyle was somehow being able to scrounge up enough money to play nude Twister with hookers in a hotel room even though you were living out of the back of a '92 Lincoln. Now believe me, I'm not saying there's anything intrinsically wrong with that, I'm just saying I didn't think it was something for which you get a bobblehead doll in your likeness.

Yes, you read that last part right. One of the many mind-bending revelations of the Lifestyle Show is that there actually is a booth featuring bobblehead likenesses of various pros, among them Greg Raymer, Doyle Brunson, Scotty Nguyen, and Phil "Unabomber" Laak. Now if you had asked me four years ago, when I was playing pot-limit hold'em with Phil Laak at the Diamond Club, to make an odds line on the Unabomber (or anyone else who played poker) ever getting his own bobblehead doll, well, let's put it this way, a $10 bet would have turned me into your indentured servant for life, since there is no way I would ever be able to pay off such a bet. I'm talking long odds.

Even Doyle Brunson, for decades as famous as you could be in the world of professional poker, looks slightly bewildered (though cheerfully so) by the magnitude of this thing and how it has grown. Here at the white-hot center, he's flogging his Internet poker site, Doyle's Room, sitting at a desk, signing eight-by-ten glossies of himself. There's a line hundreds of people long.

Mike May and I walk around while I'm on a break from signing my

Mike Muy, the author and two friends at the Poker Lifestyle Show.

book. We get our picture taken atop a Harley with two scantily clad Bodog girls; inspect special $80 sunglasses called PokerSpecs, which are endorsed (although not worn) by the Flying Dutchman, Marcel Luske, who still prefers the regular sunglasses he wears upside down that actually inspired PokerSpecs (great endorsement, Marcel!); we play poker with two more leggy trade-show girls who are promoting I'm not quite sure what; receive free poker T-shirts, hats, card protectors, and pens, while passing by booths selling poker books, videos, poker tables, chips, scented candles (for that postgame hotel-room seduction?), jewelry, rare coins, poker art, and something called the Sovereign System, an eye-scan recognition no-questions-asked safe-deposit vault where you can stash your winnings. There are also drawings for Porsches and Harleys and one for a seat in next year's WSOP (do I need to tell you that I enter it?).

Light-headed and overstimulated, Mike and I go back to the Borders table. We're showing off our shopping bags full of swag to Madeline Ungar, Stuey's ex-wife, who is still a very good-looking woman, by the way (think Michelle Pfeiffer if you're casting the movie), when Alice calls. It's the first conversation we've had since the awkward one of yesterday, and I can tell right away that her mood hasn't improved much.

She wants to know if I want my middle name on the wedding invitation.

"What do you think?" I ask, putting my free hand over my other ear to shut out the din of the convention.

"I don't know," she says.

"Well, I think we should go without our middle names, then. It's cleaner and less pretentious."

"I think we should use our middle names," she says.

"Okay. . . . Then let's use our middle names. I guess you didn't really want my two cents, after all."

"No. I did. I just didn't realize what I wanted until you told me what you wanted."

"O-kay."

Tenseness.

"Look, I had to take care of this whole thing while you're there playing poker and going to parties," she says. "You could at least sound a little more excited. Or say 'Thank you, sweetie, for taking care of it.' "

"Thank you, sweetie, for taking care of it."

"Oh, go fuck yourself." She hangs up.

Mike looks at me as I'm eyeing the dead phone in my hand.

"I probably shouldn't ask," he says.

"Not if you're considering getting married someday," I say.

He laughs.

*　*　*

There is one remaining event separating me and the more than 5,000 other entrants from the Main Event, namely the annual media-celebrity charity tournament. I have participated in this event, oh, maybe fifteen times, without ever once making a final table. This year's tournament features the defending champ, my friend Michael Kaplan, as well as an ever-expanding media horde of print, television, and radio journalists; bloggers; and Internet scribes; in addition to celebrities such as Penn Jillette, Shannon Elizabeth, Brad Garrett, and DJ-AM. What is amazing is that even in this event, the caliber of play has improved. I remember when at least half the field was absolutely clueless. Now it is probably only about an eighth of the field. Of course, with a blind structure that escalates at an alarming rate, skill is still the least important prerequisite for winning. I exit early as usual, albeit twenty bucks richer—the result of a last-longer bet I've made with Michael Kaplan, who is among the first to be eliminated.

First hand of the Main Event. I look down and find 8-9 of diamonds. In late position, I make a raise, only to have a player in a cowboy hat in early position reraise me. Since it is early, and I have the kind of hand I like from this spot, I call his reraise. The flop comes J-10-7. I have flopped the joint. My Western-attired opponent comes out betting. Big. I put on an act of thinking about his bet, and then I raise him. Without hesitation, he announces that he's all-in. I'm shocked by his decisiveness and blitzkrieg approach to the very first hand of the tournament, but I call. I mean, I have the nuts; what else am I going to do? I turn up my cards, but inexplicably, to my horror, they have changed. I am holding not the 8-9 of diamonds, but the 5-6 of diamonds. I have nothing. Not even a draw. "Wait a minute," I scream. "These aren't the cards I was dealt!" I try explaining, but my protests fall on deaf ears. Nobody cares. This is poker. Nobody cares. And just like that it's over.

I wake up from this nightmare in a state of jittery air-gulping relief. Wow. It was so real. I have been dreaming about poker frequently these past four and a half weeks, so I suppose I should be used to it. Each night, I lie in bed in the dark thinking, then dreaming, about what I could have done differently that day and what I should have done differently; often, the jabbing pain I experienced from seeing a card appear at the worst possible moment, the image of it, flashes over and over in my poor, tired brain. I fixate on it with the sick tape-loop repetitiveness of someone suffering from extreme OCD.

But last night when I got into bed, I was not replaying hands. I was not even thinking about poker. I was obsessing about the conversation I'd had with Alice, about the wedding, about marriage. It was stupid. To try and predict what the future will bring or in what manner the rest of my life will play out is like a Zen koan: I can worry about it, wrestle it, and attempt to control it until I am blue in the face, but the truth will reveal itself only in the course of revealing itself.

My writer friend Ivan Solotaroff, who wrote the piece about The Crew in *Rolling Stone,* was quite taken with an idea that Dutch Boyd liked to talk about. The idea of the Perfect Path. Boyd was thinking about poker tournaments, and how there exist in every tournament opportunities where it is possible to increase your stack without any risk; and that these opportunities arise with enough frequency that a player can gather more chips than he's losing in blinds; and how, if a player can take advantage of every such opportunity, he can get to head's up without every seeing a flop. This, according to Boyd, would constitute the Perfect Path.

To me, the idea is entirely fanciful. The Perfect Path exists only in retrospect. One can never find it in advance or even in the moment—except by accident and good luck. As for the idea of there being no risk, well, that is patently absurd. There is always risk. Every time you make a commitment, put chips in the pot, or put a ring on someone's finger, there is risk.

That is why today is a bit strange. Because I know that the biggest event in poker history is about to start, an event of which I am part, and that at the end of the day the battlefield will be littered with corpses, yet it is a certainty that I won't be one of them. That is one of the advantages of having drawn Day 1B. I will be able to watch today, get a feeling for the rhythm of play and the carnival atmosphere without worrying about my mortality or survival. I will not have to stay there, glued to a seat for hour after excruciating hour. I will be able to come and go as I please. With my media pass, it will be a bit like being the Invisible Man. Only at the end of the day, when the survivors are counted, will I find myself wishing I were one of them.

Incredibly, Shane, Mike May, and an Aussie we know from New York, Guy Calvert, have also drawn Day 1B. The four of us meet, by arrangement, inside the Rio near the doors that lead out to the parking lot. Another New Yorker, Richie Bell, an old-time underground clubber (even older than I am), also joins us. It's quarter to eleven as we make our way down the Hall of Pain, walking shoulder to shoulder, like a street gang, though no one is going to mistake us for the Latin Kings. The closer we get to the action, the thicker the cigarette smoke becomes. The crush, too. When we're finally able to squeeze into the poker room, it's a bustling, frenetic madhouse, as the 1,880 Day 1A players find their way to their seats. There are well over 3,500 people in this space when you include spectators, and there is an electric buzz that you can actually feel and hear.

By the time that Johnny Grooms kicks the tournament off twenty minutes later, saying, "Ladies and gentlemen, poker players from around the world, shuffle up and deal," the final count is not yet in. But it will turn out to be 5,619 entrants, more than double the number who played last year; they range in age from twenty-one to ninety, come from forty different countries. One of us will be the new world champion and win $7.5 million, the richest prize in all of sports, twice the prize money of the Masters, Wimbledon, and the Daytona 500 *combined*. Five thousand fifty-eight of us will walk away empty-handed.

We don't have to wait long for the first $10,000 casualty. It comes eight minutes after the first hand is dealt. "Seat open, table one-twelve!" yells a dealer. And that's that. The bloodletting has begun.

12

THE QUICK AND THE DEAD

The last time I played in the Main Event in 2001, I decided to get a massage the day before it began as a treat to myself. I was nervous and thought a massage would be a good way to relax. At the Golden Nugget spa, I was sent to a room where a muscular Swiss dude named Hans was waiting. It cost me $120 for what felt like a deep-tissue rolfing session. The muscles in my back actually knotted up, thanks to his far from gentle ministrations. And the next day, popping Advils liberally, I crapped out of the Big One after a few hours. I will not make the same mistake this time.

What I do instead, after leaving behind the insanity of Day 1A and the Amazon Room and trekking back to the Gold Coast in the positively mild 100-degree temperature (which is down six degrees from yesterday), is repeat my gym routine from the previous day, spending another Helmowitz-beating thirty-five minutes on the treadmill and following it with a dive into the pool. When I get back to my room, the red light on the phone is blinking. There is an envelope waiting for me at the front desk.

I go downstairs and am handed a red, white, and blue Priority Mail pack, which I open on my way back up to the room. In it is a check for

$500, and a note that says, "Just keep doing what you've been doing. Three cashes in five tournaments is world class. Nicky."

A while later, my cell phone vibrates in my pocket. I take it out and see that someone has sent me a text message. I push the button that says "Read."

"Ur amazing," it says. "Sorry I've been a B the last 2 days. GL tomorrow. Luv A."

Wow. I didn't even know she knew how to text-message. I call her back (since I don't know how to) and leave a message on her voice mail telling her that I love her, too, and that I'll call her tomorrow during a break. I spend the rest of the afternoon back over at the Rio, signing books at the Borders booth. The signing is followed by a television interview on the Players Network, with Nolan moderating, and Madeline and Stefanie Ungar and me as his guests. Come evening, the four of us join our agents, Greg Dinkin and Frank Scatoni, and their producing partner, Michael Roban, at Gaylord, the Indian restaurant in the Rio.

We're engaging in a little fantasy of whom we'd like to see cast in the role of Stuey if the movie of our book ever gets made, when Phil Laak and Jennifer Tilly, the Unabomber and the Unabombshell, enter the restaurant. I make the mistake of asking Phil what day he's playing, and he tells me today—which can mean only one thing, since they are here, and everyone else is still playing. I scrunch up my face, feeling their pain. "Sorry."

"What are you gonna do?" he says.

I nod in sympathy.

By eleven p.m., I'm back in my room, undressed and in bed. I turn on the tube and flip around for a while, then request a wake-up call for 8:30 a.m. and turn off the light. A lot of good players, players on the level of Phil and Jennifer, aren't going to make it through tomorrow. I don't want to be one of them. But I know I might be. The odds are I will be.

think this way. It is necessary to live in the present, at this table, in this moment.

And the moment is now—well, almost. Dragging it out just a little bit longer, Jack Effel introduces Carolyn Gardner, the 1983 ladies world champion, and we have to stand for a painful rendition of the national anthem. With that, the first bad beat of the day behind us, it falls upon Greg Raymer to issue the command we've all been waiting five weeks to hear.

"Players, dealers, are you ready?" he says with a nice dramatic flair. "Then let's shuffle up and deal!"

As the dealer at my table wheels in his seat, spinning out cards, I tell myself to savor the moment. I'm sitting down playing in the biggest poker game in the world, and I look around, just soaking it in. Then I peek at my two cards, J-3 off, grateful to have a hand that I can easily muck. Hey, at least I've survived one hand. Don't laugh—not everyone does. Over at the ESPN feature table, Oliver Hudson, son of the movie star Goldie Hawn, gets involved with Sammy Farha on their first hand. Oliver has pocket tens and Sammy has A-10, and the flop is as cruel as it can possibly be: A-A-10. The money doesn't go in until the turn, but in it does go, and Hudson is busted, out $10,000, in two minutes, in a situation that couldn't have turned out any other way. The ultimate cold deck. Poor guy. I guess he'll just have to console himself with being one of *People* magazine's Fifty Most Beautiful People and find succor in the arms of whatever ravishing model or actress he's squiring around at the moment.

As for me, on the second hand of the day, I find pocket eights, and raise the $25-$50 blinds to $150. The kid to my left, who's from Philly, and is wearing a backward visor and cargo shorts, calls. Everyone else folds. I have him pegged as a decent player just from the little bit of conversation we've had. On a flop of A-rag-rag, I bet $250, and after pondering, he calls. The turn doesn't change anything, and, feeling that he's got a weak ace, maybe A-10 or A-9, I take another stab at the pot, betting $600. When he reraises me $1,200 more, I flick my cards away. I'm down to $8,800 just like that.

For the next hour or so, every time I try to make a continuation bet, I get either raised or called, and by the time we get to the end of the first level I'm down to $6,275. I can't seem to win a pot. In fact, I haven't won one.

To quell my frustration during the twenty-minute break, I call Alice. She tells me not to get down. I'll turn it around. She says she'll be thinking about me and sending me good vibes.

"Thanks," I tell her. "I need them."

After the break, I continue playing position poker, raising from the last three spots whenever I have a hand that I think will play well from there. On one hand, after I've brought it in for a raise with 8-9 suited, I get one caller from early position. It's the skinny Middle Eastern guy in the 3 seat, who has a thick thatch of dark hair and a Zapata mustache. He's one of the more dangerous players at my table. I get the feeling early on that he's not afraid to make moves. When the flop comes A-A-A, he checks and I check back, just as I probably would if I had an ace.

It's important to think not only about what you can pick up in your opponent, but what he's reading into you. Here I am, wearing a green button-down shirt, brandishing a pen and a notebook into which I occasionally jot down who knows what, and he's got to be thinking that I'm just some sort of amateur chump. I know that's what I must look like. That's certainly what I would think if I were looking at me. And a chump, if he'd flopped four of a kind, would definitely check it.

By the same measure, I believe that Mr. Zapata might actually bet out if he'd flopped four of a kind. So I'm pretty sure that he doesn't have an ace, either.

The turn card is a nine, giving me a full house.

Mr. Zapata checks. I check back. It's probably not the best play, but

I've got him on two face cards or maybe a small pocket pair, so really, I'm worried only about paint hitting on the river.

The river is a ten.

Again, he checks. I'm almost positive that he would bet here if he had a ten or an ace, so when he checks, I'm pretty sure I was right about him having paint. There's only $400 in the pot, and I could check back and show it down, but I decide to make a $200 value bet.

He reraises me $700 more.

Wow.

I take my time, replaying the hand in my mind, asking myself a series of questions. Would he have checked an ace all the way down? Would he have check-raised with a ten on the river? Why is his reraise so big? If he's looking for a value raise, wouldn't he make it lower?

All of my questions seem to lead in one direction. Added to that is my sense of him as the kind of player capable of making a move in this spot.

I call.

He nods, tapping the table with his knuckle and turning up K-Q suited. I show my 8-9 and he raises his eyebrows in appreciation. Around the rest of the table, the reaction is mixed. A couple of players understand what they have just seen. Several others seem puzzled. It is possible I am just a bad player who got stubborn. Zapata knows better.

On another hand, soon after this, I make a good value bet on the river when a flush card hits and I have two pairs, collecting a few more chips.

By the time we reach the third level, four and a half hours in, I'm back up to even.

A player at the other end of the table gets a phone call during a hand, and standing up, says, "I really can't talk right now. I'm in the middle of playing in the World Series of Poker," which draws a laugh around the table.

The older man in the red shirt in seat 6, the guy whom I identified as a rich amateur, and whose play thus far has confirmed my suspicions about him, limps in ahead of me for $200. I've found out his name by now; it's Bill Burnett, and he's the mayor of Naples, Florida.

"Well, Mr. Mayor, I'm going to bump it up a little bit."

With A-Q suited in late position, I make it $700 to go. He's the only caller.

The flop comes Q-10-3, giving me top pair, top kicker. He checks to me, and I make a standard continuation bet of $700. He raises me $1,500.

I take a deep breath. From what I've seen of his play so far, he tends to overvalue his hands quite a bit. He could easily have K-Q or J-Q. But really those are the only two hands I can beat.

Still, I call.

The turn is a jack. He checks. Would he have really reraised me with Q-J? Probably not, but I'm feeling a little bit lost against him, so I check back.

The river is another jack.

That's not a good card for me, but it doesn't seem like a particularly bad card, either. The mayor bets out $2,500.

Now what, genius?

I stare him down, trying to figure out what he can have. When I come up empty, I call.

He turns over J-9.

Fuck. He flopped open-ended, then caught running jacks.

"Mr. Mayor, Mr. Mayor," I say, shaking my head. "You hurt me."

He shrugs. "At least you're not one of my constituents."

I'm down to $3,700.

An hour later, having grinded my way back up to $6,500, I get up and walk around, rolling my shoulders like a fighter, trying to stay loose. Man. Being poor is stressful. Broke just feels bad, but poor is constant stress. I look at some of the players at the tables around me who are sitting behind big stacks. They look relaxed and cheerful. When you've got a lot of money, you've just got fewer worries—in life and in poker.

At 6:10 p.m., the guy in seat 5, who looks a bit like a biker or a fan of ZZ Top, raises to $1,000 under the gun. The blinds at this point are $100-$200 with a $25 ante, so there's $550 in each pot before a card is dealt. I've got pocket eights but seven players to act after me. If I call and it gets reraised, I'm going to have to muck. And even if it doesn't, unless I flop a set, I'm going to be in a tough spot. My other option is to raise, but how much? If I make it $3,000, I'm basically pot-committed, so if I'm going to raise, it might be better just to move in. But if he has a bigger pair or ace-king, he's likely to call, and then I'm risking my tournament life probably taking the worst of it.

In the end, I decide that there will be a better spot for me, and I muck.

Half an hour later comes the hand that will define my day. It starts with the table folding around to the button—the older fellow in the black snap-brim beret and glasses directly to my right. I had pegged him for a rube at first sight. In fact, he's a lot sharper than my first impression, a midwestern doctor who bears a passing resemblance to Herman Tarnower, the Scarsdale Diet doctor, famously shot to death by his lover, Jean Harris, the headmistress of a girls' school. Like Tarnower, this doctor has the look of someone lean and a little mean, capable of treachery. He's been raising my blinds every chance he gets, and I'm sick of it.

When he does it again this time, making it $600, I pop him back to $1,700 holding only Q-7. He calls. That is not what I wanted, particularly since he's got me outstacked by two to one. But when I make top pair on a flop of Q-9-3, I bet out $1,500, less than half the pot, feeling pretty certain I'm good, and wanting it to seem by my weak bet as if I'm afraid. He takes the bait and calls, thinking, I'm fairly certain, that I'll shut down on the turn and he'll be able to take the pot away from me with a bet.

This is real poker. The doctor is tricky and aggressive, and either I'm outplaying him here or I've gotten myself into a jam—it's hard to say which.

The turn is a six, which apparently changes nothing. I bet $2,000 this time. Again, he calls. Now I'm feeling slightly nauseated. I was putting him on a random hand, assuming that he thought he could outplay me. But when he calls here, I have to rethink things. He could have anything. Jack-ten, for an open-end straight draw; three-six, and he just hit second pair; he might even have a real hand, like K-Q or Q-J. His call has definitely fucked me up.

The river card is dealt. A four. I've got $3,500 left. I have no idea what to do. Clearly, I can't bet again. I check. He bets. Three thousand.

I laugh. What a weird bet. If I call, I'm effectively knocked out, although I'll still have one pink $500 chip. Why not put me all in?

Well, psychologically, it's a little easier for me to call. So that would mean he wants me to call?

"Do you want me to call, Doctor?"

He doesn't say anything, but a slight smirk forms.

I continue to stare him down.

I have such a weak hand. Top pair, no kicker. He called two bets with no apparent draw out there; then he bet the river when I checked. How could he not have me beat?

I'm really giving him the third-degree stare now, and he starts getting a little edgy. I can see it. He forces a tight smile, looking right into my eyes. Three minutes have gone by. But this is my tournament. This hand. If I fold, I'm down to $3,500 and crippled. If I call and I'm wrong, I'm basically dead.

"You want me to call?" I say again.

I'm not expecting a response. But to my surprise he starts talking. He says something about how if I've been watching then I'll know what his cards are. Then he says something else that makes even less sense.

And suddenly I realize with certainty that I've got him beat. He doesn't want me to call. He's trying to talk me out of it, but he's nervous and he's not making sense, which is what people do when they're nervous.

"I call," I say.

Sheepishly, he turns up A-9 suited. A pair of nines.

"Yes!" I pump my fist, gritting my teeth, as I flip up my Q-7. I can feel the adrenaline coursing through me. I get up. *Jit jit jit.* Shake my fist again.

Periodically, throughout the day, there have been screams and jungle yells here in the Amazon Room as someone sucks out a miracle card on the river or suffers a contrastingly painful defeat. This kind of vocal display is a relatively new phenomenon in poker—and a direct result of television. With ESPN crews roaming around, looking for good drama, a little hamming it up might get you on *SportsCenter* or the Main Event broadcast.

My low-key exuberance draws not even a snapshot from a disposable Kodak. No matter, though. Plenty of time for that later. The important thing is that I put my life on the line and lived to tell the tale. By 6:45 p.m., riding the momentum, I've worked my stack up to $22,500.

But just before the dinner break, the mayor of Naples does it to me again. This time, I raise to $1,000 from early position with A-9 suited. He calls from the small blind. And we see a flop of A-K-9 with two clubs. He checks to me, and I bet $1,800. He calls.

At this point, I'm thinking that he's on a club draw. So when an eight of clubs comes on the turn and he checks, I check back, not wanting to face a possible check-raise, which I'm sure is how he would play it.

The river is a jack.

The mayor separates two yellow $1,000 chips from his stack and tosses them into the pot.

I make a crying call, expecting to see a club flush.

It's more painful than that. He has A-J. He sucked out on me again with a river jack. That's twice now. This one is even more painful. If the club hadn't come on the turn and the river hadn't been a jack, I'm pretty certain I would have been able to extract a whole lot more out of him than I ended up giving him. But what can you do? I've still got $17,000, which is about average at this point. Thirty thousand would have given me some real leverage.

During the dinner break, Mike May, Shane, Guy Calvert, Adam Schoenfeld, Richie Bell, and I all make a mad dash back to the Gold Coast for a wolfed-down Chinese feast at Ping Pang Pong. It seems like a better bet than trying to beat the crush at any of the Rio's restaurants. The food is better, too.

We're all still alive—this is amazing in and of itself—and we spend dinner comparing war stories, calling girlfriends and wives, and trying to relax a little. It's exhausting playing tournaments in general, and this one in particular. To maintain this level of concentration for nine hours, let alone nine straight days, takes a will of steel and nearly superhuman endurance.

I get back from the dinner break a little early and start chatting with the very nice Venezuelan gent who's been sitting in seat 2 all day. He has wiry black curls and a happy-go-lucky demeanor, and from what I've been able to glean a solid game. He came all the way from Caracas and bought into the tournament in cash just as I did. "It has been my dream for many years," he says. "Now I am doing it."

The doctor comes back from dinner all revved up. Apparently, he spent a few minutes at Doyle Brunson's big party in one of the convention halls. The Hilton sisters, Paris and Nikki, were there, and the doctor's friend, the one who got him into the party, told him to come back if he busts out. "The Hilton sisters," the doctor says. "Damn! I love that Paris."

Not long after we resume, with the blinds now $200 and $400 with a $50 ante, I limp into an unraised pot on his big blind from late position with 6-7 suited and get to see a cheap flop of 4-8-9.

My Venezuelan friend leads out for $1,000, and after the one other limper folds, I call.

The turn brings a beautiful, improbable ten, giving me the low end of the straight.

The Venezuelan again bets out $1,000, and this time I raise, making it $3,000.

Without giving it too much consideration, he moves in for $1,500 more, which I call immediately, turning over my straight.

"Ah, good hand," he says, turning over 10-8. The turn card gave him two pairs. No wonder he couldn't get away from it.

The river is a blank, and he stands up, nodding his head sadly. I feel bad for sending him on his long trip back to Venezuela, but he comes over and we hug it out.

Less than five minutes later, Shane goes bust two tables over, with A-K against queens in a $30,000 pot.

At the next table, an English dude with long, graying Leon Russell hair is suddenly creating a ruckus. I find out later that his name is Barry Paskin and he's a comedian, but for now all I know is that he's wearing a Beckham soccer jersey and that he has just returned from two consecutive f-bomb penalties* with a patchwork of Scotch tape over his

---

* A new rule, instituted by Harrah's tournament committee, the f-bomb penalty is an enforced ten-minute table suspension for any player uttering the word "fuck." It's a ridiculous rule in a poker game, part of the trickle-down effect of political correctness. I can see if someone were penalized for directing abusive language or behavior at another person, but to take exception to an obscenity muttered in a moment of pain is fucking ridiculous.

mouth. It doesn't seem to prevent him from talking. Or yelling. In the midst of a hand, he screams, "Don't let me do it again!" and shoves all his chips in. Then he stands up on his chair and bellows, "Call this blinking bet!" as the ESPN cameras swoop in. "Blink! Blink! Call me, you blinks!"

It works, because his opponent finally does call him with pocket fours, only to see Paskin turn over pocket aces.

Watching the drama, I move closer, but when I'm about four feet away from him, I'm suddenly hit with a smell that is like a solid wall. It is, as someone on a famous sitcom once said, inhuman, like an entity. And because Paskin is now suddenly so animated (I'm wondering where he was all day. Did his meds suddenly wear off?), the stench has been activated or stirred up, wafting off him in waves. Even sitting in my seat, which is a good ten feet away, I am suffering. I can't imagine what it's like for the players sitting next to him.

Ken Lambert, one of the tournament directors, comes over, but he can't deal with Paskin; there are too many transgressions.

"You gotta do something," someone pleads.

What can the directors do? Make him leave and take a shower?

Yes!

When Paskin shouts "All in!" again a few minutes later and there's a call, everyone in a twenty-foot radius is rooting for him to get knocked out.

He stands up on his chair again and starts shouting as the cards come out, "No! No! No! No! No!" And then, suddenly, thrusting his arms up in triumph, "Yes! Yes! Yes! Yes!"

Everybody groans. He's won again.

A new player gets moved to our table into seat 1. He's an oafish-looking blond guy in a Callaway golf hat with a mountain of chips. I can tell just by looking at him that he's a donkey. His eyes are too close together and his brow is thick. Sure enough, not two minutes after he sits down, he gets involved in a hand with the doctor, who has been short-stacked ever since I made that big call on him. Now, on a flop of 4-5-8, he moves in for his last $5,200, and is called by Callaway. They turn up their hands. The doctor has A-8, for top pair, top kicker, and Callaway has Q-7, for . . . what? Before I can even fully process how bad a play this is, the dealer turns a six, completing Callaway's gutshot straight.

The entire table groans, and the doctor seems momentarily stunned. But as he stands up, he shrugs it off. "Oh, well," he says cheerfully. "At least now I can go chase down that Paris Hilton. My friend just called. He's sitting with them!"

Having just watched this atrocity, I should be flogged for what I do next. I actually try to move Callaway off a hand. It's stupid, and I know even as I'm doing it that it's stupid, but I can't stop myself. The $4,000 I lose takes me down to $22,000.

Then, at 12:30 p.m., just before the next break, I get into another hand with my old pal Zapata, who has been up as high as $60,000 and as low as $10,000, but is now at around $35,000. He and I haven't tangled much since our earlier encounter. He's stayed pretty much out of my way, and I've returned the favor. But now, with pocket queens under the gun, one of the few big hands I've had all day, I bring it in for $1,500, and he calls me from behind. We watch a flop of 3-6-9 rainbow, which is just the kind of flop I'm looking for. I fire out $2,500, watching him for a reaction. He considers my bet, sniffing slightly, working his lips around thoughtfully. Then he calls.

This is worrisome, but not horrible. He's not the kind of player who's going to fold in that spot when I bet. After observing him for more than thirteen hours, I have a pretty good feeling for his style. He wants to see what I do on the turn. Then he'll decide whether I've really got a hand or I was just making a continuation bet. A lot will depend on what comes. Obviously, if an ace or king comes, I'm going to have to proceed with caution.

The turn is a three, pairing the bottom end of the board. It's not a scary card to me. I bet $3,500.

Zapata starts shuffling his chips with his right hand. He has long dexterous fingers, and they spider up and down, moving the chips with a wonderful liquidity. "How much do you have left?" he asks.

I count my chips for him, knowing that this is all part of the game, the intimidation, and that he is looking for information beyond the actual question. "I've got a little over fourteen thousand."

He nods. "I raise." He counts off $10,000 in yellow chips and puts it in front of his cards in two piles of five.

"What's the raise?" I ask.

The dealer says, "Six thousand five hundred."

I smile. It's an excellent bet. He knows that I have to either commit the rest of my chips here or fold. If he's on an out-and-out bluff, which I doubt very much, he's risking only $10,000, whereas a less skilled player might have moved in. This way, if I do push in the rest of my chips, and he's really on a naked bluff, he can fold and save himself $7,500. But the thing is, I think he wants me to do that. I actually think that he's got a real hand, that he flopped a set, and that he's trying to get all my money.

I roll my head around on my neck to loosen the muscles a bit, and then I say, "I guess you flopped a set."

No reaction.

Peeking at my queens one last time, I hesitate for a long thirty seconds, then bid them farewell and flick them into the muck.

Zapata very graciously flashes his pocket sixes.

"Thank you," I say.

"Kings?" he asks.

"Queens."

At one-fifty in the morning, Jack Effel comes by with a bunch of Lucite chip racks and tells us our table is breaking. It's amazing. Standing up, looking around, I suddenly realize that more than half the room has emptied out. I'm handed a little green card directing me to table 19, seat 3. I rack up my $11,500 in chips and make my way over. A change of scenery can only be good for me at this point. I'm tired, frazzled, and sick of being poor.

The second hand I'm dealt at my new table, with the blinds now $300-$600 and a $75 ante, I raise to $2,000 with K-Q suited from middle position and get one caller behind me, a dark-haired guy with hipster black-framed glasses. Despite what I just said about the change of scenery, I'm in big trouble if I don't hit the flop. I have no idea how this guy plays.

The flop is 10-J-Q. I look at it for a moment, trying to compute the possibilities. It's too hard. I'm fairly certain that even if I'm behind here, I have outs, but I'm too tired to figure out what the best play is. All I know is that there's $5,650 in the pot already, and that I want it. Sometimes, it is an advantage to be first to act. This is one of those times.

"I'm all in," I say.

Fourteen hours after we began play, I have put all my chips at risk for the very first time (if I'd lost the hand to the doctor, I'd have had $500 left). I don't know if this means I have played too cautiously up till now, or whether it means that I have played well. I just know that after all this time, all this hard work, it's not merely about survival. As Amir Vahedi has been famously quoted as saying, "In no-limit hold'em, if you want to live, you have to be willing to die."

For me, that time has come.

The guy in the hipster glasses swallows a couple of times, his Adam's apple moving up and down visibly. Then he mucks his hand.

Five minutes later, the announcement comes that play has ended for the night. "Congratulations to everyone here. Please wait in your seats until we can count up and bag up your chips."

By my own count, I have finished the day with $16,475.

*　*　*

The bagging process takes a good forty-five minutes. During the wait, I find Mike May and Guy Calvert and Richie Bell, all of whom have also survived. We're exhausted but wired. Is anyone hungry? Let's get something to eat. After our chips are counted and sealed, along with a signed form, in thick plastic bags, we head back to the Gold Coast. The Chinese restaurant is closed, so we wind up in the Monterey Room, where we order absurd things like prime rib and French onion soup at three in the morning.

I get to my room at 4:30 and climb into bed. Thank God I'm not playing tomorrow. I can't even imagine what it's going to be like for those poor Day 1C players who have to go back into battle the next day. I'm still too keyed up to fall asleep. I'm thinking, as usual, about what I could have done differently; but there's also a deep sense of satisfaction in knowing that with very few opportunities to accumulate chips, I did okay. By the time I'm finally able to come down a little, it must be close to six a.m. Somewhere around then, I drift off into a deep, deep sleep.

It is shattered, inexplicably, a short time later, by the insistent ringing of the hotel telephone.

13

THE MIGHTY CASEY

"Hello?" I mumble. I put the phone to my ear and almost fall asleep again. I'm so tired I can't even open my eyes. I'm literally blind.

"I know you went to bed really late. I'm sorry to call so early."

"Alice?" It is difficult getting my brain circuits to process even the simplest concept.

"Don't worry, everything's fine," she says. "I just couldn't wait any longer. . . . I wanted to tell you that I have an interesting item for your book."

"An item for my book?" Please, God, what is she doing? Doesn't she know how tired I am?

"I'm pregnant," she says.

My mouth opens and a sound like "What?" comes out, though perhaps I only think this. I do know that a jolt of adrenaline courses through me, but I am still so thickheaded with sleep that I have to fight for each word, plucking it from a part of my brain to which I still don't have full access. "But"—I try to complete the thought—"when?"

"In Vegas. It happened in Vegas," she says. "I was late after I got back.

I think that's why I've been so crazy this week. But I just did the home pregnancy test for the second time and it was positive again."

I know there is a way I need to react here, and I am doing my best, brushing away my shock and disbelief and the deep layers of sleep, coming up with words that convey excitement and happiness, like "incredible," and "amazing." These are sincere sentiments, but they are not complete. The truth is that what she has just told me is impossible information to metabolize or fully grasp even under ideal circumstances. I cannot have the conversation that I want or she wants, not right now, so after several minutes, I tell her that I'll call her later, that I'm incredibly excited, but right now I need to sleep.

And somehow I do fall back asleep, at least for a little while; that's how tired I am. I awake again several hours later and immediately reach for the phone. "So that wasn't a dream?" I say.

No, no, it definitely wasn't a dream.

We talk for over an hour. There's so much to consider. Neither of us can believe that the baby was actually conceived while Alice was here. She did everything you're not supposed to do. Flew on a plane. Drank lots of alcohol. Sat in a Jacuzzi for hours the next day.

"This is a miracle baby."

"It really is. The ultimate Vegas long shot."

We decide that we're not going to tell anyone about it just yet. It's too early. We need to see what happens after she goes to the doctor.

But I already know.

I say, "Now I really need to win this thing."

"Just come back in one piece," she says.

"I'll try."

Despite what I promised Alice, when I see Mike May later, over at the Rio, where we've gone to check out the Day 1C action, I can't stop myself from telling him. I have to tell someone.

"Oh my God," he says. "That's great, Peter! And it happened here in Vegas? Perfect."

"It is, isn't it?"

"So much for what happens in Vegas staying in Vegas."

On my way back to my room, I pick up a *New York Times*. I haven't read a paper in what feels like weeks. It is so easy to lose track of the real world in this place, so easy to forget that what is happening here, as important as it feels in the moment, is actually of little consequence to anyone else on the planet.

But it could be of consequence. To Alice. To our baby. It's still all I can do to get my head around the idea, around the idea of the change that is about to occur. At the same time I know that I'm holding a $10,000 lottery ticket, and I'm only 1,500 people away from cashing it. I know that nine people, everyone at this year's final table, is guaranteed a minimum of $1 million. And that's a life-changing thing, too.

I wake up Sunday morning just as the sun is rising, a blinding shiv of light stabbing through a crack in the curtains right into my eyes. Last night, before I went to bed, I read through Harrington and Robertie again—Volume 2, *The Endgame*. Now I'm obsessing about their discussion of pot odds, because something has occurred to me: We're starting with blinds of $400-$800 and $100 antes. That's $2,200 in each pot before a card is dealt. If I'm on the big blind and someone raises to $2,400, that means that it's $1,400 for me to call what is a $4,600 pot. So I'm getting more than 3-1 on my money, which means that I'm justified making a call with pretty much any two random cards.

I keep turning this over in my head. It certainly seems to make sense. As much sense as anything involving two random variables.

The seat assignments and the chip counts for the end of Day 1 have been posted on one of the doors in the Hall of Pain. I have to compete with a crush of players trying to get a look. It reminds me of my college days, when I'd go to the English Department hallway to see if I'd been accepted into a popular writing class.

There's my name. Peter Alson, table 190, seat 9, unassailable, undeniable, in black and white. The chip leaders are at the top of the list. Haakon Waerstad with $169,200. Sammy Farha in second with $156,600. And there are some notable players below me. Jeff Shulman, $5,225; Gus Hansen, $7,300 (yes, he actually showed up, despite the rumors); Chris Moneymaker, $7,575; Anthony Holden, author of *Big Deal*, $7,625. Players who were eliminated on the first day include Daniel Negreanu, Phil Hellmuth, Doyle Brunson, Chris Ferguson, Jennifer Harman, Barry Greenstein, and the Unabomber.

Before taking my seat, I call Nicky, who's still on the Cape, to tell him his 5 percent is still alive.

"I know," he says. "I've been following it on the Internet."

I discuss my pot-odds theory with him. He says, "I understand what you're saying, but I'm not sure I agree."

"Well, it makes sense to me," I say.

I do not tell him my other news. Not just yet.

When I find my table, I groan, audibly, "Oh, Jesus, you? Of all the gin joints in all the towns . . ." Richie "Bad Beat" Bell sits in seat 3. A former chef and current city schoolteacher, Richie is a New York poker lifer, a sort of educated second cousin to Ratzo Rizzo whom I like in spite of all the things about him that drive me crazy. Top of the list, no doubt, is his irrepressible appetite for telling bad beat stories. Bad beat stories, unfortunately, are the stock-in-trade of almost every serious poker player on the planet, myself included. I think that poker players like to tell you about the injustices they suffer at the hands of the poker gods not so much because they want sympathy (although they do) as because they want you to know that they're actually good players and that they played well but just got unlucky. It's a form of validation.

Richie, who is sad and misanthropic and cynical and romantic, sometimes all at once, apparently needs this validation more than most people. He can't stop himself—and no one else can stop him, either. Nevertheless, he is a member of the tribe of New York players. He is one of us. And so he is loved and accepted.

"Now, Richie, I don't want to hear any whining when I bust you," I say.

"Just my luck," he says. "I have to sit with you."

We don't have to worry, because our table is broken not twenty minutes after we sit down. Not before I manage to lose $3,500, however, trying out my stupid pot-odds theory. Why didn't I just keep playing the way I'd been playing? I had to come up with some genius justification for playing any two cards out of the blind.

My new table is in the far left corner of the room, but I barely have time to begin assessing my tablemates when I am moved yet again. We've been playing less than an hour and a half and I've had to confront twenty-seven new (or mostly new) faces. In that time I've seen no hand higher than K-J suited. Not a single pair or even a single ace. I'm down to $11,500.

Table 105, seat 6, is up near the front of the room by the ESPN set and feature table. There are mucho chips at this table. Not only that, I've got the poker legend Chip Reese sitting by my right elbow in seat 5. The blond-haired Reese, who I once described as looking like "an angel gone to seed," stopped in Vegas for a weekend on his way to Stanford Law School in 1974, and never left. By the end of the weekend, he had turned the $200 in his pocket into thousands, playing medium-limit seven-card stud. And just a few years later, he was a millionaire. The Dartmouth grad has never looked back. He is acknowledged as one of the best cash game players ever.

I can tell almost immediately that this table is playing differently from any table I've been at so far. Everyone is extremely aggressive and moving chips around. It's good for me, though. If I get any cards, I'll be able to double up. Either that or I'll get my walking papers.

I keep telling myself to stay positive as I'm forced to fold hand after crappy hand. The blinds are up to $500-$1,000 now with a $100 ante. That's $2,500 a round. After I pay the blinds twice, I'm down to $6,600 and in what Harrington calls the Red Zone, where "you have one to five times the pot." In the Red Zone, he writes, "first-in vigorish* now dominates your actual cards as the determining criteria in the selection of hands to play. If your position is good enough (say, because five or six players have folded to you) then you should be willing to go all-in with all but the very worst hands."

I've several times had hands where I had decided that if no one acted, I was going to move in. But every time, someone's stolen my thunder. It's part of the problem of having such an active aggressive table.

Now, for the first time since I sat down, it's folded around to me in middle position. I peek at my cards, hoping for something decent. Nine-six offsuit. Yuck. Inwardly, I hold my nose. Outwardly I try to look as indifferent as possible as I stack up my chips and move them in. "Guess it's time to go home," I say.

I hold my breath as one player after another squeezes his cards, looks, then mucks.

Whew. My tightwire steal of the blinds puts me back up to $9,100 but I'm still looking for something I can double up with. A couple of hands later, Chip Reese raises from under the gun. I pick up the corner of one card and then another and find myself looking at the most beautiful two cards I've seen in two days of WSOP play: my first pair of aces.

"I'm all in," I say once again, moving my unimposing $9,100 a few inches forward.

---

* "First-in vigorish," as Harrington defines it, is that if you are the first to enter a pot, you have two ways to win. "1. First way: You can win because no one else contests the pot with you; 2. Second way: You can win a showdown against the other hand (or hands) that do contest the pot."

Fold, fold, fold, fold, all the way back to Chip Reese. He quickly calls and flips up 9-7 suited. It's a pot-odds call. Still, raising with that hand under the gun? Well, he's Chip Reese—what can you say?

The flop is clean; then a nine comes on the turn just to make me sweat a bit. The river is a blank. I breathe another sigh of relief. I'm back up to over $20,000.

The very next hand, I'm the one under the gun and I find pocket jacks. Wow, is it happening? Is this the little card rush I've been waiting for finally happening after two long days?

I raise, making it $4,000. It's folded all the way around to Reese on the big blind. He moves in.

I look at him, but he gives off nothing. He's seen me play two hands, and the one I showed down was aces. I'm under the gun; I've just gotten some chips; he has to know I have a real hand. All this leads me to believe that either we're in a race situation or he's got a bigger pair and I'm dominated.

If I knew it was a race, would I gamble here? The pot odds say absolutely, but my gut would probably say no. Still . . .

I can't do it. The fact that it's Chip Reese probably swings it. I throw my hand in, knocking the table.

"Will you tell me what you had later?" I ask him. "I'm writing a book. It would be helpful to me."

This is bullshit, of course. It's not for the book. I just want to know.

"Sure, I'll tell you," he says. "I had ace-king."

I can't tell if it's the truth or not. All poker players lie. Even an angel gone to seed like Reese.

A few hands later, it's folded around to me on the button. I've got A-8 suited. I separate some chips to make a raise, but accidentally pick up three pinks and a yellow, when what I mean to do is use three yellows and a pink. Instead of raising to $3,500 as I'd intended, I merely raise to $2,500. The big blind, already in for $1,200, has an easy call. He's a big-headed guy in a Bellagio cap with tattoos on his arms. From what I've seen he plays a little bit like the way he looks. He's got about $40,000 in chips, so he's not afraid of tangling with me.

On a flop of K-8-6, he pokes one of his meaty fingers into the felt. Check.

I've got middle pair, top kicker, which is actually a pretty big hand in this spot. I definitely want to bet; it's just a question of how much. I'm already a little flustered, though, because of my betting error. This makes it hard to know what he's got, as he clearly would have called me with any two random cards. I decide to make a fairly standard-looking continuation bet of $3,000.

He starts stacking his chips up in a way I don't like, then seems to reconsider. Then he throws another curve: "I put you all in."

"Really?" I say. "Wow. You have a king?" I stare him down, hoping for something, anything. This whole hand now has the feeling of something begun wrong and then compounded. I think for that reason more than anything, I decide to muck. It feels like the wrong decision, but at the same time, I'm thinking that I'll hate myself too much if I go out on this hand. Sometimes one's own good opinion of oneself counts for too much.

As it turns out, I don't regret it, because the very next hand, down to $10,000, I move in with A-6 after the player to Chip Reese's right, a guy in a red baseball cap, makes it $3,000 from late position. He's got $80,000 in chips, and he's playing aggressively, so I just put him on a position raise. I think my ace is good. He calls me quickly, though, and I grimace until he turns up his hand: pocket fours.

Okay. It's a race. You've got to win a few races to do anything in an event like this. I look up at the tournament stats on the big board at the end of the room. We're down to 1,300 players. I've made it past 4,300 already. And here we are.

The dealer burns a card and spreads the flop. The first card off is a big, bad, beautiful ace, pairing the one in my hand. I have to sweat the turn and the river, but my aces hold up, and I'm still alive, hanging on at $22,000.

One orbit later, Chip Reese gets involved in a hand with the guy in the red baseball cap, the one who just doubled me up. Red Cap raises pre-flop and Chip calls him. On a flop of 3-7-K, Red Cap checks and Reese fires out a $5,000 bet. Red Cap reraises to $15,000 and Chip moves in the rest of his stack, about $30,000 more.

Red Cap now goes into the tank for a good long time, counts up his chips, and sees that he'll be left with about $25,000 if he calls. And then he calls.

Reese turns up A-7. Wow. Red Cap turns up K-J. Double wow. I mean, neither of them has a big hand, and they just went for all their chips and it looks as if Chip Reese is about to say adios to yet another WSOP. (He has never made it to the final table in the Main Event—some people speculate because he just doesn't care enough or have the patience. But if that were true, I wonder, why play at all?)

The dealer burns and turns fourth street, and the guy in the red cap flinches visibly—everyone does—as another seven materializes, giving Reese trips. The miracle draw doubles him up to over $100,000.

And puts the whole table on a kind of tilt.

Reese is right there to capitalize. He goes on a rush of monster proportions, knocking out two players a few hands later, when his pocket tens hold up against A-Q and A-K. He goes from $50,000 to $250,000 within twenty minutes.

To watch this, to be so close to it, is awe-inspiring, frustrating, and depressing. I'm a nonentity at this table, unable to make anything happen, and with a diminishing supply of oxygen in my tank.

Finally, a little past five p.m., after hours of hanging on by my pinkies, I find J-10 of hearts under the gun. Knowing I'm going to have to pay the blinds, which are now up to $600 and $1,200, on the next hand, I decide this is my double-up or bust spot, and I move in my last $14,000. I glance up at the big board. We're down to under 1,100 players now. The top 560 will make the money. It's almost funny when you think about it. I've come all this way, and I'm still farther away from the money than I was the moment I sat down and started playing in the Main Event in 2001.

As first one player, then another and another looks at his cards and mucks, I get a little bit closer to being able to breathe. I almost make it all the way around. But my friend Red Cap finds a calling hand. He counts out $14,000 and slides it into the pot. Everyone else folds, and it's time to show and tell. I'm expecting to see two over cards, but all Mr. Red Cap has is pocket eights.

So once again, I'm in a race. My J-10 is a dead-even coin flip. Okay. If I win this one, I'll be up over $30,000, which would be my high-water mark for the tournament. Since I've already won one of these races, I'm not feeling as though the poker gods owe me something. But I also know that to do anything in this tournament you need to win a few of these in a row. Hey, I've seen it happen. You go from where I am to chip leader in fifteen minutes. That's what happened to Chip Reese. Why not me?

I should probably seek outside help, invoke a little Vegas prayer on the order of "Baby needs a new pair of shoes." But in the heat of the moment it slips my mind.

The dealer winds up and smacks down the flop. The top card is an ace, which he slides off the top along with the next card, a three, and the last card, a king. Nothing there for me. Well, not exactly nothing. I pick up four extra outs—as one of the four queens will now give me a straight. A jack, a ten, or a queen. Jack, ten, queen. My heart is calm. I just don't want to die yet. I don't want to die.

The dealer knocks the table and winds up again, delivering the next card. A six, a stinking no-good, worthless six. Another swing and a miss. I'm down to my last strike now. Bottom of the ninth, two out, don't want to look but can't look away. The dealer toes the mound, takes aim and pitches what turns out to be the last card I'll ever get to see in this World Series of Poker—a five. I hit nothing but air.

14

THE SINGLE MOST DEPRESSING
DAY OF THE YEAR

For a poker player, the single most depressing day of the year is the
day he or she gets knocked out of the World Series of Poker. So you
figure there are a lot of depressed poker players wandering around Vegas
today. Over 5,000 of them.*

But the other thing you have to know about poker players is that
they're gamblers. And like all gamblers, they're optimists. One horse
rides out; they move on to the next.

Now it's true that I go back to my hotel and sleep the sleep of the
dead. I hibernate for sixteen hours, entering my room at the Gold Coast
while it is still light out, ordering up room service, watching television
for a while, then turning the room light off around nine p.m. and passing out until eleven the next morning.

When I do wake up, however, I am hopeful. A check of one of the
poker Web sites on my computer shows that when play stopped last

---

* One of them is Chip Reese. I never did find out exactly what happened to him,
but after accumulating what was at the time one of the big stacks in the tournament, he
was gone before the end of Day 2.

night, the field had narrowed to the final 569 players, and that both Mike May and Guy Calvert were still alive, though barely, nine spots away from the money. I am thrilled for them because they are my friends. But I am also thrilled because I have a piece of each of them. What is 2 percent of $7.5 million? One hundred fifty thousand. That'll pay for the wedding *and* the start of a college fund.

I get dressed, make sure to bring my press pass and my notebook, and head over to the Rio and the action. The area around the fifty-seven remaining tables has been cordoned off, and people are lined two- and three-deep behind the ropes, watching. Many of the spectators, like me, have more than a casual rooting interest in the outcome here, and for all of us who do, these are tense moments, separating those who will lock up cash and stay in the hunt for the millions and those who will walk away with nothing.

I slip the chain of my laminated press pass around my neck and step over the rope, finding Mike May at a table near one corner of the room, nursing a stack that is almost laughably small. He smiles—how does he do it, even at a time like this?—and says, "Well, here I am with my usual monster stack."

"Hey," I say, "if anybody can do this it's you. You're the best short-stack player I know."

"Unfortunately, that's because I have a lot of experience at it."

"How's Guy, by the way? I didn't see him."

"He's over there," Mike says, gesturing toward the distance. "He's in a little bit better shape than I am."

The decision has been made by the tournament director to go hand for hand. What this means is that each table begins playing a hand at the same time and can't start a new hand until every table has completed the previous one. The reason for this is that when players get close to the money and they're short-stacked, a lot of them start stalling, knowing that the fewer hands they play, the fewer blinds they'll have to pay, giving themselves an advantage over players not stalling. With hand for hand, there's no advantage in stalling, so it's the fairest way to proceed, especially when there's this much money at stake. Finishing in the money now guarantees a payout of at least $12,500.

Since there are so many players and tables to keep track of, the method they're using in determining when a hand is finished is to have the dealer stand up as a way of signaling that the hand is over. The effect is like a slow-motion wave or a game of musical chairs.

Usually hand-for-hand situations are instituted when a tournament comes down to three or four tables. I've never seen anything remotely close to this—fifty-seven tables. As Mike says to me, "The first year I played in the final event, in 2001, there were six hundred and thirteen players total. This is almost the equivalent of them having decided to go hand for hand from the start of the tournament that year."

During the seemingly interminable delay between hands, Sammy Farha, the Main Event runner-up in 2003, who is sitting one table over from Mike, starts picking the high card out of the muck with another player at his table, Sean Sheikhan, for $1,000 a pop.

Mike and I watch in amazement. "The idea," Mike says, "that Sammy can't sit there for five minutes without being in action says it all."

Eventually as Farha and Sheikhan's bets increase to $2,000 a pop and then $4,000, a floor man comes over. He's aghast at the notion that bets are being made in a casino and the house isn't getting its cut, so he tells the dealer that if he allows the players to touch the cards again, he'll lose his job. This doesn't faze Sammy. He plucks a quarter out of his pocket and he and Sheikhan start betting heads or tails.

By the time the next hand is ready to be dealt, Sammy has had enough. He casually flips Sheikhan a $25,000 Bellagio chip to pay his debt. Meanwhile, poor Mike May is sweating his gonads off trying to make the bottom money, which is exactly half of what Farha just lost.

Only in Vegas.

Sean Sheikhan and Sammy Farha high-carding for thousands.

The hand for hand goes on for a seeming eternity. Each time a player is eliminated, there is deferential clapping from the survivors in appreciation of the loser's pain. "We're down to five hundred and sixty-two players now, two away from the money," Jack Effel announces over the P.A.

And then, suddenly, it's over. The announcement is made that everybody still left is in the money. This time the room erupts in a not-so-polite roar.

I high-five Mike. He's got only $9,000 left. But he's made it!

Forty-five minutes later, the field is down to 498, and Mike, thanks to a hand where he was allowed to limp into an unraised multiway pot from the little blind, holding only 7-4 suited, was able to triple up by flopping two pairs. He's increased his stack to $40,000.

Guy, meanwhile, got knocked out at number 518, which paid

$12,500. Two percent of $12,500, as you can probably figure out, is not going to put my kid through college. Mike is now my last remaining hope.

As the field shrinks to 403, Mike doubles up again to $90,000. Three hours later, he is still at $90,000 and there are now only 294 players left. What an amazing short-stack player!

"You're like a cockroach," I tell him.

"Thank you, Peter. I will take that as a compliment."

As the day stretches on into night, Mike gets up as high as $160,000, falls as low as $80,000, and finishes the night sometime near two a.m., in 139th place, with $153,000. From a starting field of over 5,600 players, he is one of the 185 survivors who will get to play Day 4.

Amazingly, last year's champion, Greg Raymer, is leading the WSOP after three full days with over $1 million in chips.

Asked about his chances of repeating, Raymer says, "Right now, I make them fifty-five to one. I've got a million as of right now, but to win the tournament, I'll have to win fifty-five million more."

On Day 4, Mike May comes out of the blocks quickly, doubling up with A-Q against K-Q to reach the $300,000 chip mark. After being short-stacked for almost three full days, he's suddenly got some breathing room. That's the problem. As Mike will say later, "I start thinking, 'Hey, now I can afford to lose,' so I play more recklessly. When I'm short-stacked, every decision is life and death, so I really concentrate." On Day 3, he had been able to make Russ Hamilton lay down pocket jacks with a limp reraise from under the gun. Now, against another player, an Asian guy in sunglasses whom he had observed to be very tight, he tries a similar play. "I put the guy on tens or jacks because he made too big a raise pre-flop. My read of the *way* he played was right. I just was wrong about *what* he had. But you saw how long it took him to call with kings. He definitely would have laid down jacks."

The loss leaves Mike with $50,000. I tell him that he's right back in his comfort zone. But the truth is that having finally gotten his hands on some chips and then losing them is more demoralizing than never having had them at all. Mike doesn't actually steam off the rest of his chips; he just has the misfortune to flop top pair when a guy flops a set, but there's no question that it's prosperity that's led to his downfall, not bad luck. He's disappointed. We both are. One hundred fifty-second place pays $46,245, of which my cut is $925.

With Mike eliminated, I have no financial stake left in the outcome. As a result, the gambler in me no longer really gives a shit what happens. But the other components of me, the journalist, the friend, the fan, would like to see Greg Raymer win again. There's no argument that his showing thus far is the story of the tournament. A lot of people were dissing him coming into this WSOP. Now, some of those same people are saying that by virtue of his having outlasted 2,600 players last year and almost 5,600 thus far this year, he has already performed the most remarkable feat in poker history. The notion that he might actually win it again is nearly unthinkable—and yet everyone is thinking about it.

As he continues his run down to the final three tables, and as high-profile pros Mike "the Mouth" Matusow and Phil Ivey, as well as Tiffany Williamson, a rank amateur who is the lone remaining woman, join him, I watch the drama unfold with journalistic curiosity.

Nearly six weeks after this feverish pursuit began, I drive downtown to the Horseshoe on a blistering, nearly inhuman 115-degree July afternoon to watch the lucky twenty-seven who have made it to the final two days. Across the street from the Horseshoe, at the Union Plaza, sixty players, including Ted Forrest, Todd Brunson, Andy Bloch, and Gavin Smith, are in the midst of playing an event called the Ultimate Poker

Challenge, a $3,000 buy-in tournament that will be broadcast at a later date on various cable affiliates. The fact that the World Series is taking place less than 400 yards away is ironic only to an outsider. These are pragmatic men who do not consider such things. They are professionals. And they are gamblers. Unless they have an extremely big piece of someone across the street, the action for them today is right here.

The area in the hall outside Benny's Bullpen is mobbed with people who have flocked here to see the spectacle of twenty-seven people competing for their share of the over $40 million in prize money yet to be awarded. The space inside is so limited that the only spectators who will be allowed in, to what is essentially a small television studio, are invited guests and the press.

Greg Raymer starts the day in fifth chip position, with $3.8 million. Phil Ivey is second with $4.6. For Ivey, the day goes all wrong from the start, when Andrew Black, a Buddhist monk, outbluffs him for a quarter of his stack. Somehow Ivey, whose reads are usually flawless, keeps picking on the wrong guys. Raymer, by contrast, looks to be in great shape, particularly after he gets into a raising contest with Internet player Aaron Kanter, who calls off all his chips on the turn with nothing but a flush draw against Raymer's pocket kings.

It looks for all the world as if Raymer is about to take the $4 million pot, but a deuce of hearts on the river completes Kanter's flush, sickening Raymer and stunning the entire room. For the first time in two years in the Main Event, Raymer suffers the kind of bad beat with which the rest of us are all too familiar.

It's not long after, down to $420,000, that he gets taken out by someone named Ayhan Alsancak. Audience and players alike get to their feet and give him a rousing ovation. His twenty-fifth-place finish, worth $304,680, is by any measure an amazing achievement, but it's still an enormous letdown for those of us needing a reason to stay interested. It

PETER ALSON

gets even harder. Ivey goes next, and then Tiffany Williamson. Imagine
a final round of the Masters where Tiger Woods, Phil Mickelson, and
Michelle Wie are all in contention going in, but then all of them blow up
early, and we're left with a bunch of unknowns. That's basically what's
happened here. Somewhere, backstage in a control room, an ESPN producer is tearing his hair out. Luckily, Mike "the Mouth" Matusow, the
lone remaining recognizable pro, keeps things lively by engaging in a
verbal feud with thuggish lout Sean Sheikhan.

At the end of the day, however, Matusow's foil, Sheikhan, is gone,
too, and the Mouth is the one star attraction left, the only previous
WSOP bracelet winner. Nolan Dalla comes over to me and says, "This is
horrible. It's Matusow and a bunch of fucking nobodies. If he gets
knocked out, what happens?"

"Well," I say, "Moneymaker, Varkonyi, and Raymer were nobodies,
too, once. It's safe to say that whoever wins this won't be a nobody for
long."

I actually like Matusow from what I know of him because he's
bright, funny, fucked up, and in no way a phony. But for those hoping to
see poker's image further enhanced, the man with the thick, slashing
Groucho Marx eyebrows and Coke-bottle glasses is probably not what
the corporate world has in mind. He recently served six months in the
Clark County Detention Center on an apparently trumped-up charge
of drug dealing. He's clearly a degenerate gambler, who has said in an interview that he used real poker to wean himself from an addiction to
video poker when he was a teenager. Nothing, however, has cured him of
his addiction to sports gambling, and while he was in jail, he managed to
lose $200,000 betting on football. At least superficially, particularly in
terms of his utter disregard for money, he reminds me of Stuey Ungar.
He's not as extraordinarily gifted, but he's both extremely bright and
emotionally unstable, and whereas Stuey self-medicated with cocaine,
developing a gruesome addiction, Matusow seems to have gone a

slightly healthier route with psychiatrist-prescribed medications like Ritalin. In fact, he attributes his good play in the Main Event to the right combination of meds.

On Saturday, the last day, however, Nolan's worst fears, not to speak of ESPN's, are realized when Matusow is the first to be knocked out. With him gone, it gets harder and harder to watch the final-table action. Sitting in uncomfortable bleachers in a small, hot, airless room, watching players you don't know or care about as they bet and raise hands you can't see, is a far cry from the game you are later able to see in an edited form on television in which cameras reveal the players' hole cards and the viewer gets to play along.

I stick it out as long as I can, trying to find some reason to care. Inexplicably, the powers that be decided not to start the action until 3:30 in the afternoon, and because of that decision, at 10:45 p.m. there are still five players left and no end is in sight. This could literally go on all night. Unable to breathe, and with a fat lump of boredom in my throat, I make my way out of Benny's Bullpen. If I were a smoker, this would be when I lit up. Instead, I go downstairs and across the street to the Starbucks on the ground floor of the Golden Nugget. I carry my Mocha Frappuccino back to the 'Shoe, sipping it through a straw.

At the opposite end of the casino floor, just past the poker room, Phil Laak, wearing his trademark hooded gray sweatshirt and dark glasses, is playing a head's-up match against a sophisticated computer program sponsored by the Golden Palace online site in what is being dubbed "The World Poker Robot Championship." Laak is seated in front of a computer screen set atop a poker table, with Jennifer Tilly, in a pink wife-beater tank top that says MY BOYFRIEND CAN KICK YOUR ASS, stationed right behind him, watching. There are three different plasma screens set up on the stage, showing the computerized action. Maybe twenty people seated in chairs look on.

Laak is playing to the audience, narrating his moves and talking to the computer bot as if it's human. "You thought you had me there, didn't you? You didn't realize that I was going to raise *back*!"

It's a bizarre tableau, even more so because of what's going on upstairs, almost directly overhead. I sit and watch for a while as Laak slowly but surely grinds the computer down. He starts the audience chanting, "Let's hear it for the humans. Down with robots, up with humans!"

After the novelty wears off, it occurs to me that I am spending my precious last few hours here in Vegas watching a human play a game on a computer screen against a bot. And yet the thought of going back upstairs is equally unappealing. A little journalistic voice of conscience says, "You really should be up there." But I tell it to fuck off. My flight back to New York is less than twelve hours away, and I realize that what I really want to do right now is play poker. My bankroll is only a few dollars south of what it was when I got here. It's not too late to leave this place a winner.

I walk over to the poker room lectern and ask the brush what games they're running. The room of about twelve railed-in tables is packed, almost every table full, but there's one seat open in a $2-$5 no-limit game, and I take it. No one has much more than $1,500 on the table, so that's what I buy in for. There's a television screen visible from where I sit that shows the action going on upstairs from an overhead angle. It looks just like the screen in an online poker game or the World Robot Championship, but it's enough to satisfy my slightly guilty conscience. Upstairs, Andrew Black is ahead right now, with $20 million in chips. Joe Hachem, a former chiropractor from Australia, is trailing the field with $4.8 million.

Three hours later, near two in the morning, I see that Andrew Black has dropped to $8.2 million and Tex Barch, a thirty-four-year-old bar owner from Dallas, has taken over the chip lead with $21.4 million. Joe Hachem is still the low man with only $2.5 million now.

What concerns me more at the moment, though, is the guy sitting behind $6,000 in chips directly to my left. I've already bought in for $5,000 more, because after watching him for a while, I feel it's the right thing to do. He's about forty, I'd say, on the heavy side, with dark, thick hair, heavily tinted glasses, and a diamond stud in his right ear. His brow glistens with oily sweat. He reminds me a little bit, I realize, of the Englishman who wouldn't make a deal with me in that satellite.

In the hour that he's been sitting next to me, the Faux Englishman has run his initial buy-in up to $6,000 from $3,000. His style is bludgeoning but crude. He overplays top pairs and draws, but so far it's been working for him. We've got a little banter going, and I've lured him into believing that he can raise me off a pot at will. Somewhere along the way I'm going to trap him.

One or two more hours go by, during which time he and I get into several small skirmishes but nothing of any consequence. Then I get dealt pocket sixes in late position, and I make a fairly standard $30 raise. The Faux Englishman reraises me to $100. All the others muck their hands, and I call his raise. I don't love playing a hand like this out of position, but I'm tired of folding to him.

The flop of Q-9-3 rainbow is not a particularly good one for me, but there's $200 in the middle and I want it, and checking isn't going to get it for me. I bet $150. He peeks at his cards again, then moves one green tower of $25 chips toward the pot, pulling back two chips from the top, a raise to $450. He's seen me lay down several hands to his reraises, so I don't think he's necessarily that strong. The time has come to test him.

"I raise," I say, and sit there for a few moments, deciding how much. "Twelve-fifty total." I separate two of my green towers and put half of another on top, sliding it out with two hands.

He lets my bet sink in. At first it looks as if he's thinking about raising. Then it almost looks as though he's changed his mind and is going to muck. And then he says, "Call."

The dealer puts down the turn card—a four.

I'm over $1,300 invested in this pot with only a pair of sixes. The Faux Englishman's call has me confused, and more than a little worried. I pretty much decide that I'm done with the hand. I made my play at the pot, it didn't work, and now it's time to shut down. This wasn't the kind of hand I was looking to play against this guy, anyway. I just got a little carried away. Or impatient.

At any rate, I check.

Much to my surprise, he checks back.

So I get to see the river card free. Unfortunately it doesn't change anything. It's a seven. The board now reads Q-9-3-4-7.

It's like a kind of code, and now I've got to go back and review it and decipher its meaning. But I decide to work backward, starting with his check. Why would he check on the turn? It's such a weak play. He's giving me a free card—or is he giving himself a free card? I'm thinking that with a set or two pairs or an overpair or even top pair, top kicker, he wouldn't have wanted to let me have a free card in case I was playing J-10. He couldn't have afforded to let me draw to the straight for nothing.

But what if he's the one with the J-10?

It's actually the only thing that makes sense to me. But what do I do now? If I check, he may bet a lot and put me to the test. What if I'm wrong?

I decide to make a defensive bet of $1,500. If he was on a draw, it'll force him to fold. And if I'm wrong, and he actually has a hand, I'll at least have controlled the size of the river bet. I push three green towers of chips toward the pot.

People from neighboring games are getting up to look now because there are a lot of green chips in this pot.

The Faux Englishman doesn't fold or call my bet. Instead, he announces loudly that he's all in. He cups his hands behind his chips and pushes. A couple of towers in the front fall over and spill across the felt.

This—the gut feeling of it—is terrible. How could he raise? Would he really have checked a set of queens on the turn with a draw out there? I feel sick to my stomach, unable to fathom it.

"How much more is it?" I ask. I watch the Faux Englishman's reaction as the dealer restacks his chips and counts them. He appears to be genuinely nervous but trying to hide it.

"Could you pull in the original bets, please?" I ask.

The dealer pulls in my $1,500 bet and matches it with $1,500 from the Faux Englishman's stack. He counts up the remaining chips.

"Thirty-three hundred more is the raise."

"Wow," I say. "Give me a minute." I look around. About half a dozen players from nearby tables are either standing up or craning their necks to get a look.

It's strange. I've never been a Michael Gracz type of player, the kind who gets jollies from making the big call. It's a dangerous kind of ego trip, especially in a cash game. And this money means something. More even than it did a few days ago. But I don't want to think that way. I don't want to get to a place where I'm afraid to follow my instincts. In anything. My instinct now says that I was right. This guy has nothing. Moving in was the only way he could win the hand. I've seen him do this already a number of times.

"I call," I say.

The Faux Englishman shakes his head. He can't believe what he's just heard. "I was on a draw," he says, crestfallen, sliding his cards toward the muck.

I turn up my pocket sixes and suddenly there's a commotion all around. Exclamations from the players who were standing up looking and from the other players at my table. My heart is pounding like crazy.

The dealer counts my chips. I don't have the full $3,300. He takes $200 off one of the Faux Englishman's stacks and gives him change. He shoves the ridiculous pile of beautiful green chips across the table in my direction.

The Faux Englishman stands up, taking his few remaining chips with him. "I don't know how you made that call," he says.

"I just got stubborn," I say.

It takes me a good fifteen minutes to rack up my chips, during which time I continue to get dealt hands. I keep looking at the cards and throwing them in. I'm pretty sure I'm done for the night. After I've got the chips all racked, I leave them on the table and wander off. I take the escalator up to the second floor and wave my press pass at the guard who's still stationed by the door of Benny's Bullpen.

The World Series is still going on in the stage-lit center of the room. It's hotter and more airless than before, if that's possible. There are four players still left, the cameras trained on them. I look at my watch. It's 4:15. I see a few of the other poker writers milling around or sitting on the edge of the bleachers by the other spectators, chins on knuckles. Everyone looks bored to tears. This thing is never going to end. Nolan tells me that people are actually asleep in the media room, the old Gee Joon Chinese restaurant. I hang out for a few minutes, as long as I can stand. The names of the four are Aaron Kanter, Tex Barch, Steve Danneman, and Joseph Hachem; they're all multimillionaires; and one of them is going to be champion of the world.

I'm just not going to see it. Not today, anyway. No, today, I'm going downstairs to collect my winnings. Then I'm getting on a plane and I'm going home to see my baby.

EPILOGUE

Somewhere over Kansas, thirty thousand feet up, I began wondering who had actually won. It was weird leaving town after all that without knowing.

When I got back to Brooklyn later that day, I logged on to the Internet and found out that Joe Hachem, the Aussie ex-chiropractor, who had been low man during most of the record-long fourteen-plus hours it took to play the final table, had flopped a straight at 6:44 in the morning and trapped regular guy Steve Dannenmann into moving in the rest of his money while drawing absolutely dead. At the time that happened, I was in a taxi on my way to McCarran Airport. In the months since, I've seen the ESPN broadcast a couple of times, and all I can say is that ESPN did a damn good job of making what was like the Chinese water torture for those few spectators actually able to stick it out into something fun and exciting to watch.

As I write this now, it's March 2006, and the Internet Web sites such as PokerStars and FullTilt are already running satellites for the 2006 WSOP. Harrah's says it is expecting the field this year to surpass last year's record number by at least a couple of thousand. I know I'm planning to take a shot again, as are Nicky and Shane.

The bride on her walk down to the marital sandbar.

Nicky's rough run during 2005 continued into the early part of this year, as he struggled to find a balance between the responsibilities of fatherhood and the I-don't-give-a-fuck-all-about-money attitude that so many of the top players seem to require to be successful. Of late, though, he seems to be on a better track, at least in the cash games. He still just needs that one big confidence-building, bankroll-boosting score to get him off the rugged edge of the grind.

Shaniac hit a dry spell after his big Series score, and six months later he was nearly broke. His backers didn't lose confidence in him, though, and in February during the Los Angeles Poker Classic at the Commerce Casino, after making thirteen rebuys in a $300 rebuy tournament, and then being down to so few chips on the first day that he couldn't even pay the big blind, he came roaring back to win the whole thing and $256,155.

Alice and I got married on one of the tidal flats in front of my uncle's beach house on September 17, as planned. A hurricane was headed right toward Provincetown that day, and it was overcast and raining right up until the time of the ceremony. We had no real indoor contingency plan, which was foolish, the kind of hopeful optimism characteristic of gamblers (I can say now with some assurance that Alice, too, is a gambler. You have to be to marry one), but we got lucky. The hurricane veered off at the last moment and blew out to sea, and moments before the ceremony began, the rain stopped, replaced by a kind of wonderful pearly mist that hovered over the proceedings, giving an air of mystery, romance, and portent.

Waiting out on the marital sandbar, surrounded by family and friends, I watched my bride descend from the house. As she made her way down the stairs and across the beach, looking ethereally beautiful, her rounded belly just barely showing, my eyes filled with tears.

Six months later, at 1:31 a.m. on March 20, 2006, I wept with joy again, this time in the delivery room at NYU Downtown Hospital, where Alice gave birth to our daughter, Eden River.

Husband. Father. A lot of people would have given you better odds on my winning the World Series of Poker than on either of those things ever happening. But luck comes in funny forms. Sometimes it's in the turn of a card. Sometimes it's in a decision that you make. Sometimes it's just what happens, to paraphrase John Lennon, while you're busy making other plans. The real luck I had is that a decision that I couldn't make for the longest time wasn't made for me.

And now, because of that, because I was allowed that grace, everything in my life is astonishingly, beautifully, almost incomprehensibly different.

ACKNOWLEDGMENTS

This is the second book I have written with Wendy Walker as my editor. I hope there are many more. Wendy was a great cheerleader during the writing phase, offered wise counsel during the rewriting, and was at all times a steadying hand on the tiller. For that, her friendship, and other kindnesses, I offer thanks.

Greg Dinkin of Venture Literary was the one who originally suggested that I write a book about the 2005 World Series of Poker, and although the thrust and approach of the book turned out to be quite a bit different from what he and I initially discussed, I can safely say that without him and his partner, Frank Scatoni, this project would never have been undertaken. I thank them both for that.

Nicky Dileo, Shane Schleger, and Mike May, my good friends, all shared their time generously, contributing their thoughts and insights, as well as their memories. This book exists in large part because of them, and nothing I could say in thanks would be equal to my debt of gratitude. New York poker players rule! (Even when they're no longer living in New York.)

There are some other New York players I'd like to thank as well, whose comradeship I've valued over the years: Guy Calvert, Adam Schoenfeld, Robert Hanley, Richie Bell, Lucky Luckasavage, Levi Rothman, Tristan Baum, Bob Silverstein, Josh Levkov, Phil Laak, Ray Z., and Tonio Scali, with an extra-special shout out to Mike Tedesco (and apologies to anyone I've left out).

Nolan Dalla, my writing partner on *One of a Kind*, came through for me like the stand-up guy he is when I went to him in the clutch. You're a good man, Nolan.

James McManus has always been a good and generous friend. I am indebted to him for favors done, for favors yet to be asked, and above all for being such a goddamn good writer. Thanks, Jim. It means a lot and makes a difference.

Greg Raymer, a fine champion, thanks for taking time out of your incredibly busy schedule and always being available to give advice or answer questions. Thanks also to Daniel Negreanu, Erik Seidel, and all the other poker stars who took time to help me.

Brian Koppelman not only did me the favor of writing a foreword to this book; he actually *volunteered* to do it. Brian, thanks, pal. When you have to explain to Soderbergh why the next draft of that script was late, you can blame it on me.

Matt Strauss, friend, collaborator, advocate, fellow pokeraholic, and man of vision. Thanks.

Thanks are also due to everyone at Atria Books, particularly my publisher, Judith Curr; and my deputy publisher, Gary Urda.

I also want to thank my production editor, Nancy Inglis, for her invaluable contribution, as well as Jamie Putorti, copy editor extraordinaire Susan Gamer, and Marlene Tungseth. Thanks go to my publicist David Brown for his enthusiasm and determination. Additionally I'd like to thank Atria Books' art director Jeanne Lee, Meat and Potatoes' creative director Todd Gallopo, and the designers TJ River and George McWilliams for a fabulous cover that exactly expressed the book I had written.

Thanks are also due, in no particular order, to: Matt Klam; Sandi

Bernabei; Michael Craig; David Michaelis; Jackson Friedman; Teddy Atlas; Amy Calistri; Mike Paulle; Howard Schwartz of the Gambler's Book Club; Michael Kaplan; David Levien; Ivan Solotaroff; Brett "Gank" Jungblut; Cliff "Johnny Bax" Josephy; and Steve Zolotow.

And as always, my family: Mom, Dad, Lib, Kate, and Jay, along with the Alson, Mailer, and O'Neill clans.

But especially to my wife Alice, who endured an often absent, often crazed and harried partner during her time of greatest vulnerability and need—namely, her pregnancy—and was almost always supportive, understanding and cool about it. Thanks, Princess P.

Last, I'd like to thank my week-old daughter, Eden River, who waited and waited for her daddy to finish writing his damn book, and then and only then made her way out into the big bad world. Someday, when you can read this, dear Eden, I'll tell you the whole story.

SELECTED READING

Alvarez, A. *The Biggest Game in Town.* Houghton Mifflin, New York, 1983.

Bellin, Andy. *Poker Nation.* HarperCollins, New York, 2002.

Brunson, Doyle. *Super/System,* 2nd ed. B&G, Las Vegas, 1979.

Craig, Michael. *The Professor, the Banker, and the Suicide King.* Warner Books, New York, 2005.

Gladwell, Malcolm. *Blink: The Power of Thinking without Thinking.* Little, Brown, New York, 2005.

Greenstein, Barry. *Ace on the River.* Last Knight Publishing, Fort Collins, Colorado, 2005.

Harrington, Dan, and Bill Robertie. *Harrington on Hold'em,* Volume 1. Two Plus Two Publishing, Henderson, Nevada, 2005.

———. *Harrington on Hold'em,* Volume 2. Two Plus Two Publishing, Henderson, Nevada, 2005.

Holden, Anthony. *Big Deal.* Viking, New York, 1990.

Kaplan, Michael, and Brad Reagan. *Aces and Kings.* Wenner Books, New York, 2005.

Konik, Michael. *Telling Lies and Getting Paid.* Lyons Press, Guilford, Connecticut, 2002.

Ludovici, L. J. *The Itch for Play.* Jarrolds, London, 1962.

McManus, James. *Positively Fifth Street.* Farrar, Straus, & Giroux, New York, 2003.

Mailer, Norman, and John Mailer. *The Big Empty.* Nation Books, New York, 2006.

Matros, Matt. *The Making of a Poker Player.* Lyle Stuart, New York, 2005.

Phillips, Larry W. *The Tao of Poker.* Adams Media, Avon, Massachusetts, 2003.

Potter, Stephen. *The Theory and Practice of Gamesmanship.* Henry Holt, New York, 1962.

Shoten, Charlie. *No-Limit Life.* No-Limit Life Publishing, Las Vegas, Nevada, 2005.

Taleb, Nassim Nicholas. *Fooled by Randomness.* Random House, New York, 2004.